CONTENTS

PREFACE

"We are like gods, so we might as well get good at it."
Stewart Brand

If you track the progress of humankind, many of the graphs are exponential. The number of people inhabiting the planet, for example, hovered under 160 million until Jesus walked the earth. After that, it hovered under 450 million until 1,500 A.D., and then… hockey curve heading for the sky. Given the natural limits of the planet, this will not continue. In terms of our tribe, we are not limitless, at least not in number. There is a theoretical upper limit to what the planet can sustain. Some put the number at 200 million, others at 2 billion, but we are headed for 10 billion. If we do not stop growing, we will perish.

If you map other things like the progress of technological innovation, the rate of invention, the number of PhDs being done or the size of analogue or digital storage, you will find we continue to be limitless. You can track calories available per grain of rice, production per stalk of corn, distance of travel per litre, the cellular efficiency of solar panels, or distance travelled from "home" each year, and they all show the same limitless nature. Thank you, Voyager 2.

In almost every path of human endeavour, our progress is limitless and exponential. Consider sport. You can watch the victory times for the 100-metre race, or the speed we can run the mile, and it decreases progressively; the speeds for yacht racing or motorcycle racing; the ascent speeds for the Matterhorn or Everest—and they all display steady progress.

Some of this is due to our growing size and strength, the plentiful nature of our food sources, and our increasing co-operation. Think of the vast number of person-hours Wikipedia or Linux have consumed. But the vast majority of our limitless capacity is due to invention, technological innovation and science. These three are in the realm of the brain, our neocortex, and its limitless capacity to find solutions.

That same brain, that same neocortex, has also proven its remarkable ability to adapt and change—a function called neuroplasticity; to network and connect disparate ideas—a function called neural computing; and to solve its own internal problems—the endocrine, autonomic nervous, and immune systems. This remarkable human capacity drives self-change, self-innovation, and self-solution so that as a species we advance steadily and inexorably.

The march of personal development has been just as staggering as our technological innovation. Look at graphs from the UN examining the rates of literacy, the quantity of education as measured by the percentage of the population with a degree, the rates of numeracy, or almost any other statistic, and you will find they grow exponentially over time.

As one reads through the literature on personal development, high performance, and human potential, we find the boundaries being pushed by elite athletes, adventure sports, executive coaching, cognitive psychology, and organisational psychology. Across each of these disciplines, we find the entrée of neuroscience. Again and again neuroscientists seem to help push the boundary of human potential, both internally and externally.

It seems today that everything is "neuro." The ordinarily highbrowed, white-coated and somewhat-inaccessible field seems to have been highjacked by so many areas. To the usual suspects of neuroanatomy, neurosurgery and cognitive neuroscience, there have been added a dizzying array of new topics and their originators, including:

- neurophilosophy (Patricia Churchland),
- neuroethics (the Oxford Centre for…),
- neurolinguistics (John Grinder),
- neurosemantics (Jakobovits James),
- neuroeducation (the Dana Foundation),
- neurotheology (Andrew Newberg),
- neuroarthistory (John Onians),
- neurolaw (Michael Gazzaniga),
- neurocooking (wonderful Italian peptides),
- neuroperformance (the Colorado Centre for…),
- neurosport (Greg Layton) and now…
- neurocoaching.

There are hundreds of books about neuroscience in the market today. The vast majority of them (which I have read), and the research that supports them, is descriptive in nature. They say, "We studied this bit of the brain and we found it does so and so." That's okay for holding reader interest, but most lack the applicability or practicality we need to actually take those amazing advances and lessons being learned and do something with them. There are a handful of works that endeavour to bridge this gap, using the modalities of consulting, leadership development, business consulting, and counselling.

To this I wish to add the incredibly valuable coaching frame: neurocoaching is a blend of neuroscience and coaching. This book aims to approach personal development, change and high performance from a coaching perspective to facilitate real and tangible change, and give you a chance at real progress.

I'm not claiming to be the world expert on neurocoaching. In fact, I don't think there are any at this stage. I don't even think this collection of twenty-one topics represents all the fields to be applied from neuroscience to coaching. But it forms what I believe to be the core.

In this book, when I refer to neuroscience, I am using it in its broadest sense. It is the study of the entire nervous system (central and peripheral), which includes the enteric and autonomic (sympathetic = accelerator and parasympathetic = brake) systems. It is the head, heart, and gut brains. It is the conscious and the unconscious, and their effect on the body and the mind.

Neuroscience and, by extension, neurocoaching touches on a wide range of areas. These include reactions and reflexes, calibration to others, rapport building and empathy; multisensory integration, especially the way perception and deception occurs; how our reality is created, circadian rhythms, and libido (sleep and sex); desire, motivation, and emotional reactions; beliefs and stereotypes; learning and language; memory and mindfulness, self-esteem, and personality.

If you search for "neurocoaching" on the Internet, you will find my associates at Frontline Mind (https://frontlinemind.com), as well as some others. You may find a bewildering range of topics included and might rightly wonder what they have to do with this subject. So, let me say in advance: some of them will not. Not all of neuroscience can be related to coaching. As I have already said, much of it is simply descriptive.

What fits in? Some neuropsychotherapy (the application of neuroscience to therapy), psychology (but only that which is useful for explaining and improving human performance), neuroassociative conditioning (how the world is represented in the brain), neurosemantics (if you can get past the "self-actualisation quadrants"), and neurolinguistic programming (NLP), which is something of a misnomer. NLP is the pursuit of human excellence through modelling. It finds its way into segments of this book because NLP has often happened upon neural mechanisms by which change and improvement occur.

When it comes to neuroscience, I have to say not every research paper is created equal. As soon as researchers look for a "why," we are on the path to creating cause-and-effect explanations. When you come across "if this, then that" logic, start to be very wary. My field study on the effectiveness of coaching on reducing Post Traumatic Stress Disorder (PTSD) is an example. Through my work with the Australian Army, I have observed that coaching seems to greatly reduce the number and intensity of symptoms in PTSD sufferers. It would be irresponsible however to conclude that coaching causes a reduction in PTSD. It could be any number of variables such as empathy, attention, focused work on goals, or the very removal of the individual from war.

I have here relied on those studies and results which give the reader more options. I have included a topic if it enhances development, creates change, or helps reach an outcome or change in state. To me, that's the working definition of neurocoaching. In addition, I have looked for studies that:

- Extend the range of calibration you have on your own state (e.g., EEG/E(micro-muscular movements, micronutrients etc.);
- Have a strong scientific approach to evidence (e.g., the correct use of san size, statistics and selection of a representative population);
- Focus on outcomes, not remedies. I don't want someone's latest techniqu course or off-the-shelf solution.

Coaching as a modality treats you as the expert in your own life, so you bring the content and make the decisions around what's going to work for you. Coaching creates accountability, establishes actions, designs goals, and walks the journey to getting them. It is a judgment-free space where the coach only exists to serve your outcomes and success. It also focuses on the present and future without getting bogged down in past failure or the constant search for why you did what you did.

It might not seem obvious at first, but the use of metaphor in communication also falls within neurocoaching. We use metaphor all the time, especially visual metaphor. Metaphor and allegory are central to the way we, as a species, have passed information from generation to generation.

This book is written as a metaphor: a fictional allegory. It is a parable designed to draw out the principles of neurocoaching and assist you in applying them. It is a story designed to take you along the path to personal development, to the potential of being limitless.

In the coming pages you will meet Mark; his wife, Jane; their daughter, Lauren; a neighbour, Monique; and a range of friends and workmates all involved in helping them discover the keys they need for breakthrough. Like many of their peers, and perhaps like you, Mark and Jane have invested a lot of time, effort, and money in personal change. That change and its results have not always been positive. They have invested in:

- Dieting programs, cook books, and exercise classes to improve their heal
- Personal development and training to improve their professional performance;
- Spiritual retreats;
- Meditation experts to help them learn to relax;
- Relationship counsellors and marriage camps after a particularly rough p
- Financial planners' advice for investment strategies to manage and grow wealth;
- A naturopath, dietician and various doctors about their health.

Each worked for a period of time, but eventually the advice wore off. The Midas touch turned out to be fool's gold and after all this, their significant emotional, intellectual, and financial investments have failed to pay off. They are hungry for real and lasting change. It is time for them to move away from reliance on experts and toward self-coaching and deep personal change work.

Their story is separated into three sections. The first will introduce you to the main ideas behind coaching and personal change work, especially how they affect your brain, your state, and your being in the world. The second takes these ideas and looks specifically at how you can change your beliefs, your neural pathways, and your mind-body interactions in a lasting way so that change is more permanent. The third section then looks more closely at personality, self-esteem, and your interaction with others from a brain-based perspective.

Each chapter will cover a single topic, which will often be blended with material related to the topic. The idea will be presented to you in story form, as metaphor, and as consciously accessible research. I'd like to encourage you to just dive in and get submerged—enjoy the story. At the end of each chapter, you will find a "play along at home" section with activities for you to apply in your self-coaching.

Each group of seven chapters ends with an epilogue which contains a summary of learning and my primary, secondary, and tertiary sources for the ideas. These should provide you with ample jump-off points for your own research, should you desire. You can readily access more background material by taking that information and researching online and listening to my podcast interviews of the scientists themselves.

To make sure the story has stayed true to the science and the research, I contacted each author or researcher and invited them to tweak the content of their chapter—after all, in many cases my characters meet them "in person." Almost every one of them accepted the challenge (two are deceased, sadly) and I am incredibly grateful to them for their valuable time and feedback. I have met, been trained by, interviewed, worked with, read the works of, and interacted with each of these remarkable individuals, and have personally experimented with their ideas. Their ideas are in the book because they work.

The revelations contained in this story are based on real encounters, clients, patients, conversations, books, articles, websites, research, and people at the various universities. The experts you will meet are all real, as are all of the outcomes described. The characters however, (Mark, Jane, Monique, Lauren, Gyan, Karen, Art, and all the other workmates) are fictitious. They are hybrids and collages of people in my life.

Even though the reading might be easy and the story entertaining, the content is not to be skipped over or lightly turned aside. Each chapter ends with the family deciding upon some exercises to do to work out the material of the chapter. These are there for you to follow and experiment with. See what works for you. Don't just take my word for it—have a go. Even if it means the book gets put down for a while as you implement the concept. Take your time: it's the only time you have, and I would love you to succeed.

Please, enjoy!

Robert Holmes, PhD (candidate), ThD, PCC, CALC

INTRODUCTION

"You are the average of the five people you associate with most, so do not underestimate the effects of your pessimistic, unambitious, or disorganized friends. If someone isn't making you stronger, they're making you weaker."
Tim Ferriss

Canberra can be downright cold on a winter's night. The fog seeping in across the valley from the lake. The crescent moon hanging overhead like a song written across a sheet of clouds for anybody to read and sing. Mark and Jane had decided to move here once the new international airport was finished. It afforded them ease of travel to the various destinations to which their work called them.

At forty-five years old, Mark is still a larrikin at heart. His sandy brown hair is always cut in the latest style, making him look younger than he actually is. Mark found his way into management consulting after leaving one of the big four accounting firms. He likes people more than numbers, as it turns out. Mark works predominantly with leaders and the management teams of large organizations.

As he put the wheelie bins out for garbage collection, Mark shivered, wishing his woollen jacket was warmer. He headed back into the garage, gazing longingly at his motorbike which sits unused in the corner gathering dust. The track-day bike had been painstakingly converted from a road bike, but he'd had only a few opportunities to use it.

His wife Jane is a year older than Mark and taller too. She is an erudite and compelling individual who carries all her beauty and intelligence with ease, lightness, and humour. Jane did her PhD at the University of Queensland in neuroscience, specialising in mind-body interactions and the autonomic nervous system. Along the way, she also paid attention to biomechanics. Since then, her passion and area of research in human performance has gracefully carried her to the Australian Institute of Sport (AIS).

On this night, Jane pounded back into the garage at the end of her daily run, past Mark, and into the house. She loves running because it affords her time and space to think alone. She's even done a few half marathons and dabbled in team triathlon.

Their daughter, Lauren, is in her final year of psychology at Sydney University. One of her lecturers has suggested she continue on and do a master's in coaching psychology. Home on midterm break, Lauren is waiting for them both in the kitchen. She's cooked them a beautiful meal. Lauren has grown up in this two-parent, working family. She knows the normal ebb and flow of stress and work they are both dealing with. She doesn't resent it; that's life in Australia's second-most expensive city, where the mortgage is a killer.

But Mark and Jane are experiencing a devastating kind of emptiness, a bankruptcy of soul that leaves them gasping for air and grasping for a bottle of wine. They wonder if this is all life has to offer? They've spent a small fortune on an army of so-called gurus, and these self-stylized deliverers have failed to give them what they need. Worse still, there have been times when the expert advice of one contradicts the expert advice of another.

In Mark's consulting career he has followed Harvard's advice to outsource and then five short years later followed MIT's advice to centralize, costing the companies he consulted millions each time they obliged. Jane has gone to one gym and been advised to work on individual muscle groups. Then she attended the gym at work and was told what she needed was full-body, natural-resistance training like chin-ups and push-ups. It's madness. Madness that has crept into every single industry. The worst offenders are the diet gurus and athletic junkies. Jane was around during the Sydney Olympic Games and was shocked to see the sugar-filled, carbohydrate-rich diets the athletes gorged on. The experts contradicted one another there too… less carbohydrates, more protein; no, it should be less meat, more vegetables; no, it should be less bread, more micronutrients; no, juicing was useless—it made for expensive urine… What are they supposed to do now?

Mark had come inside and sat on the couch reading his book, one Jane had read before. He stopped with a thoughtful expression. His career had been full of swinging backward and forward between gurus, each person putting forth a cure-all. The amended words from *Lord of the Rings* sang in his mind, "One cure to rule them all, one cure to find them, one cure to bring them all and in the darkness bind them." Mark laughed out loud at his own private joke. How could any one thing work, even for a majority of people? Surely cures were deeply personal? Surely they were idiosyncratic? Surely answers could only come in the form of a model, or a hypothesis to be tested or experimented with? That's what resonated with him about this book, *The 4*

Hour Workweek.

Mark looked up at Jane, who was helping Lauren bring the green bean salad and sushi to the table. "Impressive stuff, Lauren. I couldn't make sushi if my life depended on it. Did you learn this in Sydney?" he asked. His daughter nodded.

"Hey Jane, darling, this Tim Ferriss guy is truly inspiring! I mean, I don't want to be him and I don't think I could only work four hours a week, but the simple fact that he experiments on himself… he is a laboratory for ideas… he is the benchmark and test to see if things work." He sighed, not sure where to go with the rest of the idea.

Jane nodded, smiled in agreement, and then said, "You know what, honey? Even though people treat him like one, Tim's not claiming to be a guru—he's simply being his own guru. He's leading himself, benchmarking himself." She placed dinner on the table before continuing, "We're finding his story inspiring. Sure, we don't want to be like Tim any more than we want to be like our bank manager… but we can learn from him, right?"

Mark came over, saying, "Right, yeah, right. Maybe we could replicate his example? I reckon we should bring home whatever great idea we find and just play with it, mold and model it on ourselves, see what works and then leave the rest aside! We can be our own coaches, our own Tony Robbins… except we're not just trying to become motivated. We'll try to be scientists about it… be our own laboratory and replicate the experiments." He started setting the table and pouring some sake.

As they sat down to eat, Mark shared his idea about the fault with people offering cure-all solutions, as if their strategies worked for everybody. He proposed that Jane, Lauren, and he should find out if an idea applied to them, and how it should be adapted for them. Every solution would be bespoke, every outcome personally tested, deeply personalized and therefore more effective.

It was agreed. As a family, they would start a personal-development experiment of their own. They would each bring whatever idea, inspiration, article, research, TED Talk, book, seminar content, or conference they had learned from and share it with the others. They would sift through various ideas, debate them, and find a way to try and test them, discovering what actually worked for each of them personally.

And so their yearlong adventure began.

SECTION ONE: THE BRAIN AND BEING COACHED

CHAPTER ONE: THE ART OF SELF COACHING

"Take a look at the clock, notice that it is always now."
Albert Einstein

Canberra served up a standard winter's day. The valley looked like it had been painted by watercolours. Tall, thin poplar trees lined the road, resembling broken, frosted cages whose birds had escaped to warmer climates. Mark drove in relative warmth and peace, listening to his daily dose of bad news on Radio National. Just when had he started listening to that? He couldn't remember; he was getting like his dad.

The day beckoned him to the Rex Hotel, which had been fully renovated in the last few years and so fell into the 3 ½-star rating in the NRMA handbook. This was good for the hotel because without the renovation, he was sure it would have fallen to the wrecking ball, making way for apartment towers, like all of the other buildings along the north end of Northbourne Avenue. He pulled into the car park and entered the foyer, looking for the board which would direct him to today's seminar. His boss had booked his ten senior consultants in for a two-day workshop on harnessing creativity. Mark sighed audibly thinking about it. Another touchy-feely, New Age presenter trying to help him get in touch with his feminine side no doubt.

He was not disappointed. Before him was arrayed a group of mid-level executives, all dressed as he was in formal-casual attire. At the podium stood a sixty-seven-year-old Midwestern American lady with shoulder-length, full-bodied blond hair and a bright tangerine jacket. She had aged well. This was the auspicious Julia Cameron, founder of the Artist's Way movement and author of a book by the same name. Mark knew this was going to be a day about getting creative, in the name of higher sales and problem-solving, but he thought to himself, *An artist? Good luck getting participation!*

To his great surprise, Julia worked with and captivated the class. She assisted them to write creatively in free flow, to brainstorm ideas, and took them for a jaunt to the Art Gallery to walk around and be inspired. Not much of what Mark wrote in his diary could be turned into real, hardcore sales, but Julia assured them that after forty days of following her principles they would have their creative juices flowing and be surprised by the results. He sighed.

Was this just another guru?

*

At home a few days later, Mark tried to explain what he had learned (and justify to himself the time spent). He told Jane that at certain times during the training, he had experienced an altered state. "Not like being drunk or on drugs… and not like hypnotism (not that he even knew what that felt like), but like the runner's high," he said. "Julia taught us how to silence the inner critic by writing, writing, writing; just letting it flow out of us. Eventually I was able to get to this place where I was kind of able to observe my writing without commenting. It was a bit 'third person,' if you know what I mean?" he continued, struggling to find the right words to describe his experience.

"Do you mean it felt like someone else was writing? Like automatic writing?" Jane asked, a quizzical look on her face.

Mark was a very down-to-earth kind of guy, not given to very spiritual exercises. "No, it wasn't like that, and she never asked us to meditate or anything," he said, trying to address her incredulous look.

There was a knock on the door. Jane opened it to let their neighbour, Monique, in.

Monique was a slim, green-eyed, dark-haired Mauritian who had moved in next door after her marriage fell apart. She and her Ryan, the older boy, and Rylie, the girl, had become family friends and they shared the odd BBQ on the weekend. Because Mark and Jane were business professionals, walking the dog had fallen to their daughter. But since she had left for university, Monique often walked their labrador for them. She arrived with lead in hand, ready to take the dog out for his evening constitutional.

"Hey Monique!" Lauren called.

"Hey babe, how's it goin'? You're not studying right now?" Monique said, embracing Lauren with a hug. Lauren explained her uni break.

Jane brought Monique up to speed on Mark's training, making a little fun of his "third person" experience of writing.

Monique offered her own understanding of a yoga practice called mindfulness. "Being mindful is being intentional, accepting and having a non-judgmental focus of attention on the emotions, thoughts, and sensations occurring in the present moment," she explained. "Present in the moment… being right here, right now, and nowhere else," she concluded.

"Sounds like the advice Jane gave me when we were dating!" Mark jibbed. They all laughed.

Monique shortly excused herself, collared the dog, and headed outside. The frost hadn't yet formed, but her breath misted as she disappeared into the cold night air.

The only thing Jane knew about mindfulness was a brief mention of MBSR in her degree course work. She told Mark and Lauren what little she remembered about mindfulness-based stress reduction, which to her mind had more to do with the progressive development of awareness and letting go of self-judgment. There were some natural connections with meditation, from a secular point of view, but she could not recall yoga being mentioned.

"Mark, remember how we agreed the other day to test stuff out and experiment on ourselves, like Tim Ferriss?" Jane asked, a plan slowly forming in her mind.

"Yeah, I remember. Have you got a beeline to where we start?" Mark said.

"Well, how about we start with some of this mindfulness stuff, to see if it really makes a difference?" Jane smiled and he nodded. "Any ideas on how we can actually go about doing that?" she asked.

Mark had an idea. "Yeah, honey. Can I suggest we all buy a journal and a nice pen and start journaling—just like how I learned from Julia? We'll write at least two pages a day—no judgment, no critique. We'll capture any dreams, any ideas or inspiration that come to us during the day… "

"And we can practice being present!" Jane said gleefully.

"Help me with being present, honey," Mark said, then he realized the double meaning of his words.

She caught it and took advantage. "Oh, Mark! I'm really glad you asked because I've been wanting you to learn being present to me for years!" They all giggled. "You know I meant being in the now, being where the balls of our feet are. Let's attempt to become aware of everything going on for us, and also focus our attention on those we are with," she concluded.

"Can you give me some context please, Mum?" Lauren asked. "Remind me why journaling, mindfulness, and awareness is the place we start?" She wasn't being belligerent; she just hadn't joined the dots yet.

"Well," Jane said, a little defensively, protecting her suggestion. "Your father's boss, Art, thought well enough of the Artist's Way to send him and a bunch of his workmates off to learn creative writing. They were trying to access a creative space to work better at sales," she said, but was interrupted by Mark.

"Actually, the real driver was problem-solving. One of the things Art said was that half the time we don't really know what the problem or roadblock is. This process is supposed to help us define and get clear about what's in our way, then work creatively at solving it."

"So, to Art's way of thinking, mindfulness and journaling and learning to be present go together? I think that might actually have other unintended benefits," Lauren said.

"Oh yes, like what?" her mother inquired.

"Well, if I'm present to this conversation, I'm much more likely to offer something intelligent and useful. And if I'm present to my lectures, I'm more likely to learn. And if I'm present to another person, I will enhance that relationship." She smiled.

Mark chipped in with, "Great additions, darling, and what about being present to self?" Lauren walked absentmindedly to the freezer to grab some ice cream for dessert, nodding at his suggestion. Then she said, "Oh, well, that might help me be a bit less self-judgmental. Hmm, it might lower my stress levels," she suggested.

"Well yes, as long as you are not so attached to outcomes and people's opinions," Jane chimed in.

They all pondered this suggestion while clearing the table and cleaning up after dinner. One of the luxuries Mark had insisted on in this new house was a real wood fire. They were lucky enough to have a friend with a rural property in nearby Yass, a rural town. They went there for weekends to collect wood during the autumn months. The three of them sat by the fire thoughtfully, seeking to find a way to take mindfulness, journaling, and simplify the exercises in Julia's book… making them testable as an experiment. It seemed an inauspicious beginning.

Finally, Jane broke the silence. "Okay, we'll each buy a journal and have a go at journaling like Mark said, but can we do something to take it up a notch?" They all pondered for a moment before Jane offered a suggestion: "We could take a trip to the Art Gallery this weekend, just like your company did, Mark." Mark and Lauren agreed with enthusiasm.

Jane continued, "This area has several subtopics in it. I think we put mindfulness and listening to yourself last… if we learn that, well and fine. I think creativity's going to be helpful. Problem-solving might come into it, but only if we present ourselves with specific problems. I think we should make our initial focus self-awareness."

As Jane paused for a moment, Mark continued her thought, "You can't fix what you can't see. Let's practice being present to ourselves, listening to ourselves, quietly expectant, and see what happens." And so it was agreed.

*

On Friday, they bought the journals, A5 with blank pages, and beautiful pens. The next day, they invited Monique and her kids to join them at the Art Gallery. She hesitated at first, not really understanding their purpose of journaling. Finally she agreed to come, and they also brought their own picnic lunch. The National Art Gallery sat beside the High Court and the National Portrait Gallery on the foreshores of Lake Burley Griffin, the heart of the nation's capital. It was a lovely day, hinting at the spring season to come, with a broad blue sky and almost no wind.

At Mark's suggestion, each of them had selected and downloaded a bunch of new tracks to listen to on their phones, and over the course of three hours they wandered independently through the levels of the gallery. Mark had thought that the second time through this routine, things wouldn't work for him, but he found it worked well. As he meandered through the exhibits, he didn't really see them. Instead, he felt what they excited within him. Memories came back unbidden. Choices, good and bad, were captured in the journal. His state, feelings, thoughts, and observations found expression on paper.

Jane had expected a (divine?) flow of energy, wonder, awareness, and excitement at the gallery, but instead found herself distracted by the beautiful paintings and sculptures. She brought her racing mind back again and again to the task, only to find herself wandering in thought, word, and deed. The only thing she became aware of was a rising sense of anger, and this is what her journal reflected.

Lauren, having never done such a thing before, took to it like a rabbit to its hole. She was able to dive right in, even without a real understanding or explanation, running in the dark and loving it. Lauren was by nature a fairly analytical, rational individual. But, like most people, she had contradictions. When preparing to study, every item on her desk had to be placed perfectly. The books on her shelf were coded to the subject lines on her calendar. Her bin had to be empty and her water glass full. By contrast in art class however, there was no order at all. Paint, brush, canvas, cloth, mess, and rubbish co-existed in a chaotic relationship. Sometimes she didn't even clean up. This art gallery activity must have slotted nicely into her right hemisphere, because she could handle the loose ends and unanswered rabbit-trail questions.

After a few hours, the group gravitated toward the garden bordering on the lake and sat among the giant sculptures to unpack what they'd learned. Monique was first there, laying out the blanket on the verdant lawn and fishing out the plates, glasses, and cutlery. Jane and Lauren were next, Jane looking decidedly sour but trying to put on a good face. She unpacked the basket including cheese, bread, wine and biscuits. Monique's kids were chasing each other under the reflective surfaces of the spinning-top sculpture created by Bert Flugelman, each piece twice the size of an adult. In and out they ran, their reflections dancing crazily.

Mark finally drifted in after they were all eating, carrying four coffees from the café and whistling. He had a lightness and a joy he had not felt in months.

"What's going on with you?" Jane said tersely.

Unfazed, Mark replied, "I've come to realise that with more awareness comes more choice, and with more choice comes more freedom of spirit."

Jane looked at him, a mixture of spite and envy warming her breast. "What are you so aware of now? Must be good if you're feeling freedom!" she said, her voice dripping with sarcasm.

Oblivious to her dark inner world, Mark said, "I know this sounds a bit strange but I… well, let me back up a bit. I have a performance appraisal coming up at work, and I just felt trapped. I realized today that I feel like my boss is, well, he's in charge of my life, you know? He can dictate my pay grade, my end-of-year bonus, everything. All because of a review. But I also realized today that I have choice, right? I can stay, and I can go; I'm the master." He paused to draw breath, then finished, "I could be happy where I am… whatever. Boy, I just hope I can hang onto this."

Sitting down at the picnic rug, Mark handed out the coffees and began to drink his own. Although his stream-of-conscious had been about work, his eye caught a glimpse of his tummy, rolled over the edge of his jeans, and inwardly he groaned. He'd been trying to lose fifteen kilos for months. Now he wondered about weight loss.

Jane had listened silently, but frankly this exercise had done little for her. "I have to be honest," she blurted, "I got really distracted by the artwork… and frustrated by my lack of journaling." She held up her empty notebook, looking down at the grass, only to find the ants crawling there, trying to escape human gaze. She continued, "Listening to you, darling, I feel… envious. Okay, maybe that's a little strong; jealous maybe that you found it so easy." She looked to him for help (or pity?). His grinning face held no assurance, so she concluded, "Anyway, I feel a sense of hopelessness because it's not working. This is our very first experiment."

Monique, always the emotive one, asked Jane about that hopelessness, writ large on her face. Jane explained, "It's a kind of stuck. Trapped. Boxed-in. Without options. The opposite of what Mark got."

"But at least you're aware of *that*!" said Lauren, as only a daughter could. At least her mum was self-aware! Lauren knew it was time to share her experience. After her mum's outburst of frustration, she carefully chose her words. "Well, at the risk of making your frustration worse, Mum, I would have to say I found the process pretty easy. I wrote down my responses and ideas in each zone of the gallery; ideas about my career, my friends, and my accommodation in Sydney. Coming out to the garden here, I was asking myself about the options I have at Sydney University. Toward the end of the last semester, one of my lecturers, Suzy Green, talked to me about positive psychology. Another lecturer, Sean O'Connor, advised me to go on and do a master's in coaching psychology. I've talked to Louise Sharpe about clinical psychology too and frankly I'm a bit bamboozled by the options. Maybe the word to describe that best is powerless? In the face of choice like this, I feel weak."

Now it was Monique's turn. She was nodding, oblivious to the fact that her children had basically disappeared. Jane had noticed, and got up. Monique frowned, thinking Jane was disinterested in what she had to share, unaware that Jane was looking for her kids. The tension resolved itself shortly when Ryan and Rylie came running in from the waterfront exclaiming, "Look what we found!" It was a dead fish, a carp, the body huge and distended from the sun.

"Gross!" Lauren said.

"Children! Put that down!" Monique demanded.

Jane broke the strange impasse by offering to give the children ice creams and off they ran with money to buy them.

Monique gathered herself again and said, "Well, I guess it's my turn," unconsciously smoothing out the pleats of her mid-thigh skirt.

"I've really enjoyed the day. As I wandered around, I was kicking myself that I've never come here before. It's full of the most exquisite artwork from around the world. What that gave me was an awareness that my life is impossibly full of such things. This city, this gallery, you guys, my friends, my workplace… it's just full of opportunity, alternative, and choice. My issue is that somehow, day by day, I become blind to it all. It's like I live in a rut, and the only thing I see are the sides walling me in and the open valley before me."

Lauren was crying. Monique's words touched something deep inside, so beautiful it hurt.

Jane was having the opposite reaction. Something her dad used to say was triggered by Monique's poetic reply. As Monique was speaking, all Jane could hear was her father saying, "Routine is a grave with the ends knocked out." That hurt. Jane loved routine, her soul thrived on it, and without structure she began to experience panic. One of her workmates called her controlling, and maybe she was right. Jane and her dad had never been close, but many of his sayings had lodged deeply in her heart, popping out at times like this.

Seeing Lauren's tears, Monique said, "I'm sorry, Lauren, darling. I didn't mean to upset you," misunderstanding the tears. In her family culture, it was shameful to cause another to cry.

Lauren shook her head and affirmed the beauty of Monique's discovery. "Please, go on," she choked.

In the gardens, pied currawongs, golden whistlers, and scarlet robins played in the bottlebrush, eucalypt and casuarina surrounding the group of sojourners. The winter sun lay low to the west, an early sunset broaching the end to their Saturday outing.

"I guess I never realized how many options and alternatives I have… choice feels like freedom. But you know what, I would say it's not the same thing as endless options," remarked Monique. " One of the artworks I saw in there was Andy Warhol's *Campbell's Beef Soup Can #57*, and it reminded me of the supermarket. Walking down the aisle with so many options!"

Jane laughed out loud at Monique's description. The number of times she had complained about how many options they had when shopping. It was ridiculous.

"I get a kind of option fatigue," Monique said. "So when I talk about opportunity and choice, I'm not talking about the kind of choice that gives me a headache. It's more like an open horizon, or a blue sky. Does that makes sense?"

As she spoke, the sun was beginning to set, casting its colours upon the underside of the clouds scudding across the sky and reflecting upon the ruffled waters of the lake. In the chill, they all agreed it was time to go home.

*

The family and Monique journaled throughout the week. Lauren continued to get value from it. Mark's experience dropped a little and plateaued into a regular but satisfying routine. Jane slowly warmed to the task, now that she was away from distractions. During the week, Monique was given an article at the yoga studio written by brain scientist Shelley Carson. It talked about seven creative ways of thinking and how it gives access to our inner thoughts. It seemed to her that this was a viable addition or alternative to journaling. She decided to go next door and give them a copy of her notes from the studio which read:

Connect. Also called divergent thinking. Generate multiple ideas and associations. Write down all the uses you can think of for a hammer in three minutes. Name all the flowers that have red blossoms. This sets you up to think about solutions in a divergent way.
Envision. Also called mental visualisation. Visualise yourself in someone else's space (life, work, experience) and immerse yourself in their issues. See what you can see from this new "second person" position about your own life. Imagine, see patterns and connections that you missed while you were in your own position.
Absorb. Also called immersion. Open your mind to new ideas, be aware of your environment, non-judgmentally. Eat a new cuisine. Read a new genre. Go to a new park. Take a new route to work. Stop somewhere and listen with all your modalities (seeing, hearing, smelling, touching, and tasting).
Transform. When the day has taken the energy out of you, or you are creatively stumped... if you are feeling low, anxious or depressed... funnel negative energy into a creative outcome. Do physical exercise (smash something, hit a punching bag, go for a run or just... laugh).
Stream. Flow. Get in the zone. Be totally relaxed, allowing ideas to come unbidden from your unconscious. Do some improvisational theatre. Pick up an instrument you can't even play. Write a song. Think of an issue and start doing word association exercises on it. Just —let—it—flow.
Reason. Also called logically solving problems. Work sequentially through your problem. Elaborate on an existing idea. Daisy-chain your thoughts on paper. Look at a problem and ask, "What are the next steps?" or, "What is missing?" Use mind-mapping or brainstorming techniques to get new connections.
Evaluate. Once you have done all of the other six ways, you can allow the left-brain critic in on the action to judge your creative ideas. What works, what needs to be changed or adjusted? You can practice listening to your self-talk, especially locating your inner critic(s).

Reading her list at the front door, Jane was enthused... "This is fantastic!" She smiled genuinely. "Truly in the spirit of enhancing this experiment and making the most of it. Thanks!" She took it inside, Monique trailing her.

Mark and Lauren read the list over, and each briefly shared how they were finding the experiments so far. Mark suggested they write a list of the things they were already doing (to keep track of what they were experimenting with) and add a few extra ideas for the coming week. Recalling that Monique was late to the party, he penned:

Action list

- Buy a blank journal and a nice pen, the kind you're going to enjoy using.
- Start with a stream-of-consciousness exercise, writing down anything that comes to min Write something every day—write and write and write without thinking about editing or correction.
- Write a list of twenty things you like doing that give you energy.
- Write down ten small changes you can make to bring any of these twenty things back in your life, even a little.
- Take your artist for a walk around some part of your suburb you don't normally walk in. T company if you need safety.
- Try sitting in silence, for just a few minutes, Master that and afterward practice up to half hour.
- Try listening to what is going on inside yourself.
- Try a listening exercise such as being mindful of your breathing, your heartbeat, or the position of your body.
- Be present to where the balls of your feet are.
- When you find your thoughts wandering off or taking a tangent, say it out loud. Apologis come back to the conversation.
- Practice really listening to at least one person a week.

CHAPTER TWO: THE COACHING FRAMEWORK

"Life damages us, every one. We can't escape that damage. But now, I am learning this: We can be mended. We mend each other."
Tris Prior.
Veronica Roth, Divergent

Monday morning dawned clear and glorious. Though the air was cold enough to hurt, Jane inhaled hard, running up the hill. Normally she would run with music and stay in a mindless zone, but today she was pondering the events at the National Art Gallery. Since then she had mastered the routine of journaling. Routine really helped her stay at it. She would get up, stir the fire to warm the house, then sit down and write. But this morning she got stuck again and the journaling victory ended. All the emotion of that Saturday had welled up and in the midst of it the comment Monique had innocently made about routine rose to the surface. It was actually about her father, not about Monique. Jane brooded and ran and sweated, thinking about it all. Routine… is it my friend or foe?

Last weekend she had experienced a kind of stuckness. She now felt trapped and boxed-in. She had not been able to make the journaling process work. She had walked inside the gallery, outside the gallery, with music and without music… but nothing had worked. It was terribly frustrating to have been without options. Her mind played over everything, trying to consider other alternatives. She had done the whole thing alone and fully mobile. Perhaps if she'd gone with a group, would that have changed her experience? Perhaps she should have remained more static? But then it wasn't really about journaling; it was about flow, and that went dead against her need for structure and routine. Her love for routine had been confronted as though it were a grave with the ends knocked out. Back to her father. There was an ache, a distressing hollow sorrow in her heart.

*

Lauren had spent the better part of the previous evening going over her choices for university. Now Mum was out running, and Dad was in the shower, so she secured a spot by the fire and laid all her options out on the table. She had plenty of choices… in fact, she had generated another ten options since the gallery, and her parents weren't much help. They said things like, "The right option will make itself clear," and, "You don't have to choose right now; enrolment isn't for another four months." They didn't understand. Courses like this required letters, essays, an updated resume, and besides, living in Sydney, she'd have to reapply for scholarships to help pay for living expenses. She had rung her friend Clarity, who had rather unhelpfully said, "When the pupil is ready, the teacher will appear." Nice platitude, but what do you do when twelve teachers appear?

The unfortunate thing about having generated more options was that she felt more paralysed. Choices she had; decision-making power she did not. Her research on each university and course had prompted her to draft a spreadsheet full of pros and cons. She was hoping mathematics would make the decision for her. Her laptop whirred quietly, asking for input. The spreadsheet stared at her, waiting; the cursor blinking. She created a new column for people she knew in the course, or people she admired who lectured the course. Slowly she filled out more pros and cons. It wasn't really helping because she lacked some kind of internal permission or push to actually make a choice.

*

Meanwhile her dad, Mark, left for work feeling a little forlorn. This week was performance-appraisal time, which formed the basis of bonuses and pay rises for the next year. He hated review time. Why couldn't reviews happen all year long? Why couldn't they be a conversation instead of form filling? Mark's Key Performance Indicators (KPIs) were simple enough. Each goal for his job had two or three measurable outcomes that he and his boss could agree on. But Mark and his boss always interpreted performance differently. It happened every year. Mark had worked hard at obtaining his boss's approval on project after project, but somehow he just knew what was coming: disappointment.

True to form, Art didn't see eye to eye with Mark's self-evaluations, again. Was he an apparatchik, a card-carrying member of the bureaucracy, a mere puppet of the human resources department sent to make sure costs didn't go up, no matter what the actual results were? Mark withheld his sarcastic thoughts and threw himself down on the couch in his office, thinking about the way the whole thing played out. Dave, his workmate, was cool, calm, relaxed and apparently uncaring about the whole review. He came out with flying colours. It was like magic. Even if the boss didn't approve of him,

Dave wouldn't have cared. He had been looked over for promotion several years ago and took it all with equanimity. But not Mark, no—Mark was seething.

*

Monique made her way to work near the airport. She was a facilitator in a defence organization. The people and culture team leader had booked a half-day workshop with a business coach. Jaemin Frazer was an enigmatic fellow, a few years younger than Monique, but sadly for her, he was married. Lanky and muscular, he reminded her of some of the blokes who ran with Jane. Jaemin was presenting content from his book, *Elegantly Simple Solutions to Complex People Problems*. Over the course of three hours, the group learned about fundamental human behaviour and the science of why we get stuck. Jaemin covered three main problem-remedy combinations that Monique wrote down carefully in her book, knowing she had to facilitate the team discussion later:

1) When people become stuck, it is often because they feel like they have no choice. The solution is to see that we always have choice. While we don't get to choose what happens to us, we always get to choose our response. In fact, we get to choose everything that really matters in life. We are exactly where we have chosen to be, and we can choose to be somewhere else. Choice opens up options for the future. The second and related idea here is that we have to deal with underlying beliefs because they drive our behaviour. Otherwise, we're just doing behaviour management.
2) When people act like victims, it is often because they feel powerless to do anything about it. They often live with an attitude of blame and excuse about the state of their life, convinced that it really isn't their fault. While it may be very natural to blame others, it doesn't change anything. The solution is to see that we are 100 percent responsible (not to blame) for what happens next and even for training others how to treat us by what we allow and deny. When we accept this responsibility, we have the power to change our circumstance. It is also essential to deal with the reasons we gave away power in the first place, if we ever hope to take it back for good. Why are we letting this happen, and what is our underlying reward for tolerating it?
3) When people try to use their personal power in the real world, sometimes it doesn't go well for them. Often they end up in direct conflict with those who have held power over them and can experience hurt. The way forward is to let go of needing the approval and acceptance of others as our source of significance and self-worth and replace that with an internal reference. It is to take 100 percent ownership of our own value and worth irrespective of the opinion of others. This gives amazing freedom to walk forward and see the world much more objectively, rather than experiencing everything as a personal attack. When people seek the approval of others, they are giving power to external things. The solution is to move from external measures of success to internal ones. The result is liberty and better self-esteem. However, to move forward, we need to feel safe.

*

Across town Jane had one appointment after another with athletes. Her role involved examining their patterns of performance and beginning a process of self-tracking for each of them. Most of the time a runner, cyclist, or swimmer has really strong form, but one weakness or another lets them down regularly. A good coach might pick up a mental distraction or malformed technique, but the coach could not be at every event. TV coverage was strong for the winners, but hardly ever covered the individual in third or fourth well enough to spot technique problems. Jane had developed tracking software, an app linked to Fitbit that was seamlessly integrated into the AIS camera systems.

Jane could help pick up technical difficulties. What she was less sure of was what was going on inside the athlete's head, and that certainly played a part in their performance. Most athletes denied that home life had any bearing, but she knew it did. A shaky relationship, a debt problem, or substance abuse had deep impact on performance. But they mostly hid it from her. She wondered how to get athletes to share and be honest? Their interactions wasn't exactly an AA meeting, and she was certainly no clinical psychologist. Again she felt this rising sense of having walked into a dead-end valley. Surely someone was doing this work? Someone knew about emotions and state management, but it wasn't her.

*

Lauren got up late, grabbed a snack for lunch, and went for a walk. One of the things she had learned in university was the theory Sigmund Freud had proposed about the unconscious. Underneath her conscious processes of thought and perception was a layer of pre-consciousness ready to serve up memories and knowledge she needed. Beneath that, the dark world of her unconscious mind lurked: full of fears, repressed emotions, irrational wishes, unacceptable sexual desires, immoral urges, and violent motives. It was an appealing and intuitive idea that remained in everyday pop psychology but really had little laboratory backup. Pondering this, she felt that the unconscious might actually be her friend, not just some psychopath waiting to derail her life. She had read Iain McGilchrist's *The Master and His Emissary*, which described the left- and right-brained differences between conscious and unconscious life running like a parliament. Well, if that were true, Lauren wanted access to the senate. She wanted them to vote on a future for her. Just exactly how to get that… escaped her.

Lauren flicked out her phone and called a friend. They agreed to go to dinner that night and try something new. She texted her parents and headed off on the thirty-minute ride to the restaurant district.

*

Monique had a great day at work. The morning went well and her facilitation brought out a lot to work on with her team. She drove home quietly, thinking about her wonderful life. She was content, happy with the choices she had made thus far, and the way life was working out. She ran a bit of a life audit, asking herself what wasn't working. Frankly she couldn't find much, certainly not against the model Jaemin had given her. Her marriage had sort of fallen apart, like a slow roast. She carried some regrets, especially about the children, but it was mainly his fault in any case. Since the divorce, she had given herself permission to flourish, and, at least on the surface, she was. The facilitation had been a great source of conversation as person after person identified where they were at in Jaemin's model. Perhaps she could facilitate another discussion this weekend with Jane and Mark? But deep inside, she disagreed. There was a pain in her tummy. She had no idea what it might mean.

*

When his wife came home, Mark poured out his heart about his day.

Jane prepared the evening meal, listening to his rant calmly, not interrupting. When Mark finished describing Dave's response to the review, she asked, "What do you think the main difference between you and Dave is?"

Mark thought about it for a moment, then offered a string of ideas: "Character, personality, age… he's always been the easygoing type, phlegmatic and settled, and he's ten years older, so maybe it doesn't matter so much to him because he's looking for retirement."

Jane smiled then offered, "I don't think it's those things exactly. I think it's more likely to be something that's going on inside him because of all that. He doesn't seem to care less about other people's evaluations of him. He's not constantly checking in with your boss to see if he's okay, and he goes to bed at night smiling because he gave the day his best shot."

Mark paused, wondering if that was it. She was right about Dave, even without having spent much time with him. Dave was definitely inwardly focused and self-satisfied.

"Think of it like this," she continued, "you know how the guys I run with at the AIS are all highly competitive, right?" Mark knew some of them from the BBQ they'd been to a month ago. He nodded. They were all very decent runners. "Well, one of them ran the Stawell Gift this year and in his race the guy coming first kept looking backward over his shoulder. He did it three times in a 1,500-metre race. You know what happened?" She had an inquisitive look on her face.

"He won?" Mark offered ironically.

She laughed deeply. "No, dummy, he came third! Because instead of digging down and running for his life and forgetting everyone else… "

He finished her sentence, "The guy couldn't help but keep looking at the others to see if he was winning, which meant he wasn't!"

It struck him deeply. Win, lose, or draw, looking over your shoulder isn't a very good strategy for a race of any kind. Come to think of it, measuring himself by others all the time wasn't a very good strategy for work either. His mood went up and down according to the acceptance or rejection of others—especially his boss. It really came down to whether his sources of approval came from inside, like Dave, or from outside, like him.

"You know," Mark said, interrupting his own reverie, "I consulted this farmer once. He was very rich, but he strived and worked all the harder to be more successful. Even though my work was to develop a succession plan for him, I couldn't help but notice he was never satisfied. I couldn't figure out why. So one day I asked him about it, and with a touch of bitterness he said, 'I'm gonna prove the old man wrong!'"

Mark grabbed a glass of wine from the cabinet and moved back to the couch. The dinner cooking in the oven smelled delicious.

Jane joined him on the couch, and leaning back with a raised eyebrow and a curious look asked, "I don't get it, what's the connection?"

Mark smiled slightly, enjoying the joke with himself for a moment. "Well, you see, the old man was dead. Ten years before that! No matter what he did, he wasn't going to get any approval whatsoever from the old cocky. The poor guy's entire referencing system for feeling good about himself was outside himself—and it was gone!"

Jane laughed again, her voice sweet and tingling, making Mark feel better. She remarked, "Well good God, he's stuffed isn't he? Unless he can find a way to unhook from his dad, right?"

And therein lies the problem, thought Mark. *I need to unhook from my boss like Dave has. I have to go in and talk to Dave in the morning…*

And therein lies the problem, thought Jane. *I need to unhook from my father, otherwise I'm stuck in a furrow that feels like a grave…*

*

The next day, the AIS was like a ghost town. The residential blocks were only a quarter occupied, with some students, some researchers, and some athletes. There were of course the usual staff and facilities management people. Jane found the whole effect artistic and comforting. White mist and white-grey buildings dotting a semi-obscure landscape: arching shapes of the football stadium in the distance, green swaths of grass prickled with hoarfrost, and the crunch of cold concrete beneath her heels. Quiet kneeling kangaroos in the grass pretending not to be there.

Jane thought about her athletes' state management and it occurred to her that working on her own state management might help her clients. Their domestic events impacted their athletic performance and her domestic life impacted her work with them. Observation of performance was only one part, like photographing the beauty of her surroundings. Camera, video, and eyeball could only tell her what the outside was doing. Performance had to include internal elements, but how to measure… how to prove that? She knew one of the sports psychologists on staff and decided to look him up after her morning rush was clear. She emailed Sean and asked for time in the afternoon before getting on with her day. He finally texted her back and said he had ten minutes that afternoon.

Jane found Sean in his office and broached the subject of the state and performance of her athletes and internal world with them. She asked him about his work around how an athlete thinks and whether it affects performance. Sean's first line of response was to tell her about an expert in state management and human performance, who was coming to the AIS in a few weeks. Sean suggested that she come along. His second response was that sports psychologists generally work with people to get their head in the game. They do visualization of goals, motivation, and attention focus, as well as reduce performance anxiety. His concluding thought was that beliefs very often affect performance. If a cyclist believes he belongs in the second pack during a race, then in the second pack he will stay. But if he can believe that he belongs in the front pack, somehow this affects his ability to ride harder, and he moves inexorably into the front pack. So, she concluded, underlying beliefs are important to obtaining goals.

*

Lauren had really enjoyed being out with her friends last night; it got her mind away from the more pressing issue of her indecision. Lying in her bed, her thoughts drifted back to her own baffling behaviour. *Why would I say I really want to decide which university to go to, and yet manifest total paralysis? Am I afraid of making the wrong decision? Probably. Am I afraid of losing my alternatives by choosing just one? Yep. But I've overcome things like this before...* Her brain was numb. Getting up, she helped herself to cereal, despite the fact that it was technically after lunch. She sat by the fire and flicked on the television. Dr. Phil was yabbering on about something. She turned the volume up as he got stuck into a fellow who looked dumbfounded.

She heard him say, "Listen, buddy, any time you tolerate something you keep complaining about, there has to be something about what you're doing that you get a kick out of. You've heard me say this before, but how's that workin' for ya?"

The man complained, saying, "It isn't working for me. There's nothing good about this!"

Phil didn't believe it. "It *has* to be workin' for you, or you wouldn't keep doin' it."

Lauren flicked the TV off. She'd heard this kind of pop psychology before. Dr. Phil was essentially describing the principle of secondary gain. In a class about women's psychology, her lecturer had touched on the reason a battered woman stays in her abusive home. The primary story was abuse, but the secondary story included having a roof over her head, a male to protect her kids and some food on the table. Life had probably taught her that better the devil you know than the devil you don't. Fear also played a huge role. Lauren mentally admitted her position was nothing like that battered woman's, but she could have some underlying reason for obfuscation nevertheless. It gave her pause to consider what she might be getting out of procrastinating.

*

In Mark's office, things were too busy to even have lunch. Eventually, in the late afternoon, he found Dave downstairs taking a break in the cafeteria and approached him about the way he had handled the recent performance review.

Dave was, in his usual style, nonplussed by the whole thing. He simply shook his head and said, "Why should I give a damn about the opinion of others?"

Mark shrugged, thinking, *Well, I do!* But he didn't say it. Instead, he said, "Haven't you ever felt intimidated by a boss, or worried by someone's potential rejection of you... a lover, perhaps? Haven't you been concerned about looking silly, or being hurt?"

Dave shrugged again, then offered, "Sure, I'm as human as the next guy. But I've discovered that whether my doctor, or lawyer, or boss likes me or not is not the point. I like me, and I always do the best I can. That's what matters. Sure, my heart was broken when I asked Maria to marry me and she said no the first time. But her acceptance or rejection of me isn't the end of the world." Dave paused to take a sip of his coffee, then continued to tell Mark about some public-speaking training he'd done.

The trainer had taught the class that when they felt nervous or afraid, they should think about the audience naked. In that condition they were funny, not threatening, and it also made the speaker the most powerful person in the room. Cut off your external references. Laugh at your intimidators.

Dave told Mark about a novel he'd just finished reading called *Trilby*, by George du Maurier. In it, Svengali manipulates or exerts excessive control over others. Dave finished by saying, "In your mind, our boss has become your Svengali because you let him, and because his opinion is now your source of personal affirmation. To stop being pushed around by the opinion of others, you need to wean yourself off needing their approval."

Mark nodded slowly, musing that when he found himself intimidated or threatened, he would do well to lean inwardly to his own points of reference. Mark asked about one other thing that was worrying him. "Dave, let's say I wave my magic wand and manage to create internal states of reference… how do I switch off the potential pain? I mean, how do you ignore the boss's disapproval, or someone in your cubicle area snickering. Don't you care?"

Dave considered the question for a moment, realizing that not caring about other people's opinions was making him safe. "Mark, I'm not an expert. All I can tell you is what I know, and that's that I don't care. I don't know if I'm choosing not to care, or if I was brought up that way… but people's opinions don't hurt my feelings." He shrugged as if to say sorry.

Mark said goodbye and headed for home.

*

The weekend finally arrived. Saturday was a sun-kissed day that whispered of the coming spring. No frost, no fog, and a bright blue sky. They had arranged to meet and discuss their learnings so far; the journaling, their progress, and any lessons they had learned during the week. They sat on Mark's back deck overlooking the heated salt-water pool, which was steaming in the cool morning. Jane and Lauren had laid out a fabulous brunch and invited Monique and the kids to come over. The kids were inside playing, the adults huddled under the gas-fired heater hanging overhead under the umbrella. Monique was busting to tell everybody her learning, but Jane jumped the gun and shared first.

Jane told them about her efforts at journaling, her experience of feeling stuck, and her struggles with how she felt about her father's views of routine, triggered by Monique at the gallery. In fact, the emotion registering for her was anger more than anything else. She shared her thoughts about journaling in some other ways: perhaps she should redo the experience, but instead of going to a gallery she could go for a walk in the forest or go out in a group? Wandering through trees might help. She also liked the seven alternatives Monique had given them for creative thinking. Then she shared her work at the AIS on technique and helping athletes find the extra competitive advantage. She closed with her hunch about state management and the importance of underlying beliefs.

Lauren followed her mum by sharing her frustration and option fatigue over her university choices. She chose not to tell everybody about her pros and cons spreadsheet. Out here in the cold hard light of a winter morning it seemed a bit silly to her, though if anyone had confronted her right then, she would have defended the sensibility of it. She told them about her journaling and the increasing sense she had that there must be some underlying reward for her procrastination. She self-edited the Dr. Phil reference, thinking nobody would take her seriously if she mentioned it.

Mark went next, detailing his learning from the previous weekend and his ongoing joy at journaling. Then he told them about his tough time at work, the way he had felt oppressed and hurt after the KPIs disagreement with his boss. He told them about Dave, and finding internal sources of reference for his performance. He also mentioned his need to find a way forward that kept him safe and didn't open him up for ridicule or rejection.

Monique went last and was now very glad she had waited. She described the workshop and the three-part model she had learned about opening up choice, taking responsibility and ownership of state. She also described the important aspects of discovering what the underlying beliefs are, to avoid just doing behaviour management; discovering and replacing secondary gain, so that when change comes we don't simply go back to our old ways; and ensuring that the decisions we make for the future maintain safety, otherwise we will return to what is safe.

Then Monique went one step further, suggesting that Jane's reaction to journaling at the gallery was a result of feeling stuck, and her reaction to her dad's attitude about routine might have resulted in defensiveness and shame. She proposed that the way forward for Jane was to create options and discover alternatives. Monique also suggested that Jane needed to work on her underlying beliefs about journaling, creativity, and routine. Those beliefs were affecting her performance—and this was probably a key for her at work too.

She pointed out that Lauren had exactly the opposite problem. She did not need more options; she needed personal power to make a decision, to take responsibility for her choices, and not use lecturers or her parents' opinions as excuses. Monique proposed that Lauren needed to work on her sense of owning the decisions, and the responsibility for what happened after that. She was also careful to point out that she should do some soul work around how it was serving her to stay indecisive; what she was gaining by delaying.

Mark came in for examination next and he stood up to take the floor ahead of her. "I got it, Monique, I got it. I'm suffering from needing the affirmation of others. I have placed too much authority in the opinions of others, maybe a little like Lauren, hey? But to become more like Dave, to get ownership of my life and performance, to say 'stuff what others think,' I must also find a way to make it safe. I should do some internal work around why I find it safe to have external sources of approval when clearly such behaviour actually causes me pain when they reject or underrate me."

There was a long period of reflective silence, each of them pondering their situation and need for change. Lauren cleared some of the plates and refreshed the coffee pot.

Monique wondered out loud how they might advance in the coming weeks. "Do we keep journaling, or do we put that down and move on to a new set of exercises?" She was feeling, and would later say, that even fortnightly meetings were making the pace hard, especially when they were learning so many new things.

"No, no," Mark said. "We keep journaling for sure. It's a great mechanism for self-discovery. If journaling is too hard, then we at least use some of the exercises Julia has in her book, or some of the creative brain stuff from Shelley… but we can hone the exercises more toward answering some new questions. Here, I've drawn up a bit of an action list from Monique's discoveries… "

Action list

- What's my underlying belief (about issue x)?
- What am I getting out of staying where I am?
- What's my secondary gain?
- What are my choices in this situation?
- Am I taking responsibility for this, really owning my choice?
- Are my sources of reference for feeling good about myself internal or external?
- How can I make change safe?

CHAPTER THREE: ESTABLISHING RELATIONSHIP WITH THE UNCONSCIOUS

"Compared with music, all communication by words is shameless; words dilute and brutalise; words depersonalise; words make the uncommon common."

Iain McGilchrist

Lauren was headed back to university. She loaded all her parents' love into the car; box after box of food, clothes for the coming spring, and an envelope with some cash in it. Since Saturday, Lauren had decided to make a choice which would allow her the most freedom, but also give her the deepest evidence base for her work.

These two weeks of self-exploration had been fundamentally different to her psych. degree. There she had to do intern work as a clinical psychologist and receive sessions from an experienced practitioner. Those sessions had predominantly aimed at issues which were in her past and that affected her present. They also focused on her feelings and explored her current state in order to see her clear a way to move forward. Frankly she didn't find it all that helpful, but was curious to learn more about other branches of psychology, like cognitive behavioural therapy, which would work on thought life and practical outcomes. By contrast the holiday time had been much more about improving her state, finding her goals and direction, exploring choices, taking opportunities, and thinking about her future. It had also brought in a range of coaching ideas and included a little neurology. However, Lauren was also highly sceptical of easy-believism and overly simplistic motivational solutions to problems. She was not a card-carrying member of the "if it works it must be right" brigade. She wanted to see the science and the research proving it would work for many people.

Perhaps it was the warm state she felt about being at home, or perhaps because she felt she had actually made some change, some improvement, but she had decided to choose the master's in coaching psychology at her current university. It seemed to blend the best of both worlds. The choice had a number of benefits. She didn't have to move, she knew a lot of lecturers and students there already, and she could change her mind if she wanted to.

Settled in her mind at last, she relaxed into the drive north to Sydney.

*

Monique returned to work on Monday, jubilant at the thought that the model she'd shared had given her staff a framework for change and journaling. She'd gone out and bought a journal for herself and started in on the writing tasks. For whatever reason, this exercise was much more stop-start for her than the others in the group. She found it neither easy nor difficult, but found writing to be something of a chore. As she looked over her journal entries, none inspired her, so she decided to download a copy of Julia Cameron's book and go through all the exercises prescribed there. Perhaps time would develop inspiration for her.

*

Sunday morning, Jane had taken a trip to the National Arboretum. While it had a beautiful and imposing structure on the ridgeline overlooking the lake, the rest of the hillsides were covered in thousands of saplings. The youthful state of the trees was the result of this part of the forest being completely destroyed by fire in 2003. She parked her car in front of one of the only remaining old-growth forests, a stand of Himalayan cedars backed onto several acres of cork trees. Taking her journal, she walked the cool pathways, listening to the gentle breeze rustle and moan among the leaves above her head.

The walk had a clearing effect on her mind and she pondered ways in which she might find inspiration. *Okay*, she thought, *so the National Art Gallery didn't work, but I stuck to a routine at home. I'm attempting to journal in the forest, and that's a bit creative, so I wonder what other options there are?* She sat down on a grassy verge on the ridgeline looking toward Black Mountain, the Australian National University nestled in at its base, the spire of the Telstra Tower rising from the summit. Taking out her journal, she wrote a page of suggestions for being creative:

- Walk through the Botanical Gardens,
- Use Siri to speak notes instead of writing (or Dragon Speak),
- Walking and talking the ideas (recording is an issue),
- Lunch times at work (added benefit of making sure I eat my lunch and stop work),
- Visit various tourist locations in the city,
- Go to inspiring places (cafés are a good start).

There, she thought, *I've succeeded in breaking the impasse—I just got creative about being creative!* Reviewing her list however, Jane realized that each of these would require creative time, effort and energy, and she was much better, energy wise, when she ran to a set routine. Just like Lauren studied better with lots of tight framework, Jane worked better with routine. There simply had to be ways to reduce creative fatigue; ways to reduce her choices to a minimum and form up creativity so she didn't have to be creative about every journaling decision. Then, like seaweed creeping through the surf unseen and suddenly touching a swimmer, she felt the dread and darkness of her feelings about her father touch her soul.

A psychotherapist might have said she was obsessed with her dad. A Freudian therapist might suggest she had hidden her feelings of need for him, and repressed her anger toward him deep in her unconscious. Here he was again. He would continue to interrupt her efforts at journaling because he was intrinsically a creative and artistic, spur of the moment, "if it works it must be right" kind of guy. Furthermore, he had rather cruelly jibed her, put her down and made fun of her need for routine, calling her OCD and mildly autistic when she was nothing of the sort.

He was here, in her mind, sitting at the junction between creativity and self-development, like a dragon to be slain or a mountain to be climbed. This wasn't about journaling. That was almost trivial compared to the simmering anger and self-doubt she felt. With that, she beat a retreat for home and began to prepare the house for the coming week. Jane had a busy day booked for Monday, followed by two days of appointments at Melbourne University. She needed to be organised.

*

Knowing she would be away, Mark had taken the opportunity to book in for level four of the Sydney Racing School (SRS). It was a riding mastery course run at Sydney Motorsport Park. Mark had done levels one, two and three over the last eighteen months. It was the sort of course you could take one day at a time, then go and practice the exercises on subsequent ride days.

On each of the levels he'd done so far, Mark had been really impressed by the on-track coaches. Each coach had three or four students and followed them around, offering direction with prearranged signals. After each session the coach would give personal feedback and Mark had learned a lot from this process. level four was one-on-one coaching, so his learning was set to escalate.

Mark loaded the bike onto the specially fitted trailer, locked down the wheels using straps and harnesses, and prepared for his two-day round trip to

Sydney. Racing leathers, tool kit, spare wet-weather wheels and tires, tire-warmers, a chair, Esky, and clothes in the bag. All there. *It's funny*, he thought, *in this area of my life I really don't care what others think. Not my family, not my friends, not the other riders. I mean it helps that I can ride all right, but I'm not looking for praise; I'm looking for feedback. How can I harvest that heart attitude for elsewhere?*

Mark locked up the house and started the car. Pulling onto the highway, he thought about the personal change work they had undertaken. Lauren hadn't really said much since the weekend about feeling stuck and Jane had come back from the forest with mixed emotions.

*

Monique lingered longer on these winter evenings, chit-chatting to whomever was home when she came to walk the dog. An unusually high number of times, it was Mark at home. Did she time it that way? Mark and Jane's cars were obviously different, so maybe she could see that. On the other hand, Jane's hours were never strictly nine to five. Some days she had to go in at 5 a.m. for a competition, arriving home at 3 p.m. Sometimes she left for work at midday, staying back for the summer, under-lights event at the AIS.

Bit by bit, Mark and Monique had formed a robust friendship. They shared their time, their daily debrief, the ups and downs of their emotional lives, and learned to laugh at the ironic things that happened. Monique was a great neighbour. Added to that, she was beautiful, and lonely. Who wouldn't want to keep her company? Mark didn't really see that as a problem. His compassionate heart saw a person in need. However capable and however strong she might be, Monique still wanted companionship and understanding. He never knew her ex-husband, but from what she'd told him, the guy was a real chauvinist. No domestic contribution, no tolerance of her working; he kept his wife at home with the kids. Shop-cook-wash girl. Mark knew people like that still existed, but was appalled to find out how badly they treated women. Thoughts of gender roles, gender modelling, modern forms of marriage, shared responsibility, and economics filled his mind all the way to the hotel.

He'd booked at the Formule 1 Hotel, which provided bare concrete cubicles and wood-hard beds to "sleep" on. He could touch both walls at the same time. He hadn't chosen it for the luxury but for the proximity to the track. Pulling into the driveway, he backed the trailer into a corner so the bike couldn't be stolen, then checked in and headed up to the "room." He shrugged, resigned himself to the late-night torture, and got on with calling Lauren and Jane.

Lauren had settled in at uni and had begun the tedious process of applying to her new course. She was fine, spending time with her friends and working on her study routine. Jane had arrived in Melbourne and sat through a number of meetings, then attended a consultation with the head of their Elite Athlete and Artistic Performance entry scheme. Tomorrow she had two meetings with the Australian College of Sport and Fitness (ACSF). By the time he signed off from the two of them, and thought twice about calling Monique as well, Mark's stomach was rumbling.

There was an Outback Steakhouse 500 meters down the road and Mark was partial to a good steak. He'd been reading a chapter of *The Master and His Emissary* online, digging into the conscious-unconscious relationship. The website he was on took him to an article titled, "The Affect Bridge," all about self-signalling or something. He ordered beef and prawns and was happy sitting alone with his surf and turf meal and a beer. The evening played out quietly and after acclimatizing himself to the new bed, and inserting his ear plugs, he actually slept. Before he knew it, dawn was knocking on the window and his heart rate jumped with excitement as he considered the track day. It turned out the rooms were better soundproofed than he thought. His sleep tracking app, Sleep Time, told him he'd had seven and a half hours of sleep, with three cycles of REM.

Before getting on the road again, he paused to write down a strange dream he'd had. In it there were three versions of himself. There was himself as he was today. There was an older, wiser Mark who had less hair, and there was also a younger, more athletic and thinner version of himself. Mark tried to capture the dialogue in his journal:

"You really ought to take heed to yourself, Mark. There's a lot going on in your head, in your heart, flowing around in your instincts, but you pay no mind. I have listened to the wind, to the sky, and the self, but you have not," said the older Mark.

"You sound like a flippin' monk," sneered the today version of Mark in his dream. "All full of Chinese wisdom. Listen to the wind? The sky? The self? We're in the twenty-first century, mate."

"You really should take care of yourself, Mark," said the younger Mark, poking him in the belly without ridicule. "Having too good a time there, mate. Really prospering I see. But hey, take it easy."

Touching his tummy in the dream, Mark was mildly embarrassed. He had only become thick in the middle in the last ten years, progressively wearing more on the beach at summer break to cover it and having to buy new racing leathers.

"Mate, you should really wake up," young Mark said.

"All right, I'll give it a go. I'll research some better health and see if I can lose some weight," today Mark replied.

"Great," younger Mark said, smiling. "But that's not what I meant! It's time to wake up, really… wake up!"

And he did. With all of this in the journal, Mark penned a couple of notes about weight loss, and pondered the other comments whimsically. Then he packed his belongings and headed out to the car, the gate, the road, the gates of the racetrack. A long queue of cars waited in the semi-darkness to be let into the track. Mark followed the automotive snake as it wound its way through a dark tunnel, past the skid-plate driving area and into the pits. He picked a spot, unloaded his CBR1000rr and rolled it quietly across the concrete to join the queue for mechanics to look over. Being a track-day bike, it had no mirrors, no headlight, no taillight, no stand or rear pegs. His friend, Johnno, raced in the superbike series for the Honda Racing Team (HRT) and gave him the secondhand racing slicks and wets.

Then the marshal divided people into which level they were there to drive (they could be run simultaneously) and Mark joined a relatively rare group of three riders who each had a coach for the day. He found a garage on the pit lane in the assigned area, and began the process of setting up his bike for the day. With the bike securely on the wheel stands, he wrapped his tires in the warmers and plugged them in. The day was clear and warm so he didn't bother getting the wet-weather gear out. He got dressed in his leathers, rather self-consciously pulling the zip past his protruding belly, and made his way upstairs for briefing. He wondered what younger Mark thought.

Steve, the head of Sydney Racing School, gave the usual instructions about rider safety, courtesy, overtaking, getting on and off the pit lane, and general directions for the day. Then they broke into their various groups. Level four was a much more personalized training program. He still had to share the track with other riders, but now Mark would get one-on-one time with a master coach, Adam. The other levels would do their drills together, and had one coach for every three or four people. But not his group.

"We're basically allowed to go out whenever we like, so there are no limits. But keep in mind that on a track day you'd normally have six to seven sessions of fifteen minutes. Remember how you feel at the end of that?" his coach Adam asked.

"Wrecked," Mark replied honestly. Last track day, he'd been so tired he wanted to give up on the sixth round and go home. It's hard to believe that an hour and a half of motorcycle riding over eight hours could be so tiring, but it always is. Mark had tried to explain this to Jane last time. Crossing over the bike, leaning off it over and over again, holding the bike at a fifty-five-degree lean at high speed, the adrenalin pumping, sun shining, dehydration setting in…

"Well, I want you to take it easy," Adam said. "When you're tired, come in. I don't care if the session's finished or not. You ride as much as you want, but you're useless to me tired. Got it?"

"I understand," Mark said. He had translated the instruction into *listen to yourself.* A shiver ran down his spine as he recalled the dream. "What are the signs of tiredness?" he asked.

"Cramping in the hands if you're holding the bars too tight, sore neck if you're too tense through the corners, the steering fighting you if you're trying to control it in the lean, shaking or numbness in the fingers, spots in your vision," Adam said.

On top of that, thought Mark, *just listen to your body.* Adam continued, "Concentrate on riding, not on the track or the other riders or the speed you're going. Just the riding. We've removed every other distraction for you. We've made sure you only have to apply yourself to riding."

Less chance of getting option fatigue because they've made a lot of decisions for me, thought Mark: *compulsory leather suit and boots, race prep and scrutineering removes safety questions, we're grouped according to skill level, the speedo is covered…* Mark filed that away as something to talk about with the group back home. Reduce option fatigue and creativity fatigue by removing all other distractions. Simplify decision-making.

Adam reviewed the first three days of training he had previously received, touching on all the major points of learning so they could use that language as a short cut. These drills had truly changed Mark's riding and his enjoyment of riding. He was safer, calmer and faster… and his skill level had slowly risen to the top of the advanced riders group. Next came the racing group.

Adam asked Mark about any particular area from previous training or his track-day riding he wanted to work on.

"Yeah, I want to work on the way I sit off the bike in a corner. My feeling is that I've got the bike leaned over too far, my pegs scrape sometimes, and that I could lean further off and hold the bike upright more," Mark said, thinking of the last time his bike had shimmied when the metal touched the tarmac. "And overtaking. So many times I get stuck behind someone, and a better rider overtakes us both, taking a line I think is impossible. I'd love to follow you through some overtakes and copy your technique."

"Yep, that's all good. I tell you what, since the tarmac is still cold, why don't we take this first lap to get your eye in? You just ride smooth and careful. Concentrate on technique and don't worry about anyone else. I'll be with you the whole way; I'll watch the way you ride and give you some pointers. Then on the second time round, we'll nail the overtaking, and the third time we'll go for better cornering. Cool?" Adam said. Mark nodded.

The first group was coming back in off the track by then, so Mark got ready to go out at the back of the second group. Adam was suited up and sitting on his BMW S1000rr—a fairly even match for Mark's bike in terms of racing performance. But clearly Adam was going to outride Mark, and besides, it wasn't a competition. They waited for the group to move beyond the grid then the two of them hauled it out of the pit lane into turn two. Mark took it easy the first lap, settling into the bike, the track, and the group ahead, who were graded as intermediate riders. He had already overtaken half a dozen riders by the straight. He pushed the bike up away from him and rose to hug it, the power vibrating under him, the bike willing to go anywhere he pointed. With the throttle wide open, he passed a pair of Ducati riders like they were standing still. Sweeping through turn one at over 170km/hr, he began to push a little harder.

Adam rode right behind him for the first three laps then swept past him on a right-hander and went ahead to the next corner. He pointed at the ground then dropped the bike hard into a turn through the corner. Mark followed, going deeper and wider into the corner before starting his turn. His turns became much quicker. On another occasion, Adam signalled with his right arm for Mark to keep his head more level and maintain a broad peripheral vision. Mark decided to come in before the checkered flag indicated they had to and he rolled slowly to his shed. After getting the bike settled, he sought out Adam.

"Okay, Mark, so how do you think you went?" Adam asked.

"It was pretty good. I got past a bunch of people, but you saw how I got stuck behind that group in the second-to-last lap. I had to wait until the straight. I was happy with my cornering, I took it easy, and thanks for those tips too; great reminders," he replied.

"Yeah, I'm glad you mentioned the cluster of riders. I saw about four clear, safe opportunities for you to overtake. Shortly we'll go out there and I'll show you how to take those opportunities. Don't forget the counter-steering method from level one, and the hook turn from level three. They're really essential to the skills you're trying to learn today."

Mark nodded, recalling those methods, and the video in his head of Adam doing that through the cornering. His body was moving as he rehearsed the techniques, which caught his attention. Simultaneously he was reviewing what his own body had been telling him. It wasn't much. Instead, he asked Adam about reaction times when he got stuck behind people.

"Right, great question. Most of us blame reaction times, but honestly, watch Moto-GP. Do you think you can think fast enough to react to what's going on out there in real time? Your eyes aren't even seeing a quarter of the frames per second available at these speeds. Your unconscious reactions are far quicker than thinking. By the time you think, you lose. Do you think Valentino Rossi, Casey Stoner, or Marc Márquez thought about his choices? Your body is almost in shutdown safety mode the whole time. It's terrified, and it's gonna resist the right thing to do because most of the time what you need to do is counterintuitive… that's why we do all those drills in levels one through three. Trust your training."

Trust my training? Easier said than done. He's right—I am bloody terrified, thought Mark. *And my body's speaking to me all the time about the safest thing to do.* As Adam wandered off to grab a drink, Mark thought about the article he'd been reading. Somatic signalling, unconscious control, some kind of signal should be there for him to observe or receive. So he resolved to watch for it next time out.

Adam came back and said, "In this next session let's concentrate on passing. You take the first ten people. Then I'll take the next five and you follow me through. I'll switch behind and watch you for another ten people. Then I'll take the next five and you follow. Forget everything else."

And listen to yourself, Mark added in his head. *Learn your signalling. Is it safe to go? Yes… is it safe to go? No… then wait.*

They both went back to their bikes to check them over. They were eventually good to go again.

They practiced exactly as Adam had said and Mark noticed he was much more confident overtaking on a left-hander than the right-hander and more confident on the inside than the outside. He also noticed a dull ache between his shoulder blades when he was uncomfortable, but couldn't discern any signal at all for green or go. They came back in again to debrief and take morning tea in the cafeteria area.

"So how was that for you?" Adam asked.

"Great. I loved following you through the pack. I noticed that I have a kind of signal inside myself for 'wait' but no signal for 'stop' or 'go,'" Mark said, hoping he didn't sound too weird.

Adam pondered before speaking. "Hmm, I read that Casey Stoner rides by instinct, and he just 'knows' when it's safe. God knows how he does it. Looks superhuman!"

Mark smiled. Mick Doohan in the late 1990s had broken nearly every bone in his body racing. Maybe he wasn't listening! What mattered to Mark was that he'd noticed and was paying attention. Mark made a mental note to explore "rapport with self."

Adam broke his reverie by giving Mark a few more pointers on his cornering, especially the way he tended to miss the apex on right-handers. Mark told him that he was more comfortable overtaking on left-handers than on right-handers and more confident on the inside than outside.

"Well, that's pretty understandable. Your accelerator is on your right-hand side. Most people are better on left. It's true for inside and outside too; almost everyone prefers overtaking inside because the other riders can see them and aren't going to stand up and run them off the corner. You have a vast range of experience riding a motorbike. But if all you know is insiders, then there is very little practice or confidence to go outside. Let's go out there and get more practice at outside overtaking. Same with right-handers. There are eight of those on this track and ten left-handers… I think you need to work on the way you stick your knee out and slide your bum off the bike, which involves working on your lean angle. So we'll look at that this time round as well."

Out they went, this time with an advanced group doing level three, and they were quick. Mark concentrated on his right-hand corners, crossing over the bike and finding safe overtaking opportunities on the outside of each corner. He took it "easy" and relaxed into the rhythm of the track. The bitumen was warm now and his tires were grippy, so he felt very safe. Adam shot past him to demonstrate a new position for being off the bike in a corner. Mark watched, copied, then played with it and found that he could go faster. When he was tired, they came in again and debriefed.

Before the end of the day, Mark asked Adam a question. "You mentioned practice, and getting a feel for doing things we haven't done before. How am I going to do that after today?"

"Easy. Book another level four day!" Adam answered with a smile.

Mark thanked Adam for the day and headed off to trailer his bike. When everything was loaded, he headed out the gates and off to the freeway going south for home. By the time he had reached Sutton Forest he was hungry, so he stopped for a bite to eat. He brought his journal and sat at the table, with a toasted sandwich and a coffee, writing his notes. He wondered whether food choice could be decided by having a dialogue with his unconscious self.

This week's learnings would not even be discussed until the weekend, and he was feeling like they needed more space, more time between new learning items. When he was finished the page of questions and comments, he took a photo with his phone and sent it to Jane, Lauren, and Monique with a text saying, "Learned some interesting things about the unconscious today, about unconscious and somatic learning, and about limiting choice to allow creativity. We'll debrief in a fortnight, but in the meantime please find attached my suggestion for our exercises this week. Cheers, Mark."

The restaurant had Wi-Fi so Mark jumped online to a website he had found at the University of Cambridge talking about unconscious learning. A little pop-up function offered "Tina" to chat with and answer any questions he might have. So he decided to have a go.

He popped a question into the "talk to Tina" chat box: "When you talk about unconscious learning… skills, languages, whatever, where is the unconscious? It seems to me that body learning is really important, and body signalling too?"

A moment later the chat box popped up: "Hi from the UK, and hello to Australia! To answer your question, the unconscious involves everything that we're not conscious of. The signals we feel, see, visualize come from many places. Almost never words."

He typed another comment, "Yeah, feelings, blood rushing, and muscles tightening. I've been doing lots of exercise and trying to hear my body. It's pictures and insights and instinct."

The reply again, “Don’t forget that dreams are unconscious processing too. That’s almost certainly in your head not your body, but the research is inconclusive,” Tina replied.

“Okay,” Mark agreed. “And probably that’s where déjà vu comes from too, old libraries and current circumstances.”

“Now that’s a whole different subject” Tina responded.

“Okay, gotta go, write later.” Mark signed off

“Glad to help. Ciao.” “Tina” was really Tina, the linguistics research graduate.

Action list

- Do I trust my unconscious? Do I have reason to believe it has lead me astray before? D have reason to trust it?
- What are my unconscious signals? Do I have one for ‘yes’ and one for ‘no’?
- Talk directly to the unconscious, "Thank you unconscious for keeping me safe, protectin and working on my behalf. I'd like a better relationship with you, and I'd like to communi Let's just keep it simple right now, can you show me a signal for ‘yes’?" Repeat for ‘no’.
- How else does my unconscious communicate with me? It is the entire library. How does give me knowledge?
- Reduce option fatigue and creativity fatigue by removing all other distractions. Decide as many things as possible before hand, then you only have to be creative about important things.
- Load the library with experience that fills out the filtering e.g. add more right-handers.

CHAPTER FOUR: CHANGING STATE CHANGES EVERYTHING

"When we have choice about our state, we have the best possible opportunity to achieve our desired outcomes."
Ian Snape

The weekend and the following week passed quickly, with the group practicing journaling and working on their extra questions around choice and responsibility from session two. Mark had briefed the three ladies about somatic signalling and unconscious learning after he had returned from the track.

*

Another Sunday morning crept in gloomily. Heavy cloud shrouded the morning sky, portending rain. Once again the group (minus Lauren) gathered on the deck and Monique's children played inside. A sumptuous brunch lay half devoured on the glass table. Jane had invited them to bring their bathing suits, thinking a swim might be in order. But with the rain, that wasn't going to happen. Mark suggested they take a spa instead.

Monique's eyes lit up. Before she misunderstood, Mark said, "Just us; not the kids." In so saying, it was he who misunderstood. "Ryan and Rylie?" She scoffed. "I've been waiting six months to be invited into the spa!"

"And just exactly why have you been looking forward to that?" Mark asked. But neither of them could say why being in each other's company, in the spa, made them feel nervous or excited. In Mark's gut he felt a stirring. Jane frowned. Monique said something banal, "Because it's been so long since I've tried on my swimmers!" But really, decked out in her one-piece, she simply felt… attractive.

So in they went. "Before we get started, we should get Lauren on Skype, whatdaya say, Mark?" Jane asked. He jumped out of the spa, a little self-conscious, and grabbed his iPad. Dragging the table nearer the spa, he dialled Lauren. She eventually picked up and they exchanged pleasantries while her dad brought her up to speed with what they were doing and then included her in the conversation. Mark slipped back into the spa between Monique and Jane, the three of them facing the table Lauren's face shone from.

Monique kicked it off by asking Mark for more information about the "unconscious library" he described in his text. He told them the little he knew about the way the unconscious works and apologized for not having done more research. The intervening time had been busy. None of them really had made the time to do the exercises, but instead of rendering excuses they agreed to take another week to embed the unconscious signalling exercises. They agreed to try and find something to focus on that would involve unconscious signalling, to listening to themselves internally.

"In what area are you going to try and listen to unconscious signalling, Lauren?" Monique asked cheerily.

"I can't really think of anything," Lauren said. "One of you go."

"Well, I can hardly keep doing cornering on the racetrack, can I?" Mark said. "I was thinking it would be useful for me to have a signal to tell me when I'm seeking the affirmation of others, especially at work."

"What a great idea," Monique said, a little too enthusiastically.

Jane had noticed that from time to time Monique came across as a little needy, or perhaps a bit insecure. It didn't make much sense from Jane's point of view because Monique was in her thirties, was quite attractive, educated, well-employed, and available. What was there to feel insecure about? If she could see inside Monique's heart, she'd see layers of rejection by men. Somehow in her relationships, she allowed them to dominate and she hated herself for it. It's as if she needed to be controlled to feel secure. And Monique knew that was screwed up.

The pause became awkwardly long until Jane chimed in, "I think I'm going to get unconscious signalling about my exercise. Mark explained his track-day experiences, having body signalling yes and no, and I'm really struggling with my training regime for the upcoming Sri Chinmoy event." She glanced up at the table to Lauren and nodded for her to take a turn.

"I've got something. I know it's a long way off," said Lauren. "Going right along with Mum's 'body signal' stuff, I wonder if I can get some communication from my unconscious about my study for exams. I think I take it too far, study too long, and I get stressed and anxious as exam time approaches. I can feel tightness in my chest developing and it causes me physically to stop. Do you think that might be a response or way to cope?" Lauren asked.

"Yep, I reckon it sure could be, Lauren," Jane said. "Get a signal from your unconscious so you can pull up long before that."

Now it was Monique's turn. Even though she was going last and had the most time to prepare, her mind was still blank. Somewhere below her thinking, like a subterranean cave, her identity struggle yawned darkly. But it wasn't going to be illuminated now, and maybe not ever. She was blank. Smiling warmly, she got out of the tub, excused herself to go inside, grabbed a towel, and checked on the kids.

The rest waited silently, until Jane observed, "Have you noticed that Monique hasn't really engaged in self-coaching? I mean at the gallery she was all chipper and then last weekend she walked us through the coaching framework, but she had no problems. Does she have any issues?"

"Mum! Far out!" Lauren said. "She's a single mother, she's been hurt before… maybe she finds it hard to be vulnerable!" Lauren was always willing to state an opposing opinion.

Monique didn't return to the spa or the conversation. The event gradually wrapped up and Monique hustled the children home, thanking everyone for their involvement. Her non-contribution went unaddressed.

Later that evening when she came to collect the dog, Mark stopped her at the door and asked her about it. He asked her gently, but directly whether she felt unsafe around them, whether she couldn't be vulnerable. Monique gazed earnestly into Mark's eyes and denied it. "I just can't think of anything I need to work on right now." She touched him warmly on the forearm and left. And that was that. Mark was simply confused.

*

During the following week, Mark went to work consciously thinking about his need for the affirmation of others. He watched his own interactions non-judgmentally as Julia Cameron had taught them. He observed the rising need inside as he asked for compliments and sought to get his unconscious to signal to him when it was happening. It was an odd thing because he did not have the strongly physical sign in his body such as he had experienced at the track. Instead he felt a sense of anxiety in his chest, a kind of heaviness. Checking in with himself and his feeling, he said, "There it is, I hear it, I don't really need affirmation, right, I'm fine just as I am."

However, Mark's progress in the direction of becoming more like Dave had an unintended consequence. He now found it hard to receive compliments. It seemed as though pushing back on his need for people's affirmation had become unilateral. He grabbed his lunch, sat down on the couch in his office thinking about Dave. He realized that Dave accepted compliments with equanimity. So what was Dave doing that he wasn't? Mark grabbed his journal and began drafting some ideas. He sketched a diagram with him on one side and people on the other, drawing an arrow from them to him in one colour, and wrote, "demanded, drawn, needed, and expected: unacceptable." Then he drew another arrow in a different colour, saying, "given, free, meaningful: acceptable." There were two different kinds of flow toward him, one given the other taken. He closed his journal. It was enough.

*

Lauren continued to work and study in Sydney, progressing through the second-semester material. In her case, there were assignments and smaller tests all the way through the semester and this week was no exception. Lauren's struggle was not uncommon: overpreparation driven by a fear of failure, producing overachievement and eventually (for her) a surprise grade. She really did want to do well, but believed that a "good" effort might not even produce a pass. It was irrational, especially given her track record of high distinctions (and straight A's at school).

She pondered the discussion from the weekend and invited her unconscious to give her a signal to "pull up and rest" before she got adrenal fatigue. It didn't work Saturday or Sunday, but on Monday she watched her state carefully and noticed sagging shoulders, tilting head and fading attention. At this she jumped up and went for a twenty-minute walk, going hard enough to get her heart rate up and her stress down a little. The main effect was a burst of endorphins. She went right back to study and carried on until exhaustion.

The trouble here was that Lauren didn't know when enough was enough. In her journal she had written, "Some people have called me a perfectionist. Perfection? I have high standards! Or do I? What is the standard? How will I know I have studied enough? What is good enough? Am I good enough? Perfection seems to be the complete absence of a standard. I never know when I've got there."

*

Nobody saw the struggle Monique fought with alone, not even her children. Coming out of her bedroom in the morning before they got up, she was the picture of health and interested parenting. But behind the closed bedroom door, she fell apart. Dark thoughts brooded in her mind, casting an oppressive shadow across her mind, until at last fatigue and weakness took her off to sleep. Although her depression dug deep and harrowing lines under her eyes, she covered it with makeup. Apart from that, all her crying took place behind closed doors. Her mood never resulted in sleeping in, or lethargy. She felt it in her bones, softening them like a sarcoma; a sense of worthlessness, a soul-weary tiredness, a sense of loneliness and hopelessness, a restless stirring, and a constant feeling of being unsafe.

She would wake in the middle of the night in a sweat, crying, wondering if anybody would love her again. Her heart ached to be held, to be loved. Was she over the hill? Too old to attract another? She was burdened with two kids; what man would want that? These thoughts only served to make her feel guilty, because a good mother should never wish to be without her children she reasoned. She would wake early in the morning shaking, trembling for no reason, hallucinating, sensing small creatures in the room. Things moved in the shadows, only to disappear when she turned the light on. She was becoming a nervous wreck. Nobody saw the struggle because, Monique resolved, no one would hurt her again like her ex-husband had.

*

Jane took a run, showered, and sat by the fire to journal. The absolute chill of the mornings gave way to sullen, brooding, windless days, and while they were a little warmer, it still wasn't quite spring. Jane's journal had only a few simple thoughts that day. She tried remembering the last time she had run and felt an internal resistance in the training. It was on a 10 km run the previous week. She recalled that state, then located the resistance in her body, a kind of dull ache under her diaphragm. Jane instinctively imagined the ache and asked herself, "What's this feeling about?" Whilst there were no words, she intuited a reply. "I don't trust you." She didn't trust herself? Now that was curious. She didn't know what to do next. But at least it didn't involve her father! She grabbed her journal and began to have a conversation with herself. Jane A was conscious; Jane B was unconscious:

Jane A: "Okay, so you don't trust me. I must have done stuff to make you not trust me."

Jane B: "You keep overdoing it, and you're not paying attention to my signals."

Jane A: "What do you mean overdoing it? Like exercising too hard?"

Jane B: "Yeah, like last year when you nearly had a meltdown because you refused to stop for the watering stations in the Sri Chinmoy."

Jane A: "Oh yeah, I did too."

Jane B: "I try and try to get you to stop, but you don't"

Jane A: "Like how?"

Jane B: "Like the stabbing pains in your side, like the cramping in your leg, like the pain in your foot, like your sciatica."

Jane A: "Far out. I thought that was just normal and I needed to get over it, push past it."

Jane B: "Yeah that's kind of my point. I don't trust you."

Jane A: "So how can I get your trust back? How can I listen to your signal?"

Jane B: "Well, I can tell you this: you and I together are going to get much better outcomes than just you alone."

Jane A: "Well, in the absence of one single signal, I shall just be more aware all the way through training and watch for you pulling me back."

Jane B: "And some respect wouldn't hurt either. Treat me like Jane the elder, like someone you listen to, hey?"

*

On the weekend, Mark decided to take the group out and about. One of Julia Cameron's assignments involved doing new things. He was intrigued by and a bit cynical about the value of doing so until he found an article online by Raymond B. Catrell about developing fluid intelligence. Fluid intelligence gave a person the capability to see a situation they had never been in before and start generating options. Especially when you get stuck, it helps you start looking for alternatives. Rock climbers and mountaineers use it all the time. The article laid out a range of ways to generate fluid intelligence, like doing something new (a new sport like archery), trying a new exercise (like a martial art or dancing), learning a new language (or reading the dictionary), and eating food from a different culture. He figured that to make headway on some of their issues, they might benefit from implementing something out of the ordinary. Journaling, self-coaching, and listening to the unconscious had produced a range of interesting issues, but only a few self-generated solutions. Mark thought that exposure to a new set of stimuli could help bridge the impasse.

Lauren had come down on Friday night to visit and Monique's kids were off with their grandparents, so he invited them to go with him and Jane to the city. It was all very mysterious and exciting for the others. Mark headed toward the ANU. It was still early enough that the youthful, club-going set hadn't come out yet. He parked under the Nishi apartment complex and led the troupe to Močan & Green Grout, an offbeat café, for a meal. Mark opened the conversation by summarising their progress so far:

- Mark: was journaling well. He still had a deep need for approval, needed take ownership of his well-being, and find internal sources of affirmation was getting in touch with the difference between demanding and receivir affirmation. He also needed to find a safe way to stop needing others. [H didn't mention his unofficial, off-the-record desire to lose some weight].
- Jane: did journaling well in routine, but got stuck. She had father issues around creativity and routine and needed to explore her underlying belief Her body was resisting her efforts at training, but she had at least establis rapport with self and was willing to listen to the signals when running.
- Lauren: loved journaling. Her indecision about study had been resolved, she had picked the master's in coaching psychology. She hadn't identifie her secondary gain, and needed to do this, or otherwise indecision would return. She was now working on her anxiety during study, could feel fati coming, but had no signal for stopping early. [She hadn't told them abou perfectionist thoughts].
- Monique: did some infrequent journaling. At the gallery she had experie wonder at having so many options, but in the spa had struggled to find ar issue to work on. [Monique's undisclosed issue was insecurity, anxiety, a depression].

Monique winced visibly at the last point Mark made. Not because it was delivered with any malice or anger, but because it was the blunt and startling truth. She was so different in the others' eyes, but in her own eyes she was the worst of all of them. This wouldn't come out however because she didn't feel safe.

After the meal, with Mark carefully watching the time, he led them to the Palace Electric Cinema and handed them tickets he'd purchased the day before. Mark gave them their instructions. "I've selected this movie because it's not one we would normally see. It's French, with subtitles. I want you to immerse yourself in the environment and see what it does to you: your mood, your state, and your inner thoughts. I asked you each to bring your journals to write down anything that occurs to you and we can share it!"

They went in, apprehension mixing with giddy, childish excitement. They watched the movie, and they wrote, coming out afterward with tears and laughter.

The last stop for the evening was the Prosecco Bar. The luxurious décor and leather-appointed couches pointed to the high cost of the drinks, but Mark was paying so nobody minded. He invited them to each choose a "sophisticated drink." They shared learnings from the movie and some of the things they had written down in their journals.

On the way home, Lauren said with some wonder, "You guys are such a surprise—such cool parents—thanks for including me!"

*

Monday was an exciting day. Jane got to work knowing that the whole staff had been invited to the training Sean had talked to her about the other week. Coaches, sports psychologists, researchers, PhD students, admin and support staff were all welcome to attend the training with Ian Snape. Ian was the neurocoach for the Australian Tae Kwon Do team. He assisted a great number of athletes and others with obtaining peak performance. While he worked with and accepted other disciplines like sports psychology, nutrition, physiotherapy, and biomechanics, he was here to talk about state management. That seemed a little unorthodox to most of the establishment.

Jane didn't care if nobody else was there: she was ready to learn. To her surprise, about twenty others had come to the day, from the Head of Research Science down to the assistant swimming coach. She looked around her colleagues and nodded to Sean. Ian was a wiry and intense sort of fellow. Collected, confident and highly intentional, he was the master of two martial arts and had trained and led teams for deployment into the polar regions for many years.

Ian held the room and was well able to serve the learning needs of those gathered. He started out with a background to the way coaching had advanced in sports: learning routines and patterns, body movement and repetition, strength and flexibility, and was now moving into several new areas including sports psychology and understanding the importance of attention placement. In the 1980s, many Olympic teams had focused on the power of self-talk and positive affirmations. Then neuro-linguistic programming (NLP) and neurocoaching had brought a range of new tools for human performance that helped further. One of these was state management.

Ian presented a model based on several research papers, including one from his mentor, John Grinder, that showed how the state a person was in—their felt experience, emotion, feeling, energy level—was made up from three main inputs. Jane wrote some notes to understand and explain this to the group later…

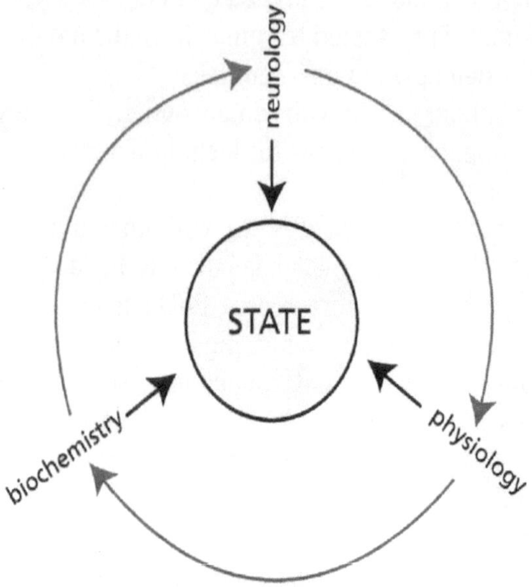

- Biochemistry is the state of our blood chemistry, hormones, neurochemis and the influence drugs and medications have on us.
- Neurology includes our entire autonomic nervous system, brain, percepti stereotypes, psychology and thinking.
- Physiology is our body, movement, energy, eating, breathing and posture

"If you want to affect state," Ian said, "you need to change one of these elements. In truth they are all deeply interconnected and have feed-forward and feedback loops, but for the sake of thinking about high performance it's useful to break them down into these separate areas."

He pointed out that modern athletes have access to a wide range of equipment and scanning machines to measure every conceivable aspect of physiological state. There are a few for neurology, but they only cover a very narrow range of aspects of psychology (like attention). Although biochemistry can be measured using blood or urine samples, they are not easily accessible for daily use. Given these factors, Ian advised that the best approach to state management for athletes would be to learn to calibrate your observations of the athlete from what they say, how they stand, and their micro-facial expressions. Jane's mind jumped ahead and she ventured a question, "Ian, given that we can help athletes with their state management, does that mean we are always aiming for a high-performance state? I mean, are we trying to be in peak state all the time?"

"Great question," he answered. "No, I don't think that's possible. The state required to get amazing sleep is different to the one required to have great sex." The audience giggled and murmured. "The state for being receptive to coaching is different to the one needed on competition day. The question to ask is, am I in the optimal state required for this activity?"

David, the head of research, put his hand up. "How do we know what state to help the athlete reach?"

"Well, it's not like you have to do a conscious process. Let me ask you, David, do you know what state you have to be in today to learn well? Now, don't tell me; you might not be able to describe it—just feel it. Can you do that?" Ian said, watching David as he closed his eyes.

"Got it," David said. "Yep, got it. I know what that is."

"Great. I invite you to adopt that state right now," Ian said.

David nodded, shifting his state and smiling.

"Now, just check for me that this state is going to serve you for the duration that you need it… " he said, and David nodded again.

"Well, there's the answer to your question. State change can be instant, and it can be done through conscious processes. In David's case, he did it through thinking about adopting a state he could visualize in his mind or experience in his body. We don't know which of the three inputs changed, but who cares? We also don't know what makes up that state: humour, anger, happiness, sexual desire… we don't know and it doesn't matter."

"The new state would then generate new neurology, biochemistry, and physiology, right?" David said. Ian assented.

"That's like the way our biathletes shift from cross-country skiing to target shooting. They're running a 200 heart rate, and drop it to 140 in twenty seconds using visualization and breathing exercises," David added by way of example.

The group worked through a couple of exercises helping them feel state change for themselves, and observed one another to calibrate state change. They had another Q&A session and Ian finished by pointing out a couple of other topics they might want to explore now they had the foundational neuroscience in place.

He told them about establishing high-performance circles and exploring flow state with athletes. But by then they had run out of time. The convener thanked everyone for coming, and made sure he had the details of the research described today, including flow state and high-performance circles.

On the way out the door, Jane collared Ian for a question. He was on his way over to the sparring matches, and invited her to walk with him across campus. She was curious about Ian's other work and asked how he applied all this.

"Listen Jane, I basically only do two things with clients. I am either helping them with state, or with outcomes. So with state they might need to identify a state, alter a state, work with their unconscious, build rapport with self and so forth. With outcomes they might need to consider more options, define one, make it clearer, consider a remedy or solution, think about why they want it, and be careful about what happens when they get it."

"Even with a high-speed sport like Tae kwon do?" she asked.

"Especially with them. We do state management during training before competitions, then on the day you might get thirty seconds for an intervention between rounds! What matters is high performance, peak state."

She was amazed. Jane returned to her office and wrote down the following notes as this fortnight's actionable items for the group:

Action list

Can you identify the state you need to be in for this activity? Are you in that state? If not, then have a go at one of the three areas:

Biochemistry. Neurochemicals, neurotoxins, hormones and chemicals in the blood affect state. These are produced in response to our environment, activity, what we eat and medicines.

- Medicines can affect cognitive performance.
- Sleep affects memory and reduced stress hormones.
- Dietary effects. You might move from a high carb diet to a high protein one. You might increase your intake of micronutrients by juicing or reduce your intake of alcohol. Watch actually notice what you eat, and then watch what its effect on you was two hours later.

Neurology. What we think affects us. Bitter/angry/resentful create a different state to thankful/grateful/happy.

- How is your self-talk?
- What sort of meaning are you attaching to events and what are they based on (stereoty heuristics and models).
- Become aware of your language, it belies your beliefs.
- You will go where are you putting your attention

Physiology. The position of the skeletal framework, the correct operation of the nerves and autonomic nervous system, the operation of the lymphatic system via movement, macro and micro muscular movements all impact or reflect the mood state.

- Correct your posture, sit or walk straight.
- How is your breathing, sleep and cleansing? Including the use of meditation.
- Facial expressions affect our state and mood.
- The speed of walking, the amount of sedentary time.

CHAPTER FIVE: FLOW STATE AND CREATIVITY

"The best moments in our lives are not the passive, receptive, relaxing times... they occur when a person's body or mind is stretched to its limits in a voluntary effort to accomplish something difficult and worthwhile. Optimal experience is thus something that we make happen."
Mihaly Csikszentmihalyi

The French-movie experience more than a week ago had really tripped something in Mark's mind. He was inclined to expand on his movie repertoire, so on Monday night he chose to watch an indie movie called *The Chef*. Jane was too tired to join him, preferring to catch up on reading and rest. As with the French movie, he fully entered the experience, letting it flow over him. The frequent use of coarse language nearly ended his experience; he wasn't a big fan of swearing. But he embraced even that, letting it push him. The movie reminded Mark about:

- The importance of using social media (which was becoming more impor in his industry),
- Getting up after having a fall,
- Listening to the right critics (that one hit close), and the kicker was,
- You are exactly where you have chosen to be.

He thought to himself, *I have chosen to be here, doing this, being paid this, stressing out about this. I am here because I placed myself here... it's not anyone else's fault. Why am I feeling miserable about work and performance? Yeah, okay, maybe I should stop relying on Art's opinion, but maybe I would also be happier somewhere else...*

His thoughts rattled on like a freight train, *I know how to make this whole feedback thing safe. Right now I am at the mercy of my overlords; they decide how to interpret my performance and they decide my financial future. My clients are always happy. My workmates are always glad to work with me. It's just Art, and frankly it's probably the culture of the company.* He continued to convince himself, *The only way to address that is by becoming an overlord, and nobody is offering me a ladder into the C-suite… I guess I could remove the guys standing between me and success.* He laughed out loud at the mental picture of taking guys out, gangster style.

But seriously, that involves, well, it involves leaving, doesn't it… starting out in my own consultancy… taking a risk. It's a risk I can afford, and a risk I like, so I guess if I mitigate risk to the best of my ability… it is also safe. Some implausible part of the thought experiment made him feel uneasy, and, just as quickly, he could hear a voice in his head say, *It's just a game, we're just playing. Like playing with the floor plans of a new house, we're not buying, we're looking. Just a game, just a game.*

He mentally drafted a list of close friends he knew in the industry, who might want to form a partnership:

- Craig. Independent, Defence background, good with IT and systems.
- Joanne. In KPMG but really sick of the big end of town, good with corpc and teams.
- Mary Ann. Loner but awesome with government, did contracting and lav
- Paul. Works in a psychology outfit: background in human performance a science.
- Monique? Defence background: facilitation, training, and HR backgroun

Monique was the dark horse of the five. Apart from the potential misunderstanding (jealousy?) from Jane because of him working with their (beautiful?) neighbour, he also didn't know the depth of Monique's facilitation background. He was willing to at least explore the alternatives. He decided to draft an email inviting all five of them to a midweek meet-up at a Mexican restaurant in the city to discuss the potential of joining forces. Some as-yet-unidentified anxiety in his chest subsided and he felt peace. Another part of him felt like he was avoiding something.

*

Lauren enjoyed her days at university going to lectures, cycling down to Glebe Point Road for a meal at the Himalayan Char Grill or Clipper cafe, visiting her friend Ming who lived in the Oaks Maestri Towers near Darling Harbour, and knuckling down to study. Today ended no differently from the rest. She made her way out of her last lecture, across the beautiful green lawns and passed the neo-Gothic, moss-stained, ivy-draped sandstone architecture of the quadrangle.

Lauren's school was at the Broadway end of campus in the Brennan McCallum building. She was grateful that the food court was directly opposite. Lauren picked up a chicken stir fry and rode back to the residences. She passed the squash courts, crossed the grassy square where ducks were chasing one another and fussing over insects. The tree-lined streets of Wesley College with their disused, brown-brick, guardian gatehouses were still bustling with foot traffic. Finally, she cut through Saint Paul's College, where everybody seemed to drive small cars like her own.

The last rays of early spring sunshine touched the red roof tiles and brown brick walls of the Women's College. The old, twenty-paned, white-sash windows exuded light from within as if to provide feeble combat to the sun, retreating from the battlefield amid a storm of rain-bearing clouds. With dinner finished and the dishes ignored, she toyed with the long black shape of the TV remote, tempted as ever to flick on some brain-numbing, time-stealing laughter. It was time for *Big Bang Theory*, one of her favourites. Then her thumb, with a mind of its own, flicked the TV on. She was aware of consciousness operating at four levels:

- There was her study work, undone at the desk, haunting the background. the time, motes of dust settled on the book on her desk, highlighted by th lamp and captured by some part of her extreme peripheral vision.
- There was the TV program running on the huge flat-screen TV in front o her, with Lauren present on the couch in front of it.
- Inside her brain there was a clock ticking a countdown to the end of the program.
- Deep within her body there was a nagging sensation, like butterflies or nervousness. It was like a tugging, a yearning hunger that grew more pai as the clock counted down and the show went on. The butterflies slowly became worms and they turned in her belly, a sickening, grinding sort of guilty movement.

The show ended and Lauren dragged herself up to the desk to study. One by one the worms extinguished and her peace returned. *I should be studying*, Lauren said to herself. Her friend Clarity had once said, "Talking to yourself is the first sign of genius." Obviously she hadn't come up with it herself; she was parroting someone. Well, maybe it was also the first sign of communicating with yourself? That reminded her of something her friend

Gyan had said. Gyan was Brahmin by birth and Western by upbringing. He was also, hands down, the smartest person on campus, but not awkward or nerdy and not a try-hard hipster either. He was full of professorial one-liners. He had once told her, "Genius is not escaping to our imagination; it is remaining fully in the world and drawing it into that imagination." So she studied.

Lauren was more aware of her state now, and the split awareness was the first of the by-products from her self-coaching experiments. She'd shared her journey with a close group of friends on campus, but very few of them took her seriously. Her generation were quite open-minded normally. They were exploring alternate spirituality, holistic medicine, and esoteric mindfulness practices and even integrative mind-body healing. Yet for some reason there was a hard resistance to Lauren's more scientific approach. It was as though they wished to simply experience and explore, but not after the fashion of experiment or accountability. Theirs was not a repeat of the sixties' "If it feels good do it"; theirs was, "If it works for you, it's okay." Lauren wanted to test everything and see, make sure it was repeatable, ask if any research had been done on it, ask what the sample size was, and it drove her friends crazy.

Well, almost all. Gyan didn't get angry. Her thoughts returned to split awareness. Often, when Lauren asked him, "What are you thinking about?" she would get no immediate reply. Eventually, after analysing what was going on for him, he would say, "At what level would you like me to answer? I am conscious of several levels of awareness and several lines of thinking proceeding at once." That would have sounded odd had she not known that he was highly self-aware, perhaps the most self-aware human being she knew. He practiced being present to people and conversations, was an excellent conversationalist and companion (probably for these reasons), not at all self-absorbed, and not stuck on his particular opinion. But she'd never expect him to lie down and give up either: he was a fierce debater too. Lauren's full attention, she now realized, had switched to Gyan and the time he had listed off seven layers of thought and awareness. She couldn't recall precisely what he said but the gist of it was:

"Lauren, at what level would you like me to answer? For many times when I share my first and second layers you grow bored… "

"Whoa, what, wait a minute: two layers?" she had said.

"Yes, for example this morning you asked me what I was thinking and I said firstly I am thinking about the layout of the campus, which is not optimised for the use of the students, being a result of historical building and growth. Second I am thinking about the locations of my exams… then you cut me off. But had you let me continue then I would have told you I had examined my exam timetable and begun to prepare my study timetable. Underneath that, or thirdly I was then thinking about my upcoming journey to India and the entire experience of being back home; underneath that I was considering the old India and my parents and arranged weddings; underneath that I was also considering the benefits of holding onto your heritage, your culture, as it gave you identity while at the same time you need to embrace your new culture and home. The strata beneath that was considering all the things I love about Australia, my new home, and how grateful I am to be here and the final layer brought me back to finances, budgeting and making sure I will be able to sustain myself after leaving home."

"Are you seriously telling me that you have seven things going on in your head right now, at the same time?" she asked, incredulous.

"Yes," he had said, "but now I am speaking to you, the strata are shifting and you are coming more into focus."

Four isn't so bad, she thought, *for a girl who's only been at it a couple of weeks!*

Lauren found that when she had a quiet house, a looming deadline to bring a little focus, a great dinner, a clear study path, silent lucidity, and the awareness of these multiple layers of consciousness, she could achieve amazing things. It was like working on speed.

After a few hours she rose to prepare (draft) herself a tisane. Lauren loved that word. To her it was a Hercule Poirot word. It reminded her of his vast Agatha Christie–created intelligence, OCD tendencies, and delicate tastes. "I think I shall have pear, honey, and mint this evening," Lauren said in her best attempt at a Belgian detective accent. Lauren had learned these past few weeks that when her belly felt like hardening steel inside, slowly cooling, slowly tightening, slowly aching, she needed to pull up for a break. She poured hot water into the pot and did a quick search on dictionary.com. "Hmm, tisane, an infusion of dried herbs, fruit, and spices used as a beverage or for medicinal effects," Lauren said to no one, and allowed it to draw and cool. The success of a good tisane, she had learned through experience, was not to let it draw too long. If it sat too long, the brew became bitter.

An idea popped into her consciousness, a living metaphor. Here was her state, working exactly like her drink, she became… well, not bitter, but… tight and unfit. The leaves and herbal contents needed to be removed, taken off the boil in order to make the drink potable. Likewise, she needed to be removed from study, taken off the hard work in order to refresh and renew. She didn't know the right amount of time, but it was less than two hours and more than half an hour. She was slowly calibrating her study to get the best outcome and keep from becoming stressed out. She had begun state management.

The main issue for which Lauren had received ribbing from her friends was the concept of secondary gain. Even though few made the connection to Dr. Phil (and Lauren didn't mind much anymore: a good idea was a good idea), they had resisted the idea that there was always something underneath a primary struggle or painful issues. They offered up all sorts of arguments about things "just being the way they are" or people having "no real control over a situation." To Lauren they now sounded like just so many excuses; people unwilling to examine their own behaviour, own it, and find out why they were doing it.

She advanced numerous case studies:

- Primary pain of abused women who stayed for secondary gain of protect and shelter;
- Drug addicts' primary gain of getting high who stayed for secondary gai employment by their dealers;
- The primary pain of being unemployed being offset by the secondary gai avoiding the taxman…

Her friends were not convinced. In the end it didn't matter. Lauren knew that her own study-till-you-collapse-in-exhaustion, sickness, and stress had been fuelled by a deeper desire to have just cause and undeniable reason to take time off. People gave themselves far too much time off in her opinion. Sickness though was excusable; everything else was lazy. Now that Lauren was working constantly on personal change, she had done some study on secondary gain and learned that it did not underlie every behaviour, good or bad. She found that it is only the behaviour we complain about, but do not change, which has underlying secondary gain.

*

Change was something Monique, by contrast, found hard. Her demons were well-known, well-hidden and kept in control. It sometimes seemed that the more she repressed and hid them, the fiercer they became. Dark thoughts seeped their way into her conscious mind, wresting with kinder, gentler thoughts, pushing them into a shadowy corner and laughing at her. While Lauren was making friends with her unconscious, Monique was terrified of hers. Dark language crept its way into her mouth, whispered in frustration or yelled when she knew she was alone. Dread terror stalked her at night, brooding thoughts of self-injury and losing life scratching at her sanity, rasping at her soul until she thought she would be destroyed.

This week had been particularly hard for her. Her ex had filed for an injunction on her custody arrangement. He only saw the kids every school holidays, and until now that had suited him just fine. He hardly fought at all when they first broke up, but now that he had met someone else, and now that they were making plans for a future, he was pushing for his rights. Monique was not an unfair woman; she knew Ryan and Rylie loved their dad, absent though he was, adulterer though he had been. What she found difficult was the fact that he was pretending to care now, and he was fighting to take those kids off her; children she had faithfully raised and self-sacrificially cared for.

In addition, work was “rightsizing” with the latest round of government budget cuts. Defence had come in for scrutiny. Ordinarily Defence was left alone, or allowed to make cuts in the long term, paring back their dreams and accepting diminished arrangements whilst the Australian equivalent of Homeland Security grew and grew and grew. Anyway, that was not her problem. She was facing the second line of cutbacks. The first round had been a series of back-room, behind-the-scenes offers for voluntary redundancy. Mainly Executive Level 1 and 2 staff had been tapped on the shoulder and some had left already. Now they were making a round of mandatory redundancies and Monique’s division was next. Stress at home and stress at work were not helping her mental battle, and it felt to her like sanity was slowly tearing apart.

Monique was not given to religious thought, but it was with marvelling wonder and impossible glimmers of hope she gaped at the synchronicity of receiving Mark’s email that afternoon. It was a bit cryptic, simply inviting her and four others to join him for dinner to discuss “a potential business opportunity.” If it meant seeing more of Mark, whom she considered to be one of her closest friends and allies, and it meant creating a path for her out of the staffing-reduction guillotine, then she was all for it. She didn’t care if

Mark put her through the mill, checked out her references, or even asked her for an investment loan… she had already decided she was in. That just left the kids and the custody battle.

Monique timed her day to make sure she saw the kids onto the bus, and welcomed them home as they got off the bus. Their school was about forty-five minutes by public transport from where she lived in Gungahlin, so they left at 8:05 a.m. and returned at 4:30 p.m. Her work arrangements were flexible enough to allow her to negotiate her own work times. It was only fifteen minutes to the Brindabella Business Park each way, twenty in traffic or construction. But today something had happened on Majura Road. Perhaps an accident, a kangaroo hitting a car, or a car hitting a bike rider. Whatever it was, and Monique never found out, she spent over an hour in the car getting home.

Being a single mum, Monique had no support network beyond Jane and Mark. Her frustration, boiling over into anger, verging on road rage, somehow produced the memory of an old Optus phone TV ad boasting 99% coverage, Australia-wide. "Ha! What's the point of a mobile phone and mobile coverage if I haven't got anyone to call?" she yelled to no one. Her kids would be off the bus by now! What would they be doing? What were Jane and Mark's movements? Should she call? That was an imposition. She could feel the small Velcro hooks of sanity in her mind begin to tear apart, ripping. Panic began to settle in, brought by an overwhelming sense of powerlessness. "Breathe, just breathe," she said out loud, and began a pattern of yoga breathing she'd learned.

Her mind settled a bit and she snatched a thought drifting past, a sliver of sanity that said, "*Text them and see if they can help.*" She wrote: one text to Jane and the other to Mark. As things worked out, Mark was still at work and Jane was home preparing dinner. Jane rang immediately, sensing the distress in Monique's terse message. She assured Monique that she would go find Ryan and Rylie and give her a progress report.

The line of vehicles before Monique snaked slowly along the tarmac path before it. Every metal joint moved over the bumps and shapes in the ground beneath it, wending slowly to the base of Mt. Majura. To her left, Mt. Ainsle obscured the setting sun. Rumour had it that the Defence Department had an installation in those mountains. She knew it wasn't true. At the base of Ainsle was the Russell Offices and across from Majura was an army training site. That was it. But the metal snake would never know the truth.

Monique's mind was frozen. From inside her brain she mechanically observed the machines moving ahead of her; breathing, quiet, simmering, counting, helpless, waiting, stuck. By the time she had made the underpass onto Horse Park Drive, Jane had called back to say her kids were not at the bus stop, and were also not at home. Punched by an invisible blow, her breath escaped her. Jane assured Monique she was looking everywhere and they were probably—*abducted, picked up by their father; stolen, dead, raped,* her mind interjected unhelpfully—still coming home. All her worst fears would be realised. Family and Community Services (FACS) would be here to investigate and take the kids off her.

At minute sixty-two, she pulled into her driveway exhausted and frantic. She ran to the house, too frightened to notice the lights were on next door. Her own house was empty, dark and cold, and after a moment of searching she resolved to go next door. Mark and Jane's house was lit up and full of laughter. To her great and tearful relief her children were playing a game with Jane on the floor. As she walked in they ran to her and spoke over the top of each other about the bus breaking down, and another bus coming, and being late, and finding Jane in the park, and coming over for muffins and milk!

Monique hugged them both, bitter tears welling from her eyes, collecting mascara and descending her cheeks to waterfall onto her black business blazer. Splashes of grey, salty relief splashed onto her yellow blouse beneath. She didn't know and she couldn't care. Deep sobs of grief forced their way up from her chest and strangled her throat, trying to get out.

From Jane's point of view Monique's grief didn't seem to match the situation. She had been through worse surely, with her divorce and the loss of everything? Wasn't this just a scheduling anomaly? *It was just a broken down piece of public transport for goodness sake.*

What Jane could not see was how this event had tapped something else inside Monique. Like a spike being driven into the ground by a mallet, cracking the earth and finding a sinkhole, today's events had opened a hole to her grief. Monique did not gather herself quickly. She was unable to even speak for a long time. Long enough for Mark to get home and be signalled silently by Jane to leave things well enough alone and go to his study.

By now the kids had taken the keys and gone home to unpack their school stuff. Mum just kept crying.

Eventually Monique calmed down. While she couldn't explain what had just happened, its very fact made her feel she owed Jane at least some kind of morsel by way of explanation. In the end she made the small admission that she struggled being alone at home; a very obvious and normal kind of lonely, as her heart yearned for male companionship: someone to protect and hold her, someone to help with ideas for parenting the kids. Presently she went home, ashamed, unrelieved, and still burdened by her worst fears.

*

Mark was in a kind of bind. It was a pretty terrible moment to tell Jane about his new business idea, and he almost thought better of it. But the thought of Monique coming over for another session, and letting his invitation to her slip before he had told Jane drove him to find the courage. They had discussed, at various times, the possibility of one or other of them starting their own business. They were financially able to handle him taking the risk.

So he walked her through his thinking, his reasons, and the way it served his need for work to be safe. She was with him all the way, right up to the moment he gave her the list of potential hires. At this point she frowned and sat down. "Mark, you have got to be kidding. Did you just see what happened to Monique? She's a nervous wreck; you can't have her on board!"

The discussion went on, long into the evening. Mark defended his original decision, saying he needed a facilitator and if her CV checked out, he would proceed. She outlined the events and her breakdown, things he'd not been privy to firsthand. He discounted them as momentary and she asked him to at least proceed with other alternatives. All things said, much remained unresolved.

*

Jane had read all the background material for the model Ian had shared on state management. Needless to say, there was a lot of science behind it, but she noticed that he hadn't mentioned the role beliefs play in driving behaviour and wondered what he knew about that. She was also very curious about the teaser he'd given on flow state at the end of the session. So she decided to contact him directly. Jane found an email address on his website and wrote asking for a chat about beliefs and flow state. Guys like him rarely answered email at all, let alone a generic one. They were usually busy with their own clients, or not in the country, but it was worth a try.

To her great delight someone from the firm answered her that afternoon and said Ian was away, but she had forwarded the correspondence and he would get back to her shortly. This was to prove a steady pattern of interaction as, over the next few months, Jane would correspond with Ian about this and one of his other passions: neurolinguistic programming (NLP).

In the end it took Ian another day to write back to her. He avoided talking about the effect of meaning and belief on state and performance, preferring instead to talk to her when he got back. In the meantime, he directed her to a book by Steven Kotler on flow state. She found it in a bookstore nearby and brought a copy of *The Rise of Superman* to read at home on the weekend. But it didn't last that long. After reading the first three chapters, Jane couldn't resist buying a copy on Audible and listened to the rest going to and from work. It was the kind of book that caused her to gasp, laugh, cry, and express absolute disbelief at what she was hearing. Jane raved about it to Mark, her workmates, and gave her hard copy to Sean in the hope of provoking some discussion.

The book searched for ways into "the zone"… a place where a person's mind becomes clear, focused, calm and zeroed in on one task. That state feels transcendent, releasing a sense of total connectedness with life, and of being high.

Kotler said, "Flow produces chemicals in the brain which are akin to those produced by drugs—nicotine, alcohol, marijuana, antidepressants and a whole cocktail of prescription drugs." Psychologists have come to call this "flow state." This is the optimal state for human performance.

Jane might be a runner, but she had never done extreme running like Ironman or marathons. It thrilled her to read about how these athletes entered flow state, moving the standards and records forward exponentially. Their incredible feats of daring and skill seemed limitless, pushing forward the boundaries of optimal human performance. She thrilled at the stories like: big-wave rider Laird Hamilton; the antics of ice-ridge snowboarder Jeremy Jones in Alaska; skateboarder Danny Way, who jumped the Great Wall of China after breaking his ankle; Dean Potter, who speed-climbed mountain faces in Patagonia; and Doug Ammond's solo kayak descent of the Grand Canyon.

Nobody had found a reliable way to access this optimal state except those dedicated extreme action-sports athletes who must flow or die. Though there was no single process, Kotler found it could be triggered by rhythm, deep meditation, and exhilaration. After establishing the Flow Genome Project, and running experiments with neuroscientists there he discovered other avenues into flow of *ecstasis* as he calls it: micro dosing psychadelic drugs (*not going to try that* she thought); deep meditation (*yep heard about that*); edgy sex (*gulp*) and team dangers were just some of them.

Jane pondered how this might apply outside the field of extreme sport and then summarized ten triggers which she felt might make this idea useful and accessible for the group at home. She wrote:

1. Intensely focus attention. Multitasking is out, single focus is in. Remove all distractions.
2. Have clear goals. Answer why first, then the how follows.
3. Get immediate feedback. In real time is best. Aim for constant improvement.
4. Balance challenge and actual skill. Find the place just beyond your current skill.
5. Maintain high consequences. Failure/high risk focus & clarify.
6. Get skin in the game. Share the risk, share the reward.
7. Work in an enriched environment. An unpredictable, novel, complex environment helps.
8. Deep embodiment is important. Physical learning is better than mental alone.
9. Don't block alternatives. Be connected. Interactions between possibilities are imperative.
10. Train yourself in pattern recognition. Exploit old techniques on new problems.

Jane got home a little earlier than Mark, switched on the computer and the coffee machine, and started to look for other information about flow state. He had showed little interest so far, concentrating instead on his coming business venture. The field of NLP seemed to refer to flow state as a "know nothing" state in which one person might follow, mimic, or copy another. The learner's unconscious programs stood available to deploy, but to learn they must not "know" anything. The learner follows, in much the same way Mark had learned from Adam on the track. John Grinder had stories of people vastly improving their performance in rock climbing, earth moving, martial arts, and driving by copying a master when in this state.

There were stories of ground breaking stunts being performed at the X Games, and then a year later nine-year-old kids were pulling off those same Guinness Book of World Records stunts. On the snow fields, the time could be as little as six months. Jane thought about that. Growing up, the most dramatic stunt at the carnival was an Evel Knievel–style bus jump. Now you could go to any event, anywhere in the country, and at least see a back somersault on a motorbike and folks thought that was a bit lame. This stunt riding was learned by copy in flow, or know-nothing state learning.

It seemed to Jane like the human spirit was indefatigable. From other fields she learned that chess players, computer programmers, recreational abseilers, swimmers, and even computer gamers have learned how to access flow state. You don't have to be an athlete or extremist, but you do have to keep practicing until your activity becomes unconscious and competent.

Jane saw that flow state was almost always the result of dogged endurance and practice which resulted in creative breakthrough. Like the first time Travis Pastrana attempted a double back somersault on a motorbike at the X Games (or Josh Sheehan doing a triple). These had taken hundreds of hours of practice—but not of the actual act—of everything leading up to it, and of the mindset. Once the time came, Pastrana "just kinda pulled it off" in the flow.

She found the story of inventor Yoshiro Nakamatsu (who has more than 3,000 patents to his name and a Nobel Prize) sitting underwater for great lengths of time, writing inspiration on a specially designed tablet. He claimed the oxygen deprivation upped his creative genius. It was probably also the risk and danger too.

Jane also read about the incredible effects of taking an afternoon nap. John Lennon would wake up in flow state (a kind of trance really) with entire songs like "Across the Universe," "#9 Dream," or "Imagine" on his lips.

The chemical signature of those experiences was all the same, and this was something she could test for at the AIS. Kotler said, "The brain produces a giant cascade of neurochemistry. You get norepinephrine, dopamine, anandamide, serotonin and endorphins. All five of these are performance-enhancing neurochemicals." That combination amplifies intellectual and cognitive performance.

Her last piece of research was for her work at the AIS on improving performance for bilateral athletes (those who use both hemispheres of the brain in competition; e.g., swimmers, runners, jumpers). She came across some very interesting games to play that worked on intra-hemispheric cooperation and required the player to operate both consciously and unconsciously at the same time. The games kept the mind busy doing one thing whilst asking the body to do another and put the player in flow. The best gains had been made by biathlon (ski/shoot), triathlon (swim/cycle/run) and quadrathlon (swim/kayak/cycle/run) players. Jane figured the lessons learned were equally applicable to her athletes and also to her friends!

*

Mark got home a bit late. He was trying to formulate his own plans entirely outside of flow state and not having much success. He seemed grumpy, and Jane by contrast was bursting with enthusiasm to discuss flow state.

"I don't suppose you've been able to flow state dinner?" he said, somewhat gruffly.

“Hmm, nope. I guess that’s the side effect of flow. Single-mindedness for the task at hand. Wanna get take-out?” She smiled warmly, nonplussed. While dinner was coming, she wrote out the following list for the group. She would explain it to them on the weekend they were due to meet.

Action list

- Select one area you'd like to master or grow and develop. Go to: https://www.flowgenomeproject.com/training
- Allocate specific time each day, even if it's only five minutes, to that task.
- Download a brain training application like Lumosity or Cognifit.
- Start playing the games and notice when there is a switch from struggling to doing a gar well.
- Watch for moments when your tasks become fluid, then from fluid to flow state.
- Get some Butcher's paper and a pen. Prepare the Alphabet Game and practise it: http://www.neurocochingaustralia.com/resources/neurocoaching/alphabet-instructions.p

Jane added a few items that she felt had been missed from the previous week, seeing as her list on flow state had been so long:

- Eat somewhere new, or try a new cuisine.
- Go to a cinema, watch a movie or hire a film you would not otherwise watch.
- Read a book from a genre you normally would not try.
- Work with your other hand. If you're right handed, brush your teeth with the left (or vice \
- Take a walk on the wild side. Take your shoes off and walk on the cobblestones and rou areas.
- Juggle, play ping pong or take up bowling to advance your hand-eye co-ordination.

CHAPTER SIX: BUILDING A HIGH-PERFORMANCE STATE

"High performance belongs to those who can use strategies to unconsciously and precisely assimilate the differences that really make the difference between the genius and an average performer."
John Grinder

The weekend of their meeting rolled in suddenly and the events of the week were quickly forgotten. Mark had gone to watch the fog as it cleared the shores of "Lake" George. In twenty years, this ephemeral sheet of water never seemed to heave itself aboveground. Well, maybe once it had. This morning Mark mused about how the lake epitomized issues in people's lives, lurking beneath the ground, whispering of its existence, but not supporting life or change. Malignant, malodorous and marking the ground of our lives, issues always came forth when there was enough rain from above.

He sat on his haunches, his mind a predator pondering two very odd experiences. Yesterday Mark had been sent urgently to the shops by Jane with a shopping list. The last item of the list was "Spicy Red Sauce" and he had stood in the aisle where the sauces were. He'd gone from top to bottom and left to right but couldn't find it. Then Mark asked a shop assistant to help and neither of them could find it. So, he stood right back against the opposite shelves and said to himself, *Okay unconscious, we've walked down these aisles a hundred times before. Where is it?* In the moments following, his feet shuffled left three times and he raised his right pointer finger and there it was! One single bottle on the shelf, crouching back in the shadows, willing itself to remain unfound. His conscious mind might only be able to ingest four (plus or minus two) bits of information per second, but his unconscious was pulling mountains of information into its library! Only Mark had never before attempted to access the library, and it turned out he owned a key—and the key worked!

The second curious incident was a dream he'd had last night in which he was hunting full stops. Yes, full stops. *What on earth?...* he thought, shaking his head. Hunting three full stops to be precise, and that was crazy. It haunted him, like a task undone: like an assignment given by an undercover agent.

Mark couldn't let it go. All he could think of as he stared at the retreating mist was that he had been editing a proposal for work last night, and figured it was something to do with that.

Once the first wave of cars had fled Canberra for the vineyards and the coast, Mark headed home with as much speed as caution and liberty would allow. His car nudged into the driveway just as Monique and her kids crossed it to come inside. It was brunch time. Before things could get underway, Mark rushed unapologetically to his laptop and fired up the offending document. Starting at the beginning, he painstakingly went through the fifteen-page document he had finished last night. Sure enough, he found three missing full stops, each one located within a quotation. This was remarkable, simply remarkable, and he told everyone so. Monique called him Sherlock Holmes. Jane said that he'd always been intelligent like that but as far as Mark could recall he'd never done anything even remotely like this before.

Though the spa beckoned, they ate inside around the large oak table, the smell of freshly brewed coffee lingering in the air. Lauren Skyped in again, this time mirrored off the iPad onto the TV in the dining room. It was Monique's turn to bring the food.

In the spirit of trying new things and expanding their horizons, she had prepared a range of dishes from her youth. Tuna in béchamel sauce, stuffed into a crusty loaf; Mauritian Chinese egg foo yung, which she had made as an omelette; gateau piment, a kind of Indian dal fritter; and avocado smoothie. Monique's children had eaten all of this before, so they had no hesitation hoeing in. The three adults chatted to Lauren as they grazed and Monique answered curious questions about the food.

They shared their key learnings from the Palace Electric Theatre. This was their first catch-up since the French film and dining out two weeks previous. It already seemed like an age. Mark shared his learnings from the second film, *The Chef*, especially the revelation that he was where he had chosen to be (and perhaps they all were). Lauren told them of her learning around how every behaviour we complain about but continue to tolerate is fuelled by a secondary gain. This was something they had heard before but it was good to be reminded. She also shared her definition of perfection: the complete lack of a standard.

Jane dragged them even further back in their journey and asked about how they had done at managing their state. She reminded them about the biochemistry, neurology, and physiology model.

Prompted by what had happened after her kids' bus had broken down (and so had she), and aware that Lauren might not know, Monique surprised them all by sharing the backstory to her breakdown. She waited until Ryan and Rylie were out of earshot, watching telly in the other room, then took them back to her drive home, and being stuck in the snaking traffic. "I became quite hysterical; it felt like I was losing control. I calmed down, only briefly, by practicing a breathing method I learned in yoga. That was a physiological intervention." Everyone leant in, silently approving of her depth of vulnerability. She smiled. But she went no further.

Mark went next. "Well, I've had two exchanges with Art recently, and each time I made sure I walked down the corridor to his office tall and straight. Actually, this might sound funny, but I read an article about how raising your hands and smiling can really affect your state, so I did this right at his closed door! I took a few deep breaths and smiled like a Cheshire cat, then went in with a great state. I guess that's all physiological too."

"That's funny, Mark; what if someone had seen you!" Monique said breathily. "I'd go and do it in the bathroom!"

Jane went next. "I've been working on my internal beliefs. I think beliefs alter behaviour, so I've been looking at those. I haven't got far but I reckon my hang-ups about creativity, journaling, and flow are all bound up in my beliefs about them, formed by my relationship with my dad. More later. In addition, I've been working on my self-talk in the car going to work. There's this whole status fight in the research department and it slams my self-esteem. So I've been giving myself a pep talk about who I am and what I've done and I do feel better. I guess that's a neurological intervention."

Lauren finished the round by talking about her state management during study, listening to her state: the butterflies and worms in her tummy when she's doing the wrong thing, and the cold-steely feeling when it's been too long at work. Then she told them about her tisane revelation, not staying in study too long and becoming bitter. Everyone applauded Lauren, knowing her struggle with this. This promoted her to continue and tell them about her four layers of awareness and the conversation with Gyan (who had seven).

Unwittingly this led Lauren to raise the spectre of what might be lurking in the unconscious, which was rather too close to home for Monique, who winced physically and hunched her shoulders in reaction.

*

"Freud says the Id is animalistic, base, and socially unacceptable," Lauren said. "My friend Gyan says we carry a lower instinct, a sinful nature… and I know that's there. Psychologist Carl Jung called it the shadow. This has caused me to kind of question just how wise it is to trust our unconscious… you know, the signalling stuff, Dad? Isn't the unconscious potentially 'bad', and if it is, how can you trust everything it says?"

Jane was the one to answer. "I think Freud's model was right, but his interpretation was off. There's so much evidence now for the unconscious, but it isn't the monster he made it out to be. The unconscious is you, and it loves you, and it's protecting you. Tolle said its intelligence is directed primarily at survival. Gyan's right, we do have a propensity toward evil; you only have to visit a jail to see the truth of that, but I don't think of the unconscious in those terms. Those feelings might not always be the most effective way of dealing with things, they might be old or childish responses. They might even be responses you learned when you were little. They probably served you really well then, but are not helpful anymore."

Mark continued, "The key question is whether your conscious (or unconscious) desires are resourceful or unresourceful (is that the same as sinful?). Will this response get what you want?"

"So you are saying the answer is simply to question everything? Test it, see if it's resourceful?" Lauren asked.

"Well yeah, but even more importantly, you should be having a conversation with your unconscious! Build rapport with yourself and work together, like I was trying to do on that track day," Mark said.

Lauren seemed satisfied with that. She was still a little sceptical, but okay to go play with it. Once they had cleared their learnings around state management, Mark decided to get in before Jane gave them a rundown on what she had learned about flow state. He told them about his research on creativity fatigue and his lessons about limiting their decision fatigue (the way the Sydney Racing School did for their students). He sent them all a link to an article he had stumbled across by James Clear, another coach Monique had learned the coaching model from: https://jamesclear.com/willpower-decision-fatigue

Jane finally jumped in and took the floor. She summarised her learnings from reading *The Rise of Superman*. Her enthusiasm was both obvious and infectious and they buzzed when she showed them a YouTube video of Danny Way jumping the Great Wall of China. Then she brought out the to-do list she had developed around flow state and gave them a week to go and work on it. They started immediately.

Monique replenished the coffee, refreshed the food dishes, and reset the table while they read reviews of, and downloaded various brain-training applications onto their phones. They downloaded the Alphabet game and discovered that there were a range of other New Code games (so called by the NLP field to distinguish them from older attempts), like Colours and the Ball game. Well into the afternoon, the company disbanded wired and excited.

*

The warm afternoon spring air drifted over the hills behind Gungahlin, breathing out the scent of pasture and life. Families played in the parkland, middle-aged fathers flew quadcopters while their dogs and children chased one another. Ducks cared less for flying and more for swimming. Spring was here.

Mark and Jane opted for a bicycle ride to Black Mountain and afternoon tea at the Botanical Gardens.

Monique would have joined them, hungry for company, but she knew that might look desperate. She chose instead to take the kids to the Stromlo Forest Park to watch the cross-country mountain downhill practice. Monique had recently gotten into amateur photography and had bought herself a mid-level DSLR camera and three lenses. It was a good start. Two workshops, some online training, and a Flickr account made her feel like she could explore and have fun. Photographing action on a mountain trail turned out to be harder than she expected and the kids got bored quickly. A gentle melancholy touched Monique's soul as she followed the winding road back to Belconnen and home. She had no one to share this with and no one to argue with over parenting decisions. As quickly as that, she decided to raise a profile on a few dating sites and find someone. Or at least date a few times. She could at least go out. Even once. Maybe.

*

Monday rose a splendid day, except for the traffic. To Mark it seemed like a crapshoot. Some days the roundabout at Barton Highway flowed beautifully and some days it was blocked like a sewer. Today was the latter and his patience was wearing thin. "Time to practice state management, I think," Mark said to himself. Biochemistry was out. He'd already eaten and slept and he wasn't going to grab a beer or eat sherbet either. Physiology was out; he couldn't get out of the car to stretch and breathing exercises were not going to help his stress much. It wasn't his thing. Neurology was of limited use at such short notice. Reframing his situation as an opportunity to build his business plan seemed difficult to reach without a notepad. Self-talk around being a good person, or a more patient person took weeks, not minutes. "Well, if I can't push and pull those elements… what can I do?" He pondered for a while.

Then Mark remembered something Jane had told him from the seminar Ian did, about jumping to state. Athletes can find the state they need simply by focusing on that state. If the athlete could just think of the state—without a name; just a feeling—then they could get into that state again. "If you can imagine the state you'd need to be in, then you can go there?" Mark had asked Jane. She had replied that of course you could. Her boss, David, had in that seminar. Ian had them think of the state they'd need to be in to learn at a seminar and another for a university lecture. Two, three, or four states could be merged simply by thinking of them at the same time. Jane had told Mark how easy that was.

Come to think of it, immediate state change happened all the time. He had entered this car in a great mood, and now he was in a terrible state. He recalled times when he was feeling amorous and climbed into bed, only to have Jane start offloading about her day, her emotional upheaval, and trouble with her boss. By the time she was finished Jane was raring to go, and Mark just wanted to hurt himself. It was a state killer for him, but sharing was a state maker for her. So states were unique and highly idiosyncratic to the individual.

The traffic inched forward slowly and his hope rose a little. He glanced at his wristwatch. Time was ticking. Okay, time for a self-experiment. Mark thought of the last time he was relaxed, carefree, and happy: slow heart rate, low stress, no troubles. It was on the weekend, watching the fog clear from Lake George. He'd never been one for yoga or relaxation techniques, but that morning had been… almost spiritual, really contemplative and restful. So he started to think of that state, willing it to return. It began to, but it was weak, so he thought of another time when he had been driving his car (he loved this car) along a back road in the countryside: sun on his face, stereo playing his favourite music. Thankfully his car was parked in the traffic jam at that moment because he had closed his eyes, fully experiencing that state again. The experiment was… tremendous! Mark felt both states merge and he was absolutely inviolate to the traffic now.

As if yielding to his state, the traffic began to inch forward again, clearing ahead of him. Mark determined to maintain this state all the way to work. He wondered if he could create a way of holding it, or helping someone else in the same way. He wound his way around State Circle (the irony of the name wasn't lost on him), the beauty of Parliament House rising gracefully on his right.

By the time he had pulled into a car park, quite distant from his normal position, and grabbed his work gear, the state was wearing off. But a pause, a quick recall, and it was back. He noticed that he didn't even care that Ashley was parked in his designated spot. He let it slide as easily as forgiving Lauren when she made a spelling mistake. It was nothing to him right now.

Going to his desk Mark searched on the Internet for "state management" and got a bunch of programming, IT, health care, and hypnotherapy stuff. He searched for "high-performance states" and found a treasure trove of information from people in the "neurolinguistics" field. Whatever that was, he didn't have time to learn. Mark just wanted a way of sharing his learning from today's commute with an executive client he had to go visit after lunch. He finally hit the jackpot when he came across Circles of Excellence, designed by John Grinder to assist clients develop high-performance states. Mark read all he could, borrowed a "script" on how to run it, then headed off to visit the client.

*

Mark's client, John, was a clinical psychologist. His work sometimes involved corporate meetings and negotiations, some of which involved highly confrontational conversations. The problem was that under pressure, John tended to stutter, clam up, sweat profusely, and sometimes become physically ill. John had engaged Mark months ago to help get through his difficulty doing presentations and hard or confronting conversations. Mark had already spoken to him about having fierce conversations (Susan Scott's idea), holding stage presence (à la Olivia Fox-Cabane), and clearly preparing his presentation (per Carmine Gallo). This time Mark intended to help John manage his state more effectively. In Mark's mind, he could see the process.

Step one would be to create a state of "being able to handle confrontation", just like he had created a state for calmness in the car this morning. Once there, step two would be to help John make further physical, mental, and biochemical changes to cascade back down and help him maintain higher performance.

Arriving at the building where John worked, Mark parked underground and bounded up the ramp. Going through the ground-level atrium, he waved at the friendly reception staff and ascended the glass and steel staircase. The foyer of John's company chambers was to his right and there John greeted him eagerly, hoping that the exchange today would be effective. John was a ruthless businessman, who had fired far more people than he'd kept, and Mark was one such survivor. Mark was still around because his advice actually worked.

Mark realized that step one was the high-risk part of his plan. Mark's mind worked on how to build a bridge to the "circle work" he wanted to do. He went over their past lessons and asked John what he had learned. After that, a little sheepishly, he said, "Do you mind if we play a bit of a game?"

"No, go ahead. I trust you!" John said enthusiastically.

"Do you want to do this sitting down, standing, in your head or what?" Mark asked.

John indicated he preferred standing.

"All right, well, what we are going to do now isn't something you can use on the spot, or fire off under pressure, though I suppose we could get there with some practice. What you will learn today is something you will do before the meeting, at the door, in preparation. We're working on state, on how you feel when you're under pressure, all right?" Mark asked, raising one eyebrow.

"All right," John agreed. "I'm going to use this before the meeting, before the confrontation."

"Yes, awesome, yes… " Mark agreed.

Mark asked John to imagine a circle on the ground in front of him. "Okay, John, so now recall a past experience where you had great rapport and good conversational state." Mark instructed him. Once John had done that, Mark pointed to the ground and said, "When you step into that circle, I want you to download that state and experience it now. Okay?" John nodded, then stepped into the circle and the state. Mark then instructed, "Okay, stay there and really experience it: sights, sounds, feelings, memories." John nodded. "Now turn up the volume, the intensity of it… and… step out of the circle." The chatted for a bit then Mark asked John to think of another time he had great rapport and was confident. "It could be anything at all, personal or corporate." John nodded. Mark had him step back into the same circle.

"Add that in right now, along with anything else you need, any resource that will make this awesome and perfect: feelings, insights, sensations, beliefs, information, visual images, cues, or metaphors as well." John nodded.

"Right, step out of the circle… and tell me what you're having for lunch," Mark said, and John laughed. After a brief pause, they continued. "We've broken out of that state so we can test it. Let's try it out again now. Step back into that same circle and fire it off," Mark said, growing more confident with the process. John's performance state was heightened. The two of them repeated this a few more times until John was sure the state was "all there" and then Mark tested John's ability to move the circle by doing the exercise in another room. Finally, they tested its potential application to a scenario in the near future; namely, the upcoming meeting where John knew there would be a confrontation. John imagined the confrontation and, just before his stress level peaked, Mark invited him to step into the circle. To John's surprise, the stress dissolved. He was amazed at his own ability to make that happen simply by creating state changes.

"What's this process, this result based on?" John asked, incredulous.

"The natural human ability to anchor a state to an input like smell or sight. We're just doing it on purpose. You and I change state all the time, but now we're connecting it to a circle, instead of, say, a song or a smell."

Once John had mastered accessing his desired state, they role-played confrontational conversations and John's confidence continued to grow. It was time for step two. Mark walked John through the three-inputs model he had learned: physiology, neurology, and biochemistry. They identified further strategies for changing his mood quickly and easily—by recalling fond memories, for example, or by gently applying pressure at the spot where his wrist formed a crease with his hand (an acupressure technique that helps relieve anxiety and tension)—or by breathing slowly, controlling the flow of speech, and standing tall.

Their time was now a little more than spent and Mark had to leave promptly to get back to the office. They said goodbye and Mark waited eagerly for the results.

*

The next day, John was able to take his new high-performance state to work with him. There he stepped into it and handled the confrontation beautifully, perhaps for the first time in his life. It changed his confidence forever. John now had a designer state and a corresponding set of actions (triggers) to access it. The more he practiced, the more routine this reaction to stress became, running like an automated program.

*

The group had allocated four different brain-training applications and three different New Code games to one another. Lauren was working with *Lumosity*, which seemed to be an all-purpose brain game app that measured speed of reaction time, memory (instant and short term), attention (single and multifocus), flexibility of thinking, and problem-solving. Lauren was enjoying it and found that, especially during the speed games, she could find flow after a few turns. She was also allocated the Alphabet game to create a high-performance flow state and, while at first she failed horribly, by practising just ten minutes a day she mastered all three levels by week's end and snapped into flow state rapidly. She noticed that when flow didn't happen, she really sucked at it.

Lauren shared her journey with Gyan, who lived off campus with his family in Newtown. He rode to his lectures and sometimes invited her back to Newtown either to eat with the family (she liked Indian food) or at one of the local restaurants. Truth be told, she really liked Gyan, but figured that given his heritage, his future relationships would be all sorted out for him. Despite being a forward-thinking, twenty-first-century, urbane guy, he was also Brahmin and stuck with what he had. As proof of this, Gyan was headed back to India to visit the extended family.

Gyan was booked to leave the following week. He'd miss some lectures, but Lauren was sure his grades wouldn't suffer one iota. An iota incidentally is a very small amount, a fraction, a tiny portion, and the ninth letter of the Greek alphabet. He had told her that! They'd been discussing the merits of reading fiction, which to her seemed like an absolute waste of time and energy. He had argued that fiction was often the very best mode of communicating truth. To illustrate he mentioned the parables of Christ, the teaching allegories of Buddha, Aesop's fables, and children's fairy tales.

He challenged her to read at least one book before he got back, and she took up the challenge by choosing the book he'd just finished, *The Rosie Project*. The result was… profound. She was shocked at the effect the book had on her. Gyan's conclusion had been, "The aim is not to get lost in a book, but to find yourself in it." He really identified with Professor Tillman, the main character who had Asperger's.

*

Monique was allocated the brain app *Elevate*, which seemed to be much more of an academic game, more suited to Lauren than to her. It ran her through various English-, maths- and science-related puzzles. She was also allocated the Colours game and found she could make the intermediate level okay, but plateaued. She never accessed what she would term "flow" state or the zone. This was probably because in the background Monique's unconscious was trying to find a way to get her to work on the cavernous darkness that was enveloping her soul. In her conscious mind, this manifested as a desire to find a better state for parenting.

It occurred to her that when she was angry, her reward-punishment system became more punitive. When she was depressed, she became more permissive and passive. So, without the insights Mark had gained on Circles of Excellence, Monique simply asked herself, "Is this state working for me?" It wasn't. "Then what do I need for good parenting?" For her, this began with mindfulness: practising being more present and emotionally accessible to her kids. She became more present, but was still pushed around by their reactions and behaviour. She tried breathing exercises from yoga and closing her eyes. This posed a new problem; she began to really go into herself then and was no longer "there" for her kids. It was nice, but countereffective.

*

Jane had been allocated the *CogniFit* (brain training) application. She had never played this style of game before, games like whack-a-mole, mahjong, balancing, and movement tracking, and audio-visual matching games. Initially they were a struggle, but as the week wore on she grasped them more deeply, and she was so satisfied she ended up buying the full version.

Jane and Mark had together been allocated the Balls game and spent ten minutes a day tossing a juggling ball back and forth while doing various cognitive skills. It was a lot of fun, and Mark turned out to be better than Jane in switching off the thinking and getting into flow.

At work, Jane had begun doing EEG observations on her athletes. This was not an area traditionally part of biomechanics or performance observation, but Jane was curious about flow state. She had cyclists, runners, football players (not part of the AIS, but there because of a research grant), and two biathletes. Jane was asking, "What state do you need for high performance? When you're in flow state, what manifests?" The AIS had recently purchased some wonderful helmets that could do the EEG on moving athletes. Jane's findings were consistent with other research.

It seemed that when an athlete expressed some sense of flow, of unconscious competence, of their perspective opening up and their performance skyrocketing, the EEG reflected a baseline alpha pattern interposed by a spike of gamma activity. When she had to explain that later to Mark in layman's terms she said, "Their brains were simultaneously at rest, relaxed, and lucid, while also bringing together disparate thoughts and problem-solving. All at lightning speed." At least she knew what flow state was now!

*

Mark was allocated the *Fit Brains Trainer* app. He was blown away by the 400 unique games and puzzles which seemed to be aimed at stretching and improving mental agility (although he was also frustrated by the brevity of the instructions). Throughout the week Mark made good progress through the sessions, which got harder as he improved. He also enjoyed playing Balls with Jane and was so good at eye-hand coordination he started trying to juggle the ball set he bought to play the game. By week's end, he could take his attention off the balls and get into a kind of flow state to juggle. He noticed that as soon as he started trying, or working, the state failed and the juggling balls began to hit the ground.

*

On Wednesday Mark brought the group of potential partners in his new business together for a meeting in the city. He had chosen the Beach Burrito Company. The shop was resplendent with sugar skull artwork done by some Willy Wonka who celebrated the Mexican Festival of the Dead in fluoro-colour, psycho-religious, heavy-metal art. Around the table were Craig, Joanne, Mary Ann, Paul, and Monique.

None of them knew one another previously, which would prove a difficult hurdle to overcome. The group were all quite surprised by the conversation instigated by Mark, more surprised by his decisiveness and apparent risk-taking than the business idea itself. Mark proposed making a new company that was not just about consulting, but more about human performance: organisational design, change management, business psychology, group facilitation, coaching, and consulting. He gave them an idea of the direction, the potential markets, and the way the team might work. They asked about income protection, profit sharing and projects. Most of them gave a noncommittal ascent to Mark and would play a wait-and-see game. For example, Mary Ann wanted to hedge her bets and stay employed where she was presently, offering to contract from time to time. Mark wasn't surprised, and he also wasn't affected. Of course they needed to see some real contracts, some actual work.

Driving home from dinner with Monique, they had time to discuss the future. She was effusive about the potential. He listened, heartened, and a little giddy to be getting her on board. He also thought about what was going to happen to Dave from work. Mentally he added Dave to the list of potential hires.

*

While they were out, Jane's dad had called to say he was coming for a visit and Mark found Jane in a rather miserable state when he got home. Jane's dad was hardly what one would call an exemplary figure. He may have been a creative genius, but he was prone to bouts of depression and driven to days of madness. That madness included high-risk behaviour like gambling, with its commensurate level of debt, doubt, and shadowy dealings. This had often led to loans being given and empty apologies rendered. Jane did not like the prospects of him "coming over."

Given that Jane didn't really feel like talking, Mark decided against telling her about the outcomes of his meeting, choosing instead to draft a to-do list on building a Circle of Excellence, which he emailed to Lauren, Jane, and Monique before turning in for the night.

Action list

Pick an area where having a better state would be useful.

- Build a Circle of Excellence for that state.
- Add in all the resources you need.
- Check that it is transportable.
- Utilise additional state management techniques.
- If you haven't already done so, download brain training app.
- If you have not already done so, play a New Code Game.

CHAPTER SEVEN: GOAL SETTING AND ATTENTION

"We spend a considerable amount of our time engrossed in following deceptive brain messages until we begin to see them for what they are and value our true emotions and needs."
Jeffrey M. Schwartz

The cold, white grip of winter was steadily pried loose by the sprightly green fingers of spring. The barren trees were starting to bud, the brown garden beds pushed forth the tips of flower bulbs and the air, though still cold, warmed through the day. Mark and Jane had taken their first swim of the season and on their regular bike rides they were being joined by an increasing flow of fellow peddlers.

Spring had a way of lifting the spirits, but for Jane it only lasted so long before the impending doom of her father's visit loomed over her like the shadow of a grave headstone. He certainly knew how to work the system. He came a day early, catching her off guard. Jane was coming into the driveway, thinking about her workday, when she looked up and saw him sitting on the front stairs. Jane loved her family, including her father, but seeing him brought a mixture of warmth and cold, love and resentment. Like the bitter aftertaste of a good coffee, she enjoyed his creative rush but despised the effect he had on her.

"Hey Dad," she began weakly, "you're early."

"Hey honey, of course I'm early! I couldn't wait to come visit," he replied, reaching out to hug her. She tensed up, unconsciously pulling back at the same time as opening her arms for the hug. He stood in his suit and waistcoat, looking for all the world like an exotic entrepreneur, but she could tell from the dark lines under his eyes and the shake in his hand that things were not going in the right direction for him just now.

They proceeded inside the house, his eyes darting around the walls, examining the artwork; evaluating the throw rug, the piano, the quality of the interior decorating. Though he might have been short on cash, he was rich in appreciation for their fine art. Jane thought he bordered on being an art snob. After all, wasn't art a matter of personal taste and societal popularity? Picasso and Pollack were both celebrated in their time; Gauguin and van Gogh died as paupers.

She showed him to his unmade room (she'd intended to do that tonight), apologizing for the state since Lauren had left it. She excused herself, went to her bedroom to get changed, and closed the door behind her, breathing heavily. How did he get to have so much control and influence on her state? She changed into casuals and paused for a moment to collect herself.

Dad was helping himself to a drink in the kitchen when she came out to ask, "Dad, how long are you staying for?"

"If it's okay with you, I'd like to stay for a while… " he replied.

A while? How long is a while? She thought of having lunch one day in a restaurant when the waitress had said, "There'll be a bit of a delay on your order, we're really busy right now." What was supposed to have been a helpful comment turned out to be a major frustration. Jane thought "bit of a delay" meant ten to fifteen minutes. The waitress meant forty-five at least.

"So, what do you think a while is, Dad?" she asked, trying to frame his stay with proper expectations.

"A week, ten days, or something," he said noncommittally.

"Dad, a week and ten days and 'or something' are three completely different things," Jane said, beginning to become exasperated.

He shrugged.

Framing had an amazing effect on state. She recalled a time when she was walking with Mark and Lauren on the beach. He had said, "Let's go for a bit of a walk; it's not far." They had headed off down the beach and pretty soon little Lauren started to complain. Ten minutes later Jane started to complain and Mark, exasperated by them both, said, "Oh, for goodness sake, it was always going to take half an hour to get to the end of the beach and half an hour back! I told you it wasn't far!"

In her mind, Jane decided to frame her father's visit as two weeks, thus pacing herself for a longer stay. That way, if he left earlier she'd be pleased. She made a mental note to tell Mark when he got home. After that, the evening went smoothly with Mark home, dinner made, some light chitchat, and no confrontation.

That is, until Jane's father, who employed a keen sense of observation, decided to remark on her behaviour. "Jane darling, you're fun to watch; you haven't changed a bit. I love the way you prepared the salad tonight, all those little julienne vegetables lined up by colour. And the way you pack the dishwasher, all the spoons lined up, all the forks together… "

Without even thinking, Jane defended herself, unaware of Mark's nonverbal signals to avoid his purposeful prevarication. "Dad, how else will I be able to balance the ingredients? Every meal has a recipe, weights, and quantities… and the dishwasher is most efficient when the cutlery is put in correctly, and the bowls are lined up!"

Dad had jumped up out of his chair and, careening into the kitchen, threw open the cupboard to discover the contents all labelled in opaque Tupperware containers, neatly stacked and everything lined up. "Yes, darling, you're right! The cupboard is the same too," he cajoled.

She missed the ribbing, taking it for praise. "Darn right! Now you're talking. You'll find the bedrooms, the hall cupboard, and the garage are the same!" Jane said, elated.

"Yes, yes," Dad said slowly, rubbing his chin thoughtfully. Mark could see it coming; he'd seen it dozens of times before, "and these artists, Monet, Dubois and Renoir… you have lovely prints of theirs. I see they're neatly framed and hung, but, oh dear… something's wrong. Monet seems to think the world is made of dots. Dubois paints with a certain… liberty of interpretation, don't you think? And Renoir, oh dear, hmm, very impressionist, yet you seem to like them all?"

Jane looked across at her hallway of prints, deflated. "Art and science are not the same thing and you know it! Packing a cupboard or a dishwasher is a science, painting and drawing cannot be compared, come on… Renoir? Really?"

"Yet here you are making food using a recipe—science being applied to art! Cooking by the best chefs is done from the heart, from the heart, my dear, not the head," he said buoyantly. He loved this game.

The discussion ended simply, with Jane saying "arghhh" and storming off to the bedroom. Mark knew better than to follow her. He stacked the dishwasher, her way, and turned on the TV. Jane realized tonight that she needed her father's approval, and when she didn't get it she reacted with rejection and despondence. Tonight, though, something else also happened. Something snapped inside, and she rejected him; his opinion, and his attitude. *Do I need his approval? Well yes I did, but no, not anymore. I'd like his approval, I'd prefer we get along, but you know what?… If he doesn't give it, if he behaves like a pork chop, well… that's his problem.*

Eventually Mark came to bed, and she was busting to tell him about her revelation. She explained that when she is needy, she becomes vulnerable to others' behaviour and opinion. When she wants or has a preference, she can laugh when it doesn't happen the way she thought. This somehow gave her great relief about her need for routine, structure, pattern, because those things could never reject her, or give her approval. He had a preference for art and mess, and she for order and science. They were just preferences and everyone had those. It wasn't life and death. Now she could own it, not be ashamed of it. Need. Want. Prefer. It made all the difference.

*

With Gyan overseas, Lauren found herself leaning on Clarity and Ming for company. She had suggested they start a book club. They were both shocked at the suggestion, feeling pressed for time already. Lauren was incredulous because she studied harder than either of them (though perhaps less than Gyan). They found time for drinking and swimming down the beach and seeing their boyfriends… but not reading? To her mind they were making choices, but they complained like they had no choice, no time.

She tucked into *The Rosie Effect* by herself and laughed and cried at how similar Professor Don Tillman's behaviour was to Gyan's. "Find yourself in the book," Gyan had said. Of all the characters there, she was drawn to Rosie, but began to find herself challenged. Rosie was far too free, boundary pushing and nonchalant for Lauren. Rosie knew how to challenge Tillman; did Lauren know how to challenge Gyan?

But Rosie wouldn't leave her alone. Like a scene from *Lizzie McGuire*, with a cartoon version of herself rising up from the page to discuss a matter with Lauren, Rosie now became a feature of her conscience. Lauren sat down to study and the imaginary Rosie/Lizzie/cartoon sat on the end of her desk, saying, "You know your current-state management strategy only works as a warning against burnout? What about helping you last longer?" It was a thought she'd had briefly before, obviously. Lauren considered this for a moment, pondering "extenders" to a good mood. A good playlist of her favourite music would be a start. "How about an incense stick or something?" the cartoon suggested. *Oh, come off it!* she thought. Clearly Rosie didn't know her very well. "Come on, you love those oil candles at Ming's place!" *Darn it, she's right.* Lauren added regular tisanes into her "extenders" list and got down to work.

*

At work, Monique had a growing sense of malaise. Knowing Mark's offer was sitting out there waiting, and knowing the stirring she had in her heart to help him with it, work became more bleak. At home, Monique had made small progress on her parenting state and none on her internal world. It had felt good to talk to Jane that night about her meltdown, but circumstances had not opened up another opportunity. In loneliness and making good on her self-promise, she went to the computer and typed in "dating apps" on the search engine. Up came a dizzying array of options: *Tinder, eHarmony, Bumble, Zoosk, RSVP, Be2… Where do I start?* she mentally asked herself.

Without thinking, she drifted next door to ask Jane, who wasn't home. She asked Jane's dad, who hadn't used dating sites at all, but certainly took greater than normal interest in her. An awkward silence hung between them. Neither of them knowing what to do, she smiled and left. Without advice, Monique decided on downloading Tinder. She found making a profile easy, even taking a selfie wearing her nightdress. She found a selection of people who lived within her area and did the "like-then-talk" process. If the photos were to be believed, there were plenty of good-looking guys to be met.

Maybe Monique was a bit too desperate, or maybe Tinder was designed for something else, but the first five guys she chatted to came on way too strong. She ditched it and tried Bumble, which seemed oriented toward having the girl chase the guy. She was down with that… and she decided to say yes to one invitation to have a date which proved to be terrible. It was probably not the website's fault… she hadn't carefully worded her biography and she hadn't vetted her selection by running them past someone who knew her well. Reading the "safety guide" hadn't help avoid the tragedy and so she gave up only one week into her experiment. Well, gave up was probably too strong a sentiment. Monique still wanted a companion; she just gave up answering the steady flow of interested emails.

*

Mark was blown away with early success using the Circle of Excellence, and he used it again with another client, a lawyer who became nervous as he approached a court date. He continued on with his business planning, but was sorely tested by the lack of buy-in from those he had invited (Monique was the beautiful exception). Mark had a thought, wondering if changing state would give him access to different outcomes for his business than he had before.

He had a whiteboard in his office and on it he drew up the various theories for goal-directed behaviour:

- Setting a big hairy audacious goal (BHAG), then adding a time line, milestones, and measurable achievements (thanks, Jim Collins),
- Set up SMARTER goals and keep a goals book (thanks, Peter Drucker),
- Place your attention and focus on things you can control, not on things you are concerne about (thanks, Steven Covey).

He stood back and wondered about the role of state in any of these. Surely, if one lacked resources, then the BHAG was unreachable; if one felt unmotivated, then you would not make many goals, or make them and not look at them again. If you were highly stressed or distracted or tired, you might tend to blame others or fail to pay attention. In other words, some actions were accessible in one state but not in another. Jane was a perfect case in point. At the gallery, her state had locked her out of the goal of writing creatively. All her attention went to her poor state.

Then pop, his unconscious delivered him three words: be, do, have (probably his unconscious grabbing a book from his library, maybe Napoleon Hill's Think and Grow Rich). The state we experience is all about the being: the mood, the condition, and the place we find ourselves. Doing, well, most goal-setting models have that in spades. Having, well, that was goal attainment now, wasn't it? In his first-world, high-paid world that was really just materialism. He sat down at his desk and played with the three words… Based on where you started, you got a different state or outcome:

Have-do-be: when I have the time then I'll do the work then I'll be happy, (a victim for sure);
Do-have-be: if I work harder, do more, I'll have the resources, then I'll be happy, (a worker);
Be-do-have: if I am happy then I have access to better actions, then I'll have what I want, (winner).

The key here was to manage state. Doing that had given him the confidence to confront his boss and obtain permission to advance a project Art had rejected previously. Doing state better had helped both his clients access behaviour that was, up until then, locked away from them: confrontation for John and confidence in court for the lawyer. No amount of stress, or noble effort, or powerful thinking or goal setting would give them access to those outcomes: only state would. He immediately rang Jane at work and shared his insight. She listened earnestly, agreeing that his experiments with clients were right, but she remained concerned that it wouldn't work with her athletes. She shared her ideas about belief underlying behaviour, and they both came away now wondering about the place of each other's ideas.

Mark wanted to continue to understand how state, attention and goals worked together. Attention had a powerful influence on state, as their experiments with mindfulness had shown. Being present to one another created a very different experience of being heard, understood, loved and valued. Being present restricted the level of distractions and focused attention on here and now. As Mark researched attention, he came across some guys at the Boston Harvard Medical School doing work on state. They were working with a Zen Buddhist monk on the effect of meditation on afferent (felt) pain, and the effect attention had on pain management. "Self and attention are like a cup and its contents. You can place your attention all outside the cup (self) or you can place it all inside the cup. Changing your attention will have a profound effect on your experience (of pain)," said the monk.

Not only did attention affect state and one's experience of pain; it also changed the kind of goals you could actually see or conceive of. You could pay full attention inside yourself, seeing the goals you wanted to go after; or you could place all your attention outside and lose sight of what you want and only see what is currently available to go after, or what others were getting. One of the things that seemed to really get in the way was distraction. The mind is easily taken away from task, dragged toward the most attractive (glittering, mesmerizing) thing nearby. Certain things were almost irresistible, because they drove right at the survival mechanisms of interest circuits in the brain (look, a red berry!). Things like the ding of an arriving message on the phone, the notification that you have email popping up on the desktop, and the smiling face of a friend's message on Instant Messenger or Facebook are irresistible to the modern mind.

Mark found some work Elliot Berkman had published at the Neuro Leadership Institute on the neuroscience of goal pursuit and attention. Firstly, he learned about how goals are represented in the mind. That picture could come internally (who I should be; what I want to have) or externally (what others say I should obtain; what social norms are). The reason you want to accomplish a goal can be intrinsic or extrinsic too. Do you want to lose weight because you want to feel good about yourself (intrinsic), or so other people like the way you look (extrinsic). He actually thought about his car, wondering if he had wanted it so much because it filled an internal motivation (this car is for my state management) or external (it's a status symbol to others). He jotted down some ideas like: the best goals are multi-dimensional: visual, auditory, tactile, and especially come with a feeling or emotional desire. The best goals appeal to both the left and right side of our brain, the logical and rational part and the creative and emotional part.

There appeared to be a goal hierarchy: from abstract and concrete… from "why" something is important first to "how" you're going to go after it, and then "what" the goal is. Mark had seen this before somewhere. *Maybe Simon Sinek's Start with Why*, he thought.

*

He decided to practice attention placement to discover where his attention actually was, inside or outside. So he closed his eyes, right there at his desk, placing his attention inwardly. Sight and sound diminished, external feeling too. Then he waited just a moment, and for the second time today his unconscious served up a thought, *pop*. It was an image from Start with Why that showed this in concentric circles. Apple's "why" was being a rebel and going against the mob. Their "how" was by pursuing creativity and beauty. Their "what" just happened to be computers, tablets, phones, and watches.

In terms of pursuit of goals, Mark learned that attention can only be placed on one thing at a time. So what was the proposed answer to where you should place your attention? This idea again nagged at him; he was sure he had heard something similar. He took a deep breath, paying attention to his imaginary internal library, scanning its shelves for a helpful source and *pop*, number three occurred… Dan and Chip Heath had written about this in *Switch*. Give clear instructions to the rider (the will), give clear and compelling reasons to the elephant (the emotions), and then clear the path: remove resistance, make goal-directed behaviour easy (the environment). Mark quickly hunted for the book online to try and recall the ideas he'd read, and found a quote from the book instead. He jotted down:

> What looks like laziness is often exhaustion. (Mark: better state gives access to better outcomes);
> What looks like resistance is often lack of clarity. (Mark: pay attention to one specific and clear goal);
> What looks like a people problem is often a situation problem. (Mark: clear the path, make it easier to get to the goal).

The working day ended and Mark made his way to the carpark, musing about his work. How was he going to take this to his lawyer or his psychologist clients? It was not for their clients necessarily, but for themselves. As he started the car and let it warm up he summarised in his mind this way: it starts with state. Great state opens up your available options, your actions and goals. Attention helps you select the goals, paying attention internally and externally and it also makes sure you focus on one thing at a time… multitasking is out. Goal setting comes in a hierarchy from why to how to what.

When he got home he shared with Jane about his afternoon of research. He had completely forgotten that her father was home. Then he appeared, walking into the room, cutting Mark off mid-sentence. Mark scrambled for his train of thought, but it had derailed. Instead of being upset he laughed and declared, "Right there, see I'm a victim of attention deficit! Cut off and cast asunder. Hold on for a moment!" He retreated to the front door, to walk in again. The stream came back, the train re-railed and Mark lit up and continued his dissertation.

*

Jane's mood declined and she closed up. The meal, which was to have been a nashi pear salad and Japanese marinaded beef strips on rice was now headed toward a green bean salad with steak. His creativity was being sucked into a deep dark hole, Mark persevered, pouring them all some wine and giving her a back rub while she cooked. His effort paid off as Jane brightened a little and he continued to share his ideas from the day. As dinner was served Jane asked a question.

"You know, I think state, attention and goals would all best be served by the whole self and not just a part. I mean, you can't just place your attention on something, your mind I mean, if you are starving hungry. And if your body wants or desires chocolate for example, that doesn't just make it right to eat it, if your goal is weight loss. You see what I mean?"

Mark nodded, looking to her dad who was finishing his plate and looking disinterested. "So the exercise needs a 'whole of self' consideration? Does it align with your values, can you go after it single-mindedly, is your heart in it… and I suppose it would pay you to listen to your unconscious in all of that too." Inwardly Mark was saying, *Come on brain, there's a word for that, come on*! but the more stressed he got the further away the answer got.

*

Saturday morning. Mark mused about *ecological* as he squatted on the "shore" of Lake George again. In the distance, a ridgeline stood proudly covered with the huge propellers of wind turbines. Green energy, he laughed; those turbines were just so much green marketing. They only produced energy twenty-five percent of the time, when the wind was just right (so said eco-warrior Stewart Brand). The rest of the time the wind was too high, so the energy was lost, or too low, so the grid used coal-fired power anyway. Ridiculous. What looked like an ecological decision turned out, well, not to be so much. Fracking was exactly the same. For all they knew the Canadians were creating a massive future problem for themselves. His mind leapt naturally to his father-in-law.

The group were left with the quandary of whether to continue their self-coaching meetings with Jane's dad around or delay them until he left. But when would he leave? Lauren would normally come visit at least once a month, but with her grandfather staying in her room, she could hardly come down. In the end an odd compromise was made. Lauren came down and stayed over at Monique's house, and Jane's father agreed to go to Piallago looking for mop-top robinia trees to plant in the garden.

Catering was Mark's job this time, so he set to defrosting raspberries, blueberries, and a cheesecake. He went out to grab croissants, and presented them toasted with ham, cheese, and tomato. From a Lebanese Bakery he brought back the circular awamat, some baklava (which everyone would recognise), and mafroukeh (a kind of semolina and sugar cake). In the spirit of his set homework from two weeks ago, he made everyone take off their shoes and socks, get in touch with physical reality, and walk to the kitchen by way of the rock garden near the pool, in danger of falling in of course.

The fragrance of chai tea greeted them at the door, along with green tea for the kids.

They each caught up on progress, particularly enjoying having Lauren with them in person. She told them about Gyan's departure to India, hinting at her hunch about his being forced into a prearranged relationship. She mused, "I don't know why, but it hurts my heart having him away. He's a really great friend, and I miss him."

"Are you sure it's just the pain of a friend being away… or something more?" Monique asked.

"Why? What do you mean? Like what… like the prearranged marriage thing? Of course I don't agree with it, in this day and age!" Lauren could honestly be so clueless sometimes.

Her mum and dad rolled their eyes.

"Yes," said Monique, being patient with the only person who didn't get the joke. "Lauren, what if that was it? What if him being away was causing you pain, what if it was about the prearranged marriage?" she asked gently. "What would that mean? What would it mean if you really listened to your pain and figured out what it was saying?"

"Hmm, nice point, Monique, like me listening to my exercise pain and really hearing what that's about. It's a pity we don't have some interpreter for that," Jane said encouragingly.

"Hey, how did we all go with flow state?" Lauren said, changing the subject abruptly, and conveniently. The group went with it, sharing about each brain-training application and New Code game they had used.

Jane shared her learning about gamma state mixed with alpha state in the brain, and nobody else got it (having never used or seen an EEG machine). "Think of it like being stressed out, really under pressure, and then suddenly dropping into a relaxed state right in the middle of it. Boom, you've got this high-pressure way of things mixed with this relaxed way of thinking. Or think of being in the middle of a high adrenaline push for the finish line, but instead of running harder you are handed a cup of tea and a biscuit. Think what that would do to your brain, right? That's kind of like gamma and alpha. Only it's heaps better than that. It is divergent thinking grabbing disparate thoughts, converging with a new application, in a relaxed state of mind, operating at high speed." Jane looked around. Some understanding was dawning.

"That brings me to Circles of Excellence... did everyone get my email?" Mark asked, and everyone nodded. Mark reiterated the value of having a Circle of Excellence as a state-changing tool and told them the story of what he did in the car to illustrate. Then he asked about their progress with the homework for Circle of Excellence. Mark and Jane had worked on them together, so Jane had no trouble getting hold of it. But Lauren and Monique both admitted that they had struggled, so they decided to take a crack at it right there and then in the living room. When they were done, they refreshed their plates and glasses and went to sit down again.

"This week I've really been thinking about how to use this idea with my clients, and take it further in the corporate world. I've gone to things like state, attention, and goals... I've been discussing this with Jane, but I want to make this our homework for this week," Mark said enthusiastically.

Then he brought them up to speed on his research and pointed out that both state and Circles of Excellence were almost always defined by an occasion: a meeting, confrontation, event, competition, or challenge.

"This highlights the need for clearly stated goals," Mark said. "Let's call that being clear on outcomes. Usually just one outcome, one thing you need a great state for." He told them about John and his objective for one confrontational meeting (which he nailed).

"Once you have that in place, then it's important you place all your attention on that outcome, and check in with yourself on why that's important… listen to your pain, listen to your heart, listen to your unconscious. It's like you take a step back and get clear about your intentions. The truth is, when you do this you may find an even deeper intention behind that."

He used the lawyer as an example for them… Why was being confident important to his lawyer friend? Because he wanted to win. Why did he want to win? Because of his reputation. Why was reputation important? It affected his earnings. Why was earnings important? Family. Why was family important? Well, it just was. End of the line.

"Once you are clear about those intentions, it's important to check what happens if you actually get that outcome… is it safe? Does it work for everyone involved? How's the ecology? Let's call that getting clear on the consequences." Mark explained the idea of ecology as an environmental review to see if getting the outcome was all right all the way round. Lauren nodded as she drew a rough diagram to depict what she thought he was saying.

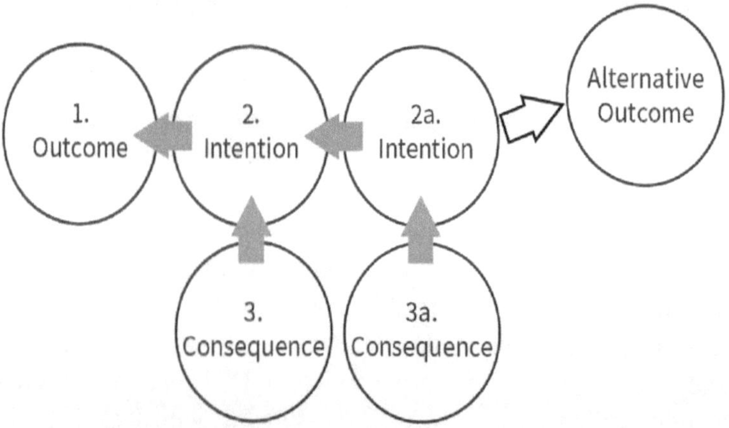

"When I did this for my objective of starting a new firm, I found that behind everything lay another related outcome—I wanted freedom. It was connected to both the reasons I wanted the firm. When I got one, I got the other… and my motives were the same for both," he said. "So here's what I reckon we should do," Mark said, delivering his to-do list. They'd already covered state so he left that out, starting now with outcomes (goals), intention (attention), and consequence (ecology).

Action List

- Choose an outcome you would like. Make sure you can experience or imagine it multi-dimensionally with all senses. Does it come with emotion, feeling or visuals…
- Check that you can access the required state for that outcome. Deploy the Circle of Excellence as necessary.
- Choose a way of enriching your outcome. Here are some options:

1. Brainstorm the outcome. Use the SMARTER goals framework to ensure it is complete, formed and clear.
2. Try doing it physically. Imagine a circle on the ground and stand in your outcome. Fully envision it, experience having it, upload the sense of it.
3. Work physically, by using cups on a table, circles on a page or circles on the floor.

- Step back and consider the intention, the reason for the outcome, why you are paying attention to it, what you are paying attention to.
- Is there also an intention behind your intention?
- Step to the side and consider the intention and the outcome. Check the consequences, ecology, what happens when you get that outcome. Sometimes you might want to make intention your new consequence.
- Additional resource: Goal Setting That Works – a summary of the work of Tad James in Line Therapy' http://www.neurocoachingaustralia.com/resources/neurocoaching/goal

EPILOGUE: SECTION ONE

"Live as if you were to die tomorrow. Learn as if you were to live forever."
Mahatma Gandi

Well there's the first third of the ideas to be presented in this book. Let's just sit down and take stock shall we? A lot has happened since Mark and Jane started off on their journey sixteen weeks ago. It was late winter in their lives and in their city. Their daughter Lauren and their neighbour Monique joined them on a journey of learning and self-discovery, kicked off by the example of Tim Ferriss, who experimented on himself.

Mark and Jane were sick and tired of spending money on gurus, in every field of their lives (dieting, personal development, spirituality, relationships, finances, health) and decided to look for personal coaching and self-transformation ideas themselves.

They rejected normal self-help guides, choosing instead to look for change processes that were evidence based, scientifically backed and testable by experiment. As you will see, much of what they have learned has been based in both psychology and neuroscience…

1. The art of self coaching. The first thing our characters played with was the creative benefits of journaling and working through writing exercises which shut down their inner critic. Researcher James Pennebaker contends that regular journaling strengthens the immune system. But it also helps problem solving, creative thinking and expanding your horizons. People like Lauren found it easy. People like Mark find it works well and are rewarded. People like Monique get into it after doing absolutely every exercise provided. Others who are like Jane continue to struggle. Mark raised the issue of suffering from creativity fatigue, and ultimately learned that frameworks can really help reduce that fatigue. What were our sources for learning here?

Primary: Julia Cameron, author of The Artist's Way (2002), gave us the exercises we used in the book plus 42 more in her book. Well worth the investment if you think journaling is going to help you.

Secondary: Shelley Carson wrote the incredibly helpful, Your Creative Brain (2006), which gave us the seven exercises we can do to build creative talent.

Tertiary: John Kabat-Zinn was the inventor of the scientific practise of Mindfulness Based Stress Reduction (MBSR - 1979) based on secular Buddhism. Many Yoga practices now include mindfulness techniques in their courses.

2. The coaching framework. Monique attends a life coaching seminar where she learns that when people feel stuck, as Jane did with her journaling. Finding choice and options give them hope. Jane started to examine the role of belief. When people feel a sense of disempowerment, as Lauren did with her option fatigue, they can play the victim. Lauren raised the question of secondary gain underlying it. Mark by contrast was struggling with feeling oppressed by Art, and his workmate Dave sought to show him how to laugh at his Svengali. What were our sources here?

Primary: Jaemin Frazer in *Elegantly Simple Solutions to Complex People Problems* (2015), outlined the hope, power, humour model for overcoming being stuck, being a victim and being oppressed.

Secondary: Iain McGilchrist in his book *The Master and His Emissary* (2009), lays out the ground work for the way the left and right hemispheres work together in a conscious and unconscious way. My only criticism would be that he does not give enough credence to the mind/body interactions.

Tertiary: Dr. Phil McGraw gave us the famous quote, "How's that workin' for ya?" The science underlying it is quite well established on secondary gain being the reason people adhere to patterns of behaviour they say they want to change. Fishbain, D.A., Rosomoff, H.L. et al., (1995). "Secondary Gain Concept: a review of the scientific evidence," *Clinical Journal of Pain*. 11(1):6-21.

3. Establishing relationship with the unconscious. Mark learns more about the relationship between the conscious and unconscious, especially yes/no signalling on the race track. People need to build rapport with the unconscious because they have been ignoring its signals all along, like Jane and her body's resistance to running. She needs to learn to listen to her pain. The unconscious does not usually have words, but speaks somatically and through emotion or visual memory. To be fair the founder of the California Superbike School (upon which the SRS is based), Keith Code never imagined these insights being taught at his school, and they crept in more by serendipity. Thanks go to Steve Brouggy for separating the track day teaching from the psychology. Lauren discovers that perfectionism is not the presence of very high standards but in fact the absence of any standard, she could have read the work of Randy O. Frost and his twenty years of research on it. So how about some references…

Primary: The ideomotor reflex and use of it as a conscious/unconscious signalling phenomenon was first described in 1971 by J. G. Watkins in, "The Affect Bridge: A Hypnoanalytic Technique," The International Journal of Clinical and Experimental Hypnosis, 19(1):21–27.

Secondary: The concept of building rapport with self, or more specifically with the unconscious was first posited by psychotherapist Milton Erikson who said that, "the reason people come to therapy is that conflict has arisen between their conscious and unconscious." Right on.

Tertiary: Adam Raffe was my instructor at the California Superbike School. Where he learned his insights… he doesn't recall. In fact he doesn't recall telling me much of any of this, so hey, maybe I made it up.

4. Why changing state changes everything. Mark discovers that one of the best ways to adapt and change to circumstance is to try new things, and thereby develop fluid intelligence (that's definitely Cattell - see below). Staying soft and fluid proves to be useful for the group again and again as they try to break old patterns and connections of thinking. Jane learns about the three forms of input to change state: biochemistry (neurochemicals, neurotoxins, hormones, medication and chemicals in the blood), neurology (entire autonomic nervous system, brain, perception, stereotypes, self-talk, psychology and thinking) and physiology (body, movement, lymphatic, energy, eating, breathing and posture).

John Russon brought together the existential, phenomenological and the ontological as an explanation of human 'state' (neurosis and everyday life) in 'Human Experience,' (2003). Although he won't confirm it, I think Grinder was relying on Emmanuel Kant's model, which is more elegant, and easier to use that Russon's. Kant envisioned the human mind as the central organiser of reality (perception and representation).

Primary: John Grinder is ostensibly the creator of Three Inputs to State Model (2001). You will not find reference to this fact online. Many NLP schools simply include it as part of the package without proper attribution.

Secondary: Ian Snape designed the State Management Techniques you see used in this chapter, published for the first time in his Neurocoaching Manual (2014), as part of Process Oriented Coaching.

Tertiary: In 1963 Raymond B Cattell proposed the "Theory of Fluid and Crystallized Intelligence: A critical experiment," Journal of Educational Psychology, Vol 54(1):1-22.

5. *Flow state and creativity.* Mark initially discovers (from watching a movie about a Chef) that he is exactly where he has chosen to be. Monique has a breakdown about being late and discovers there's a lot more going on under the hood that she's willing for anyone else to see. Jane goes berserk on the research of flow state and thinks of the incredible ways normal people could access this, including the use of New Code games, which take advantage of intra-hemispheric activation and down-regulation of conscious control. You know by now this had some basis in research right?

Primary: Steven Kotler, who himself relied on the work of Mihaly Csikszentmihalyi in Flow (2008), gathered much excellent research on flow state amongst extreme sports athletes in his book, The Rise of Superman (2014). Steve goes on to explore the themes in his sequel Stealing Fire (2019).

Secondary: Mihaly Csikszentmihalyi (pronounced Chick-sent-me-high) wrote, Flow: The Psychology of Optimal Experience (2008). This was not a book so much as a summary of two decades of research.

Tertiary: Consciousness operating at multiple levels forms part of many belief systems including the Hindu Chakra. However at least one neuroscientist proposed the brain can think at several layers at the same time, and can measure it using EEG. Partha Mitra wrote for the Scientific American in "A New Method to Measure Consciousness Proposed," (2014).

6. *Building a high performance state.* Mark discovers that you can jump to state, and researches further on anchoring and state management using the Circle of Excellence. He discovers the process by which you can create a high performance state and then deploy it at will to change your performance in a given situation. Jane discovers that flow state is made up of alpha (relaxed) and gamma (under pressure) EEG signals to make up a brain state which can see disparate pieces of information and join them together to solve

new problems. Lauren questions whether the unconscious should always be trusted, and learns that it is more about a relationship of honour and respect. Here's where the ideas all came from…

Primary: John Grinder is the source of the "Circle of Excellence Model" though this was really only recognised officially by Collingwood, J.J.P. & Collingwood, C.R.J. in the NLP Field Guide; Part 1. A reference manual of practitioner level patterns (2001).

Secondary: I learned the "Jump to State" technique from Ian Snape during personal mentoring in 2015.

Research by Amy Cuddy has shown that standing in a power pose for just 2 minutes increases testosterone and reduces cortisol (curling up in a ball does the reverse). Cuddy, A.J.C., Wilmuth, C.A., Carney, D.R., (2010). "The Benefit of Power Posing Before a High Stakes Social Evaluation," Harvard School of Business, 13(27):1-20.

Tertiary: *1. Listening to the pain:* The concept of listening to your pain was ostensibly coined by Sufi Rumi 800 years ago when he said, "These pains you feel are messengers. Listen to them." More recently Dr. Ben E. Benjamin has applied this to health coaching with relation to actual pain.

2. Anchoring: This idea also comes from peak performance athletics and sports. First trialled in the Olympic Games, and now popular in tennis and other high speed sports anchoring can be very useful for personal state management. For example public speaking, interviewing or high stress financial trading. Hypnotists and performers use positional anchoring to trigger the audience. The applications are endless. Have a read of Performance Coaching: the handbook for managers, HR professionals and coaches by Angus McLeod (2003).

7. Goal setting and attention. Initially Jane attempted to manage her experience of her father's visit by framing her expectation. This worked until he crossed her unconscious rules and she stuck because of her need for his approval. She discovers the power of moving to want and prefer. Mark separates being from doing from having and sees three pathway options. He explores starting with why, moving to how and finishing with what. Ultimately he discovers the power of designing your outcome (goals), examining your intention (by paying attention) and being careful about the consequence (the overall ecology of the goals). So what's the research behind this?

Primary: I was first introduced to the OIC model by Ian Snape, who referenced the work of James Lawley and Penny Tompkin (who provided the PRO model) relying on the work of David Grove. But my research indicated that John Grinder may have furnished us with OIC and Grove gave us PRO.

Secondary: The concept of be, do, have was first proposed by Patrick Lencioni in his award winning book The Advantage (2012).

Tertiary: *1. Goals:* Elliot Berkman who studies social and affective neuroscience wrote about goals in "The Motivated Brain: understanding the pursuit of goals," Psychology Today, (2014).
2. The layering of goals: Why, how and what was proposed by Simon Sinek in his book, Start with Why, (2011).
3. Elephant and rider: Chip and Dan Heath are credited for their excellent three quotes from Switch (2010).
4. Timeline therapy: Tad James developed the timeline script you are given in this chapter, although the original idea for Time Lines was part of New Code NLP developed by John Grinder.

Spring break is upon Lauren, as Mark and Jane decide to take two weeks annual leave. Monique doesn't have the luxury, having to fend off a legal battle for her children and work hard to pay off the fees. However this period of time gives the four of them adequate space to practice the exercises learned in the sixteen weeks which have passed so far. They are able to go through the exercises they have come up with, refine their learning and see which practices work, which don't and which will stick. Almost all of them have found the brain training games helpful and can remember people's names better, recall disparate information for work projects and stay focussed on task. But the neurocoaching has not been a cure all by any means.

Monique is still hiding her dark depression and poor self-image. Lauren is still haunted by anxiety and stress during her study and exam periods. Jane and Mark are both becoming more conscious of their health, he with his weight and she with her form in running. Jane has learned to deal with her need for her father's approval, but is still deeply affected by his antics. Mark is learning to free himself up from his boss's opinion, but remains totally unaware of the three limitations Art wishes him to address.

Each of them had made some progress toward their higher selves, and each had an immeasurable distance to track to their glory. Their potential, and ours remember, is immeasurable. Each graph that measures human progress and performance drifts along in a steady and slowly climbing path until it tilts upwards, and heads, parabolically and exponentially toward limitless.

So let's return to their story as they approach the end of the holidays.

SECTION TWO: THE BRAIN AND ITS ENVIRONMENT

CHAPTER EIGHT: LEARNING ABOUT LEARNING

"How you do anything is how you do everything."
Zen Buddhist Proverb

Monique was just heading out the door when Jane's father arrived home from shopping. Her kids had already crossed the verge and headed inside. Mark and Jane had not followed her outside. The two of them met in the driveway. He had all the charm of a King's Cross spruiker and she reacted, well, exactly how you'd expect. Stepping back, her path home now blocked, Monique engaged in small talk about the gardening trip and the state of their two lawns. He commented on how young and full of vitality she looked. Stunning. In more ways than one really. Words failed her, and he, behaving like a gentleman still, made way for her to go home. She felt a mixture of hope (from escaping) and queasiness.

Monique was vulnerable, a wounded fish in an ocean full of scent-smelling predators. Her on and offline dating experience had proved that there were real dangers out there. Jane's dad may not have been harmful, a whale shark perhaps, or a basking shark, but he still cast a big shadow on Jane's world and made Monique feel uncomfortable.

He took his shopping from the car and went inside to wash up. Lauren was about to leave; she was picking up Gyan from the airport on her way back to uni. Lauren took her supplies of tea, candles, bath oil (a new idea for relaxation), and some food in a box to her car. Her parents and grandfather waved goodbye and she made her way out of the rabbit warren of streets to the highway.

She decided to buy the Heath brothers' other book, *Made to Stick*, on Audible, and enjoyed listening to it on her way home. Gyan had said that books were a gateway to the world and to the soul. They were able to bring the outside in and the inside out. How did a science major get to be so… philosophical? Before she knew it, Lauren was pulling up at Sydney Airport and walking across to the international arrivals area. Gyan's plane had been delayed, for no good reason as far as she could see, and she went off to grab a coffee. She had an ambivalent relationship with coffee. She drank it, but didn't like it very much, and really only wanted a very, very good coffee. She had become a coffee snob at Sydney uni.

She did a state check: nervous, her heart beat tangibly in her chest, butterflies wandering round her tummy, and adrenalin making her skin itchy. Then she went to the toilets (again). Was her nervousness based on the trip from Canberra? On second thought, it was probably the coffee. She wandered over to the cafe area and sat down. The little cartoon apparition of Rosie appeared again. "Nope, on third thought, it's Gyan. Really, it is; why can't you admit it? It's not like anyone's here to worry about… hey wait… is that him? It's him! IT'S HIM!" Lauren felt like a teenager! Of course, she still was a teenager. Hormones flooded around her body, irises wide open from familiar attraction, neck and cheeks flushed as she ran to embrace him. Gyan for his part reciprocated… but more coldly. Call it internal conflict, call it a process-oriented relationship style, call it being an introvert… he struggled.

They talked and talked as they made their way back to campus. Rude drivers, slow traffic and poor service at the restaurant did nothing to dent their enthusiasm and hours of conversation did nothing to slake their thirst for each other's company.

Lauren was a very fluid thinker, and willing to tolerate much misunderstanding too. This played to her favour because the conversation was very male-female stereotypical. He was trying to fix something and she was trying to connect and share. Her hunch was right about the intention for the trip. His parents had tried to arrange a partner for him. What was funny (to her) was the way Gyan handled it. Obviously he had said no, or at least that's what she assumed, given his amour and expressions of unrequited desire to spend time with her.

Gyan explained what had been going on in his mind when in India. He had a spreadsheet of pros and cons for the arranged marriage deal as a whole. Then he balanced his impressions of the girl when he met her; the village, the elders, the dowry, and so forth. In all, the arrangement had been quite in the negative, despite the girl's beauty, education, and ability to speak English (at this Lauren had to laugh). Then came the part she wasn't ready for. Gyan, without any fanfare or even much visible emotion, explained that a significant part of the spreadsheet had been a comparison of the girl with Australian alternatives, which spawned a new spreadsheet of pros and cons defining relationships.

At first he tried to hide that it was a spreadsheet about Lauren by saying,

“My thoughts about having another kind of relationship… here in Australia… were with other students on campus.” This broke down when his unconscious forgot to mask it, and he said “You’re like” and “You and I are… ” Lauren almost coped with it, but his problem-solving, automaton approach spooked her and for no very good reason, as far as Gyan was concerned, she left in a huff. She was NOT to be spread-sheeted.

*

Back in her dorm, Lauren tried to think of the Circle of Excellence stuff from last week. Would it serve to bring her back to a better state now? Probably not; it was made for study, not for love. Besides, she was too angry for that. She absentmindedly started to play a brain game on her iPhone. It helped a bit. Lauren ran a bath, lit a candle, and soaked herself in tears. She lay there and thought about dealing with Gyan. Until arriving at the airport, she hadn’t really admitted to herself she LIKE-liked him. She considered her future relationship, and his cold tendencies. He had a heart, he had emotions, but nothing as portrayed in Disneyland. When she had finished, dried off, cooled off, and had a cup of tea, Lauren thought about what she wanted from a relationship. Well, from the relationship for after all she wasn’t about to spread-sheet him against the alternatives. What were her intentions? What were the consequences?

Lauren thought it funny that anger and love sat so close together on the emotional bench that you can scoot down by just one position and be yelling, or kissing again. She had always wondered how people could have make-up sex.

Though it was getting late, she knew Gyan would still be buzzing from his international flight. Jetlag was her friend, so she ran to his dorm and knocked on the door. He appeared at the door rather sheepishly, knowing Lauren would be the only person bold enough to call after midnight. “Gyan, listen, I’ve been thinking… I’m sorry for the whole run-away-from-you thing just now… I just… ” But before she could finish he simply leant down and kissed her. And that was all the discussion she needed.

*

Mark’s boss, Art, sat silently in his office, perplexed by Mark’s resignation. His large mahogany desk reflected the ambient light from the floor-to-ceiling glass windows in his office. The leather in his chair creaked underneath him as he rocked backward and forward, pondering. Mark had been a fairly model employee: on time, hard-working, billing more than sixty percent of his time.

His sales skills were good and his technical knowledge was always growing with the research he committed himself to. Mark had steadily progressed through the ranks, but he would never advance until he had learned at least three things.

The first was how to take negative feedback. If he wanted to be a leader, he would have to groom a healthy self-scepticism and get feedback from others. Academics called this getting "peer review." That was not withstanding the second weakness… the necessity to fight for his opinion, which Mark hardly ever did. At Bane & Co, Helmsmen, Synergy, and especially McKinsey, the art of debate was paramount. You had to fight for your point of view. Lastly, Mark was well able to see practical and tactical layers of work, but he lacked a strategic perspective for clients, and they intuitively sensed this in their interactions with him. There was no way senior management were going to have him along if he couldn't do strategy.

Mark wouldn't be the first person to leave a consulting firm, and he wouldn't be the last. But Arthur actually cared about Mark's future and whatever he went off to do would fail without addressing these factors. He had tried numerous times to tell Mark these shortcomings, first in his performance reviews, then in boardroom debate, and finally, as plainly as he could, last Friday. Perhaps that's what sparked this resignation? Mark always seemed to take things so personally, as though Art were picking on him, setting him aside for attack. The human resources department was already appraised of the situation (by Mark) and of course it was Arthur who was in danger of reprimand as the perpetrator of office bullying. But it was nothing of the sort.

Should he approach Mark? If so, how? Mark was so defensive and now he was on the way out; Arthur could hardly conceive of a way to address him. Then slowly a plot hatched in his mind. There was a course starting tomorrow on Action Learning, a process the company wished to deploy more fully with its clients. Despite the very recent training with Julia Cameron, Art resolved to dispatch Mark to the course as a last-ditch effort to communicate with him there. Art was already enrolled. The two of them were going to learn about learning, and in the process have a nice dinner, some wine, and… a chat.

*

The next day Jane continued to think about the role belief plays in performance. Since Mark had talked about the book Switch last week, she had grabbed his copy and started leafing through it. She found the 1995 study about Molly Howard, principal of Jefferson County High School, where eighty percent of the kids came from poverty and most were failing their grades. Molly decided to remove D and F from the grading system and instead award NY, which simply meant "Not Yet." Students were told to continue studying toward getting a grade. In other words, the school redefined the student's experience of failure, making it impossible. Students interviewed later said that their teachers believed in them, believed they could do it, and so they did! In 2008 Molly was voted nationwide Principal of the Year for the improvement in the school's standing (from a crowd of 48,000 principals). Here was the evidence Jane had been looking for! Belief affected behaviour (at least in the learning environment) and this seemed to give the students more choice, more of a foundation to change their learning behaviour. In the end, this affected the entire school's grades.

Jane thought of some athletes she had taken through the lab with David. In his vaulted, glass-walled office he had a machine. The athlete stepped into the machine and was handed a two-kilo weight for each hand and asked to lift them up to shoulder height. The electrodes measuring muscle strength then indicated actual endurance (say five minutes), but the athlete almost always gave up before that… way before that… at say, minute three. Then David would tell them that the mind has safety buffers that limit exertion in order to maintain longevity, but they stop you far before damage to the muscles. After mental-endurance training (on a bike-race simulator) and muscle strength programs (only mental training), the athletes would come back and retest. The results would almost always rise, this time into the vicinity of four minutes, but rarely five.

Jane knew the same had been learned in long-distance running and marathons. Breaking the so-called "pain barrier" was all in the mind and had to be experienced to be understood. But ultimately it came down to belief. Normally you ignore physical signs at your own peril. She had learned firsthand the consequences of ignoring your unconscious. But here was a contrary example where belief was limiting performance. On her desktop Jane had an article open which was titled "Mobilizing Unused Resources: using the placebo concept to enhance cognitive performance." She cut and pasted a quote from professors Ulrich Weger and Stephen Loughnan into an email addressed to Mark. It read, "People have significant psychological resources to improve their well-being and performance, but these resources often go unused and could be better harnessed." The key? Knowledge and understanding about their beliefs, about their actual capacity. This was certainly not easy-believism, and neither was it "fake it till you make it." This was hard core science at its best.

*

Meanwhile, Mark was busy processing his current work situation. He wasn't sure if Art was trying to get him out of the office, or whether this was really the season for incredibly relevant training for his department, but Mark found himself on the way to another three days of training. He pulled into the car park at the Hotel Kurrajong in Barton. It was raining lightly and the car park, surrounded by ferns and overhanging greenery, seemed a fitting frame for the moss and lichen-etched tarmac he had to cross to get to the front door. Tucked away behind rows of shining government offices and private businesses, the hotel was architecturally typical of many older hotels in Canberra. Opened in 1926, its rambling, apricot brick walls and red terracotta tiled roofs reflected traces of Edmund Barton, wooden tennis racquets and the Anna Pavlova, the ballerina after whom the uniquely Australian dessert derived its name.

Stepping into the foyer, Mark became somewhat disoriented. A beautiful restaurant stood welcoming visitors with its timber floors. A well-appointed front desk to one side and a maze of corridors leading away to what he presumed were either the rooms or the conference area. Then he saw Art and had a churning, confusing response. What was he doing here? Was this a joke? Why hadn't Art responded to his resignation? Mark's mind felt like he was a sea creature attempting to escape hunters, only to be forced ashore to flounder on a beach. His thoughts stranded: *Art doesn't have my back… Art has it in for me… Art never understands me* and lay helpless, gasping for the ocean, attempting desperately to roll back into the sea.

A smiling face behind Art greeted Mark. The facilitator, John Sautelle, very efficiently signed him in, tagged him with a name, and swept him into the room to meet the other participants. The usual accoutrements of training were arrayed about the room: tea and coffee, biscuits, a white board with pens, a stand with butcher paper and Blu-Tack. Strangely, for eight participants, there were three large circular tables, each able to seat eight. Mark mixed and mingled, his sea creature floundering, thoughts chasing one another helplessly across the beach until John called them to "Table number one." Once they were all seated, John gave them an overview of the training.

"You're here to learn how to be an Action Learning Coach. You will applying a well-defined, structured process to small groups working on urgent, important problems, or opportunities and learning while they do so. The process we will be using was developed by Michael Marquadt, founder of the World Institute of Action Learning (WIAL). It can be used for problem-solving and leadership development," John explained. As Mark would come to learn, John was always measured, listening and calibrating his people. He was highly intentional about this.

"It's used at Boeing, Coke, Microsoft, NASA, and many other firms," John continued.

Before getting into the detail of the how it all worked, John explained the process of learning, writing notes up on the board and a rough diagram of the learning process:

For a thing to be learned, you step through four stages:

- You begin unconsciously incompetent, you don't know that you don't know.
- Then you realise you don't know and you start to try and learn, you are consciously incompetent.
- Bit by bit you master the subject and become consciously competent.
- Finally you master the content and become unconsciously competent, burying the new learning into autopilot.

Mark had previously seen the cycles of learning model (sometimes called the 'quad-loop learning model') which concluded much the same thing. It also said on first pass we learn the 'what', the rules and way of a thing. On second pass we learn 'why' it is important, and we try to tinker with the rules. On the third pass we really master the material, the nitty gritty of 'how' and become able to pass it on to others. On the fourth pass, by which point it has become instinctive, we start cross applying our learning to other areas and bringing other learning to this field to change it. In his mind it looked more like this:

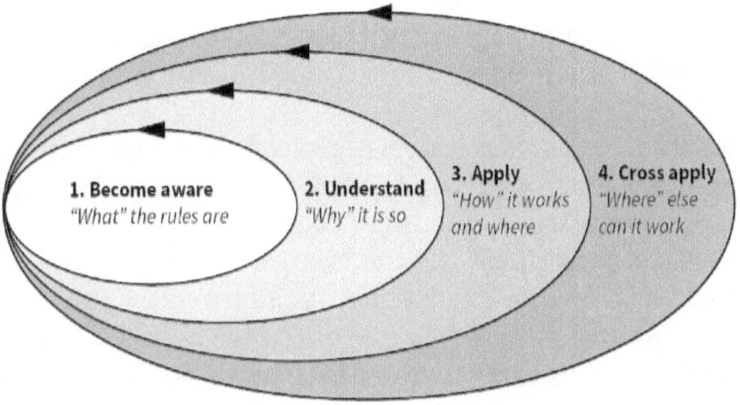

While Mark thought of all of this, Art asked if he could add to what they were learning. John gave a clear five-minute permission. Art shared his learnings on the subject of the unconscious with the group, from reading David Eagleman's *Incognito*. The surprise for some perhaps is that the large majority of our being is running on autopilot, Art shared. David put the figure as high as ninety-seven percent "below the water" in what Freud termed the unconscious. This had got Art really fascinated about how much unconscious programming we had, so he read *Conscious and Unconscious Programs in the Brain* by Benjamin Kissin, who said the unconscious is like a parliament of automated programs, about 10,000 of them by his count.

"These are automatic, routine, familiar, habitual, and handle the most common needs without thought," Art said. "Things such as holding a glass, walking, language rules and emotional response to stimuli. Each of these are embedded in the unconscious as you become competent at them, just like you're saying, John."

"Yeah, but the problem comes when, later in life, you find that the program you have isn't what you want," said Mark, non-combatively. "You may not want some of them, or may wish to improve others. You know, like becoming ambidextrous to do sea kayaking, or amending a childhood tendency to say 'them' instead of 'those.' I have a friend who says, 'Can I have them biscuits' instead of 'those biscuits.' He really fights hard to change that," he concluded.

John smiled. They had stayed right on topic. John invited them to move to table two and from there he launched into training the Action Learning process proper. He drew diagrams, handed them all manuals, penned illustrations, and fielded questions. After a short break for coffee, he moved them to table three and they practiced the skills for the first time. Art pointed out that they had moved to stage two, consciously incompetent and experimenting!

John had them adopt several perceptual positions: participant presenting a problem, a member of the problem solvers (who asked questions much the same way a coach would), group coach (who held the group to the reflective questioning ground rules), and observer (who tried to mimic the master). John was uncompromising about the rules, facilitated as they were by the novitiate and also about the way they were to debrief. All debriefing took place on table one. There they were to ask, "What did you do well?" and "What would you do differently?" The process always started with feedback from the participants, moved to the facilitator, and ended with the observer. Just about everyone struggled to discuss what they did well. Most were highly critical of themselves, but John would have none of it.

Soon it was lunch time and they broke training to answer texts, return calls, and generally hustle to the restaurant for lunch. A babble of conversation broke over the group as people interacted about who they were, where they were from, why they had come and so forth.

Mark just had to know why they had three circular tables, so he broached the subject with John over lunch. John resisted answering, inviting Mark to ask again in the next session for the benefit of the group. And ask Mark did. As soon as they were seated at table one, he launched with his question. "John, I have just got to know, why are there three tables? I've never seen anything like it!"

"Anyone got a theory?" John asked, always the proponent of self-driven learning and discovery.

Mary Ann, the accounts manager from Melbourne, spoke first. "At least one of them is like a practitioner table, number three I think, where we did the actual exercise." John nodded. She beamed.

Joanne, the psychologist from Human Resources at RMIT, spoke next. "I think table number two is a learning table, but more like theory; that's where you have the whiteboard set up." Again John smiled and the student glowed. Mark opened his mouth to speak and Art beat him to the punch, "Then table one is for debate, questioning, debrief, the place we are allowed to review and discuss?"

Again John seemed pleased, though this time, leaning forward, he added wisdom to knowledge. “Right on three counts. It doesn’t really matter what you call them, what label they have. Each exists for a purpose. They are separate learning positions. One table is where you learn experientially; it’s the action table. Another table is where you learn academically, theoretically, about the action space. The third space is where we learn about the other two spaces. It’s the reflective space. These also mirror three perceptual positions identified by John Grinder and Richard Bandler, first person (self), second person (other), third person (observer).”

They all pondered what had just been said, then considered the merits of physically separating those three positions. As though reading their thoughts, John said, “Human beings anchor very easily. Mood to song, place, or person to perfume. Because I want you to learn at conscious and unconscious levels simultaneously, learning the subject while experiencing the subject, I separate them physically.” Through this process they were learning both mentally and physically, coding the learning unconsciously; taking up the information without conscious effort.

“Can you see that this is a layer-upon-layer learning process? Underneath the conscious learning, there are layers of unconscious learning. I’ve told you a number of stories about clients, trainers, practitioners and seemingly unrelated stories with my own anecdotes. Further down still, I’ve been constantly using metaphor. David Grove, a clinical psychology researcher, once observed that, ‘Metaphor mediates between conscious and unconscious processes.’ It is my understanding that metaphor also opens up to a person’s internal landscape, which David found was self-organizing.”

John then took a few minutes to teach them how to write down their learning in bullet point and story, or what others have called micro-narratives.

Mark had recently been reading John Grinder’s work around state and it occurred to him that what John Sautelle had done here with learning was analogous to constructing a “know nothing” state. High-speed, high-performance learning from a master involves synaesthesia: the use of multiple channels of input (sight, sound, touch), including and especially involving the body. It involves knowing nothing else but what is directly in front of you, putting away the conscious “know-it-all” that likes showing off and needs approval. High-performance learning is almost all unconscious. Sitting off to one side are the various programs you already have, waiting, willing, and ready to serve what you are about to learn. Mark felt like he still had a lot of growing to do in this area, but resolved to share everything he had learned with Jane. This was surely useful to her athletes!

This ability was probably analogous to the flow state she had learned about from Kotler's book. This was beginning to peer into the spectacular state of boundary-pushing, achievement-smashing athleticism that extreme sports was finding access to. More, much more than Csikszentmihalyi (God bless his Hungarian name) went looking for in his pursuit of happiness and peak states of wonder.

*

Art left the Kurrajong that day wondering when he'd get a chance to address the three issues with Mark. Mark left the Kurrajong that day wondering why Art was there with him and intuitively preparing for an confrontation. Come hell or high water, he was leaving the firm. Jane left work that day wondering about the effects of belief on performance. Dr. Martin left work that day wondering why the biomechanics researcher was paying such close attention to his machines. Gyan left his lecture that day wondering what Lauren was thinking about his kiss last night. Lauren left her lecture that evening wondering if she could act on her lecturer's advice. He had told them all to take the day before the exam off. Recent research had shown that rest and a full night's sleep produced better results than cramming. Monique left work wondering how she could avoid the affections of Jane's dad. No scratch that, how she could avoid the man all together.

Mark realized that they hadn't made any attempt at arranging a weekend catch-up. This coming weekend was the October Labour Day long weekend. Mark and Jane had booked accommodation down the coast to get away and refresh. So Mark wrote an email to everyone asking them to write an account of what they had done with last weekend's homework on outcomes, intentions, and consequence, plus any other learning they had. Then he summarized his learnings from the first day of the Action Learning course and sent them all this week's proposed actions.

Action list

- Pick an area of learning: a tool, a skill, a new area you wish to advance in.
- Consider the four layers of learning from unconsciously incompetent to unconsciously mastering the area. Mark down which state you think you're at.
- Download http://www.neurocoachingaustralia.com/resources/neurocoaching/loop-learni
- In the loop learning model, journal about whether you are at the what, why, how or wher phase. What is the next step for you? How much practice is involved?
- In what ways have you actually applied yourself, in action steps that you can be account for?

- Is the experience synaesthetic (using multiple input channels)? How can you make your learning more tactile and multisensory?
- Is there a master in the field you can be tutored by? Can you adopt a know nothing state
- Set up your learning environment so that you separate learning from practicing from revi and critiquing your progress in the area (like the three tables).
- Arrange a time when you can examine your learning in this area from three perspectives

1. The learner,
2. The teacher, and
3. An independent and disinterested observer.

CHAPTER NINE: BEING FLEXIBLE ABOUT NEUROPLASTICITY

"If you want to change your life, you need to change your brain."
John Arden

Mark and Jane, like so many others who lived in the nation's capital, owned a house at the coast. Well, perhaps "house" was a bit generous. Since the late nineties, house prices at the coast had soared and what they could afford was a little weatherboard three-bedroom shack. The cottage was tucked into the seaside village of Barling's Beach. They were glad to see the cottage after battling traffic, accidents, and the police on the Kings Highway. Lauren had asked if she could join them and somewhat cheekily neglected to tell them she was coming in Gyan's car… with Gyan.

October was still a mild month, cool in the evenings, which kept the mosquitoes at bay. The usual rigmarole of unpacking and preparing the house left Mark and Jane without much time to catch up about the self-coaching. Normally Mark would drive (he loved to drive) and Jane would attempt, unsuccessfully, to stay awake. So no talking took place. Just as the first street light flickered on and Mark finished preparing the meal for three, Lauren arrived. But the horn which sounded didn't sound right and Jane's curiosity was piqued. Looking out into the driveway, they saw a small Volvo three-door hatch and came out to see what was going on.

Lauren climbed out of the passenger side and smiled, shrugging and calling out, "Hey," somewhat sheepishly. Despite the fact that Lauren had worded Gyan up on things to avoid and social etiquette in this situation, he simply gamboled out of the car, up onto the deck, and shook the hands of both Jane and Mark. Smiling broadly, and with his beautiful Oxford accent (he had been educated in an international school in his home state), Gyan said, "A pleasure to meet you both; a real pleasure. We brought dessert!" And that was that.

Jane made up the guest bedroom, situated next to the room Lauren was staying in. Jane was neither angry nor unsettled. Although she was shocked at first, her logistical mind ran fast over the accommodation and food arrangements. She was now thinking how pleasant it would be to have company. "Gyan, please, bring your things into the guest bedroom; dinner will be served shortly."

Mark found himself put out. He never considered himself prudish, and frankly he never really thought about Lauren's love life because she didn't have time for a boyfriend and she lived in women-only accommodation. Now his mind turned to the darkest things; suspicious, envious and protective of his daughter. He needn't have worried over all that; Gyan was even more demure than Mark was.

*

Monique had come home on Friday afternoon inwardly expecting a weekend catch-up. She was caught unawares by Mark's email telling them that it was too late for arranging one. Furthermore, they'd taken off to the coast for a long weekend. Her iPad was balanced on the kitchen windowsill where she prepared the vegetables and watched over the kids playing in the backyard. Out of the corner of her eye, she saw what looked like a snake. Just a shadow flitting in and out of the fence palings between her yard and Mark and Jane's. She looked away to read more emails, then saw movement again, turned back and nearly jumped backward into the open pantry. There at the window stood Jane's father, smiling.

She opened the back door, but not to let him in. Instead, she blocked the way and asked him, "What do you want?" taciturnly.

"Well I was hoping to borrow some honey, you see they've left me behind in the house, to mind it, and have taken the honey with them to the coast," he explained, rather weakly.

Any pretence to see me, she thought cynically. "Wait there, I'll get it." But rather than ingratiating himself to her by playing with the children, or even doing as she asked, (in order to build trust and rapport), he came up the stairs. Having got the honey, Monique was turning around to bring it back to him when she saw his invasion. She froze, rigid. Her heart pounded in her ears, her cheeks blanched white and her teeth clenched. The horrible scenes of her ex-husband's behaviour played back to her in full, multisensory, deeply somatic, phobia-level recall. She was having a panic attack.

From her throat a growl, then she found her voice. "Get out, get out, get out of my house Mathew, you snake, you lying bastard, GET OUT!" she hissed. Trembling, she advanced toward what she thought was her ex-husband and instead of offering Jane's dad the honey, she flicked her right hand sideways to grab a baseball bat standing there against the refrigerator side.

Jane's father had no idea what to do, or what he had triggered in Monique. Her self-defence program had kicked in. Now he was in very real danger. "Fine, fine, Monique that's fine," he said, holding his hands up open and empty. "I don't need the honey, honey, don't go crazy now." Those were the last words he could remember.

Mathew used to call her honey and now he was calling her crazy! She raised the bat in fury, and he backed out the door at the exact moment one of her children had knelt down on the patio to take off her shoes… and over he went… headfirst… to the concrete below.

Her son only saw half the event and would later tell the ambulance driver that his mum had clocked the old man with the baseball bat. The police were never called because, apart from surveying the scene and the injury, the ambulance driver would have backed Monique's self-defence in any case. He'd seen this kind of thing too many times before, only the woman was the injured one and the man was the one making up the story.

Jane's dad needed twelve stitches and an overnight stay in the hospital. Monique needed company.

She rang Mark's mobile phone number and told him all about the events. She hadn't eaten yet and really hadn't calmed down either; she sounded so upset. He did the only thing he could think of. He invited them all down. Monique hesitated, thinking he meant Jane's dad too, but once that was cleared up she accepted. Mark handed the phone the Jane, who'd been listening in quietly. As Monique fielded Jane's questions about what happened (minus the whole internal, mental drama) she also realised the coast house wouldn't have space for her kids. So she made arrangements for them to stay with the grandparents again, grabbed a sandwich and coffee for the road, and made haste to the coast.

*

Morning dawned a juxtaposition: tranquil setting—disquieted hearts; gorgeous sunrise—monochrome mood; songbirds—silent, bath-robed acolytes. Jane was the first to try and draw things together. First she went for a pre-breakfast walk with Lauren, which actually turned into a jog along the beach and back. By the time they were ready to climb the headland, Jane asked, "So why the study break, and why the boyfriend?"

"Well my lecturer told me the latest neuroscience on study, taking a break was best for recall on exam day. Cramming rams short-term memory full and reduces access to long-term recall. Okay, I'll admit he said take a day, but I figured Gyan and I could do with three days off. And as for Gyan, he's not my boyfriend, yet. He is my best friend, so, no Mum, we're not sleeping together."

As a reflection of her saintliness, Lauren prepared breakfast: fresh fruit, yoghurt, fruit, toast, coffee, herbal teas, and the traditional coast breakfast of bacon, avocado, asparagus, spinach, chicken, and eggs (Dad did a real mean poached egg). Meanwhile Jane knocked on Monique's door, and was quietly welcomed in.

"Jane, I'm so sorry," she began in fear, but it wasn't necessary.

"Monique, listen, I'm not here to attack you or correct you or anything like that. In fact, if you had attacked my dad, I'd be here thanking you. No, that's not it. It's something you said on the phone last night that has me thinking." Jane was soft and gentle, carrying her concern carefully. "It felt to me like you were having a dissociative episode," Jane said. She pre-empted the next question by saying, "That's an event where your brain blocks you out of reality and runs you a different reality. You think you're reacting to one thing, when in fact it's another."

"Am I losing it? Am I going crazy?" Monique asked, worried.

"Well, no, in fact your unconscious is doing a great job protecting you. The issue here is that there's stuff going on underneath that someday you're gonna need to deal with. This incident with my dad was running on another track, an old track. I guess I just wanted to know if you wanted to find out what that was?" Jane asked, super gently, and aware that breakfast was coming.

"Yeah, yeah I do. I don't like that I could check out mentally like that," Monique said, hanging her head.

Jane thought quickly about her options. She had been taught the first, second, and third person framing method at university, but it was a bit of a jump from here, so she said, "You remember the three tables Mark told us about at 'day one' of the training he just did?"

"Ah, kinda… the trainer had three circular tables. They were for, ah, doing the stuff, and um, learning about doing, and then reflecting on learning and doing." Monique lifted her head.

"Brilliant!" Jane enthused, "so how 'bout we do the same thing? We'll play first, second, and third tables for your experience. But let's grab some breakfast first, especially some coffee!"

Jane decided to ask Monique to simply imagine everything that had happened, from third position. That gave Monique the ability to review the entire thing dispassionately and come to the realization that she had confounded her ex-husband and Jane's dad. All her rage, her pent-up desire for justice, her violence had come out against (or almost come out against) Jane's dad. This had the effect of clearing Jane's dad of high treason and also separated Monique from the pain of guilt about what happened.

Just as well too because the phone rang and it was the hospital. Dr. Franklin wanted to speak to Jane; her father had fallen into a coma. Evidently he had tried to get up in the middle of the night and had fallen in the bathroom, cracking his head on the tiles. Jane didn't know whether to laugh or cry. Either way, he was hospital-bound until he came to and she wasn't rushing up there to hold his hand. Monique was relieved at her own response, free of the sense of being responsible. Lauren didn't even seem to mind, which was odd because she was normally very caring and sensitive about people getting hurt.

*

Breakfast turned into brunch and the group plus Gyan debriefed about events thus far, including Mark's email about his learnings at the training. Monique appreciated the three-table, three-person exercise Jane had made and Gyan raised the distinct possibility that Monique's experience might relate to neuroplasticity. This was cause for discussion indeed. How was the brain changing, learning, adapting, making new neural pathways, and how had Monique been hijacked by old pathways?

*

Jane went to town to do some shopping on her own. Lauren and Gyan decided to take in a movie in Bateman's Bay, which left Mark and Monique by themselves. A little self-conscious in the house alone, they went to the beach to enjoy the unusual spring warmth. They undressed and Monique asked for help sun screening her bikinied back. Mark obliged happily enough and they sunbathed and swam.

Monique asked, perhaps prematurely, for more sunscreen to avoid being burned. Unfortunately this coincided with Jane arriving down at the beach.

Mark greeted her warmly. Jane greeted him coldly. "Let's take a walk, Mark," she suggested, her tone hard enough to cut through the fog of attraction.

"Sure, darling, a walk would be nice," he agreed, sensing something was wrong.

When they were out of earshot, and never one to mince words, Jane said, "There's a line, Mark, a fine line, between friend or colleague and interested romance… and you, my love, have crossed it."

"Oh, come on, Jane, really? We're at the beach. You guys took off. We're here in public, not the house, mind you, and look around you; who else is there to do the sunscreen?" he said defensively.

"Oh, don't be so naïve! She's hunting for affection, she's hurt and confused, she wants your, you… I don't know, but it isn't right!"

"Okay, honey, okay. I see your point. I'm not really sure what else I was supposed to do; there was nobody else to… " Jane shot him a hateful glance. "But here we are. Okay, I'll be more careful, okay?" he said, shrugging.

And that was that. Monique knew something was up. She guessed it was about Mark and the coconut oil, but it didn't matter to her, not unless it affected her future aspirations. She smiled quietly, redressed, and headed to the house with equanimity.

While they were out, Gyan and Lauren fetched take-out. With dinner served, they all sat down to watch TV. They chanced upon a rerun of Todd Sampson's Redesign My Brain Series One and they decided to watch all three episodes. Todd's premise was to learn, grow, innovate, adapt and learn. He attempted the World Memory Challenge and then he escaped from chains underwater.

They watched, laughed, and gasped, desiring the brain changes he was talking about. It was fun watching Todd and being provoked to think about neuroplasticity… they were particularly taken with the way the producers had given four simple steps in each episode for personal change.

*

The next day, as serendipity would have it, Mark received a very timely email. After reading Tim Ferriss' book, he had signed up to the 4 Hour newsletter and this latest email was promoting a podcast Tim had just done with Adam Gazzaley. The episode, "The Maverick of Brain Optimization," was about the work Adam had done on neuroplasticity. This field was, of course, broad and full of different projects. Monique was entranced with neuroplasticity and went online to study it further. Here's what she learned…

Neural networks are like highways, with many off-ramps to link with regional roads, back roads, and tracks. Even with congestion, information always prefers the highway. New behaviour requires new pathways. In neural terms, she learned, it takes at least three days to create new neurons (that was a Japanese study from 2011). It takes two weeks for new paths to be laid down by fresh neurons (said an American Neuroscience Nursing study from 2012). But it takes six to eight weeks of practice for those pathways to become new highways (that was an Australian study at UQ in 2013). Then the new "ways" had a chance of taking the traffic away from the old. All this time, Monique had been trying to build new roads for her life, behaviour, and thinking, but lurking in the dark background were older highways used to taking abuse and still angry at men. That was her default network.

It didn't take Gyan long to look through a list of potential Kindle books about neuroplasticity and select a copy of John Arden's Rewire Your Brain. By midafternoon he had ploughed through it and offered his notes as a starter, including actions:

STATES. Neurons that fire together, wire together (that was from Carla Shatz back in 1992). Long practiced states become personality traits.
ACTIONS—Priming: use the right body language, actions and language that matches the mood or state you require. **Exercise:** is a more effective antidepressant and anxiety reducer than any drug on the market because of the release of endorphins and creation of new neurons in the BDNF region of the brain. Serotonin also stops stress before it begins in the system.

MOOD is affected by environmental variables. [Note from Gyan: The genome project only took us so far, epigenetics (what the environment does to the genes) takes us much further].
ACTIONS—Eating: A proper diet with vegetables (for micronutrients), fruits (with natural sugar), wholegrain carbohydrates, protein and small dairy will give your brain a heavy dose of the neuropeptides it needs. Increase water consumption for easy access to the bloodstream. **Go outside:** melatonin helps the immune system. **Socialisation:** Don't get socially isolated. Get out of the house or office, meet real people in real life. Socialisation reduces anxiety and depression because it works the mirror neurons in the TPJ area of your brain. When these are not exercised we begin to spiral downward.
Try labelling: label the emotion you are feeling and become more aware of your state, take action to learn that those emotions can be overcome.

MEMORY is a 'use it or lose it' proposition (said Beth Azar, 2002 in relation to Alzheimer's). Work on it, practice improving it, pay attention to it and your memory will improve.
ACTIONS—Learn: look up memory methods, play memory games, work on remembering 40 things by linking them to eight things and research the loci method. Emotion is a powerful link for memory.
Sleep: Proper, uninterrupted sleep helps you moderate hunger. Natural sleep is better than sleep modulated by drugs or pills. During sleep your brain trims the glial cells, processes memory, consolidates thoughts and regulates cortisol and adrenalin in your blood stream – which are key to reducing stress.

Even though he was a science major, Gyan hadn't been exposed to the human sciences much. Of course he'd come across neuroplasticity before (who hadn't?), but actually applying it to everyday life? That was new. This little family had popped a bubble Gyan didn't even know he'd been in. They were possessed of an idea, the self-application and self-experimentation of ideas that aimed to create personal development. This idea seemed so rare to him, so remarkable, that he had to tell Lauren. He waited until everyone was packing up, clearing, and cleaning before he spoke.

"Lauren, do you realise how unusual it is, this thing you and your mum and dad and Monique are undertaking? I mean, I can understand a group of nurses or doctors trying to master a body of knowledge for an exam, or for surgery… but this?" Gyan spoke softly, in measured tones.

"Well, I guess I've never thought about it. It just seemed to be the thing to do," Lauren said, looking deep into his rich brown eyes.

"No, but think of it!" he went on, "most people read a book, or watch a TV program and they say, 'Hey, that's pretty cool,' and they grab a beer and wander off to the next thing. People just don't take something and try to use it, really use it, for goodness sake, even with self-help books! That's why the industry works so bloody well: by the end of the book they either forget what was being said, apply it to someone else, or find someone to help them implement it. Bingo, next sale!" He shook and nodded his head sideways as he spoke, in the customary Indian mannerism.

"I think we've always been that way, Gyan, willing to learn, hungry to grow, prepared to change," Lauren said, pondering her little family and their history.

"I know I haven't had much exposure to all this, but I think I can improve your process in at least two ways," Gyan said thoughtfully, and when she nodded, he continued, "The first is that this growth, this hunger for change… you have no real way to measure it. You say you're being scientific about it, and that's true in the loosest sense. What you are doing is based on science. But you have no measurement and you don't know if it's working, or how well. If you had a starting point and watched progress or failure… it would work better." He looked askance at her, and she nodded, pondering.

As she looked at her watch and calculated the time to get home, he rushed on, "And secondly, it seems that there's no accountability either… from what you told me in the car coming down here, you just catch up socially. You tell one another what you're doing and kind of trust the journals you've written to help you. You should help one another. You should have the freedom to tell one another when you're just having yourself on, right? To speak up and say,

'Fair go, mate, you're not trying, what's that about,' and so forth. Like your neighbour and her issues. Like a football coach really pushing his players along."

Lauren could see the reasonable nature of his argument and the good intention he had. But still, she had to stop, take a deep breath, close her eyes, and think happy thoughts before answering. For starters he had stopped cleaning up, and in their discussion Monique had already waved to them and driven away.

She accepted the idea of measurement, and agreed that they had not been strictly scientific about their experiment. This was an idea she would later share with her parents and Monique and it would improve their chances of success: each action would have a starting point, a goal and measurement of progress. But on the second point she said,

"However, I have to disagree with you about accountability, at least the way you describe it, Gyan. The power of this experiment is the way it's self-driven. We each become accountable for where we are. We own it, we're responsible, no one else. I think it's fair to ask 'how are you going?' and to look at the actions they agreed to take… but I'm not responsible for whether Monique has her stuff together, or if she's sorted it out with Grandad. The motivation has to come from inside her. Just the very fact of meeting acts as accountability. You know people are going to share, and you'll look like a fool, like a non-player if you have nothing to say. But we are not their partner in getting it done."

Gyan didn't disagree. In fact, he was pleased she had listened to him, and at least considered his suggestion. He happily took the rubbish to the council bins at the end of the street and by the time he got back to the house, both cars were packed and ready to roll out. It was a happy weekend, all things told.

*

Tuesday arrived like a shipping container, fully loaded with burdens and work from Friday. Mark was off to the second day of his Action Learning course. Art, it seemed to Mark, stalked him like prey all day. They and the other participants practiced Action Learning and continued to learn the facilitation skills required. Art was disappointed with Mark's evasion of him (running as he was on an old track, and not knowing that Art really intended him good). Art determined to take him out for dinner the following night. At the conclusion of the third day, John Sautelle invited the participants to do something Mark had never seen before. He invited them to look directly into the eyes of a person, and thank them sincerely for who and how that person was during the training. John insisted they find something specific, an example of their conduct, choices, behaviour or decisions. It was a time of appreciation and acknowledgement of strengths, and more than one person cried.

Art finished the circle by choosing Mark. He said, "Mark, you are one of the most insightful, caring, present people I have ever known. On day two, when you facilitated the group solving my problem, and we deviated off course, you handled it skilfully. I appreciate you.'

When Art finished speaking, Mark didn't know what to do.

The group said their goodbyes and John started to pack up. Art approached Mark and invited him out to dinner to debrief. Mark, whose heart was softened, accepted. He texted Jane telling her he'd drop in on her dad on the way home and he'd be late. They went to Figaro in Kingston and ordered dinner, Arthur's shout, and they chatted about the training while the entrée came.

After a glass of Chianti, Art raised the matter of Mark's resignation. "Mark, I don't want to be awkward and ignore your resignation. I got it, I read it, I thought it was pretty stupid… and I decided to send you to the training with me," he said carefully. "So here's the thing… I wasn't trying to buy you off, or even convince you to stay. The training investment will be worth it whether you stay or go because you're an excellent consultant and frankly, I've come to see you as a colleague."

Mark paused before answering, "Yeah, I was kind of wondering what happened to the resignation… so you mean to say this training was on purpose, not pre-booked?" Mark didn't know what to make of that and he had no clue what was coming next. Entrée was devoured and they waited for mains.

"Mark, I've known you all these years. You remember when we went to the Arbinger Institute training?" Art began.

"Yeah, leadership and self-deception!" Mark remembered it very well. "That was a classic! Angelising self, demonising others, making out our own behaviour to be better and theirs worse… "

"Well, I think your resignation might be based on a bit of that. I think you may have demonised me and angelised yourself. Actually it's more to do with the second half of the book, not knowing yourself quite as well as you think," said Art, hoping to prompt Mark to self-examination.

"Yeah… I remember it… the book says the best strategy is to be open to 360-degree feedback. That others know you and see you better than yourself," Mark said, and now he knew what was coming. Dinner arrived. They had both ordered pasta and wine, their side salads sat beside their massive white plates. "Okay, Art, hit me," Mark said with resignation.

Art shrugged. He'd hoped Mark might think for a while, examine his own history. But that is the nature of self-deception: you can't see what you can't see. He began, "Okay, Mark, stay or leave, but you're gonna face a number of issues. These have never been resolved because, well, because we've never really had this kind of discussion. I fear for your future, mate, if you don't deal with some things… "

"What things?" Mark said a little defensively, talking over the top of Art.

Art took a deep breath, then started in. "Like taking negative feedback. You love positive feedback, but you've never taken negative feedback from anyone." He looked to see if this was reaching Mark. "You gotta learn how to reframe your experience, be more mentally agile, look at it as self-improvement." Art took another deep breath and let the comment sink in.

Mark inwardly agreed; he hated negative feedback. So he kept his defences down and asked Art how to do that, how to reframe. They discussed some strategies then moved on.

"The second issue is that I always feel like you're managing the news with me. Like you check to see if it will be well-received, acceptable, reflect well on you. That's politicizing and you know it. At your level of seniority, you should… well, by now you should be able to speak your mind, mate. You should be able to come forward and tell it like it is," Art said and again, to his surprise, Mark took it on board. Dinner was cleared, dessert and Sambuca were ordered, and their discussion carried on. They had both read Fierce Conversations by Susan Scott and Mark knew very well not to politicize his conversations.

"That's 'a couple of things,' but is there more?" Mark asked and Art nodded. "Are you saving the best for last?" Mark asked.

"Of course! The pièce de résistance is this. To survive in consulting, Mark, you have to, have to, be able to think strategically. In my opinion, you're a tactician and an implementer, but to rise, you need strategy. All the Lords of Consulting have mastered strategy, and… well… it's not in you right now. I want you to survive, I want you to thrive… but you're gonna have to play with the big boys and learn to think up."

Mark readily acknowledged this, at least in his heart. Most everybody is a practitioner: the doer, the player, a front-line soldier. With promotion a person learns to become a tactician: the manager, the team coach, even a CEO or a commander. Very few are asked to, or required to become a strategist: the chairman, the club owner, a general. Those guys have to think environmentally, globally, politically in the long term, they have to handle ambiguous environments and make decisions without all the information, only a strategic instinct. That was something Mark had always struggled with, getting out of the business, the game, the battlefield to see big picture.

He was also amazed at the truth that people can see us more clearly than we can see ourselves. Dessert and alcohol made the whole thing easier to take, but still, Art had given him a lot to think about. At the core of this lay his need to learn new ways of thinking and new ways of perceiving. That demanded neuroplasticity.

When Mark got home he flicked on the laptop and in came an email from Gyan. As well as his list from the book he had read on the weekend, which Gyan had already typed up and distributed, Gyan had read John Arden's other book *The Brain Bible* and penned a few more action items:

Action list

- Eating: Start photographing everything you eat. Track it with a calorie counter, or at leas watching what goes into your body (every packet has a breakdown of the basics).
- Exercising: Start out with ten minutes. Get on that Elliptical Trainer you bought a few yea ago or go for a walk. Build slowly from there. Aim for 30 minutes at least.
- Education: spend less time passively and more time actively, even if it means cooking th meal or fixing a shelf. Determine to learn something every day. Play 'Words with Friends Whatever.
- Environment: Make sure you stop for lunch and meet with human beings, and join a new or group – not online – in the real world!
- Sleep: Become aware of your sleep cycles. In the evening you will feel a wave of sleepir come over you every three hours. Catch one to bed.

CHAPTER TEN: WHO SPLIT MY BRAIN?

"Aberrations of the human mind are to a large extent due to the obsessional pursuit of some part-truth, treated as if it were a whole truth."
Arthur Koestler

Despite her calm outward appearance, Monique was quite messed up. The makeup and her natural demeanour helped to hide what was actually taking place after the drama of last Friday. The work she had done with Jane around taking a third-person position, dealing with guilt, and the confrontation over being at the beach with Mark had all taken its toll. Underneath all that were her failed dating attempts, which only served to further erode her confidence and enlarge the dark, hollow space gnawing away at the foundations of her sanity.

Monique was a mystery to herself. She was reviled by her ex-husband, a man who just five years before she'd adored. She was desperate for company but failed in all her search for love. She wanted so much to be part of Mark's future company but seemed attracted to him, or at least to behave in a way that compromised the integrity of Jane's trust. She had two beautiful children who were turning out well, but she liked to be with them less and less. Her desires seemed to pull simultaneously in two or three directions.

One of Monique's closest confidantes at work was the Defence psychologist Karen (pronounced car-wren). She rang Karen and made a professional, not social, appointment for the following afternoon. Monique wasn't really sure how much to tell Karen, who had already given her a lot of advice as a friend. She had yet to confide in her about the fight for custody of her children, or the brooding anger she still felt. It was all so unsafe.

At home that evening, she put the kids to bed and brought out the double list of actions from the weekend at the coast. Letting her eyes wander down the email from Gyan, she noted her progress. Actually, she thought, *I should use this as a bit of a guide for tomorrow with Karen.* The to-do list compiled from John Arden's books had nine points, next to which she wrote her activity:

States. (I've practised this state I'm in, it's become a trait, that's why I want to see Karen)
Mood. (I'm quite isolated, labelling my emotions will help, ask Karen)
Memory. (Do I really want to go back? This feels unsafe)

Learning. (I'm certainly doing a lot of that with this group)
Eating. (I already track everything on the Lifesum app)
Exercise. (I walk the dog every day, except today)
Education. (What do I need to know if I'm going into a consultancy with Mark?)
Environment. (Have lunch with people every day, yes I do) and
Sleep. (My sleep is terrible, this really needs work)

She wandered into Ryan and Rylie's bedrooms, kissed them good night, and went out into the evening. The vapour trail of a late plane traversed the night sky and intersected the full moon, hovering opulently overhead. There was just enough moisture in the atmosphere that the moon cast a circle, an eerie and vaporous rainbow around itself. The overall effect was hauntingly beautiful and made Monique's heart ache.

*

Driving home from the coast, Mark and Jane had spent quite some time travelling silently. Mark was still ticked off at Gyan and Lauren, but couldn't place why. At one level he really liked Gyan, who was honest, intelligent and treated his daughter with respect. At a deeper level he felt fiercely protective, even aggressive. There was some old track in his brain there, but he wasn't sure what it was.

Jane, for her part, was still brooding about Mark and Monique. Well, mainly Mark actually. Jane trusted Monique more than she knew… Monique was just a needy, broken girl. Mark should have known better. At another more cerebral and disconnected level, she was angry at herself because this all felt like she was being judgmental. It was possible the two of them were innocent and she was just the one being immature.

Jane, tall and elegant even in the car, interrupted the silence and said to Mark, "Honey, I'm sorry I got angry at the beach. I wanted to justify myself, but when I do that, I remember I basically never gave you the chance to defend yourself. I was just, am still just, simmering," and having ended her confession opened the door for him to speak. "Is there anything you want me to know?"

Mark bit his lip. He wanted to say, "I've been faithful all these years" or "It was honestly just innocent" or repeat the words on the beach about him having little choice. Instead, he waited. Finally, he said, "I don't know, honey, it's confusing, isn't it? Not knowing where to go, I'm foggy, and I doubt, well, I just wonder if, not seeing clearly, we might jump to conclusions. Don't you agree?"

Confusing, well yes, it certainly is, she thought. Foggy, doubtful, and unclear? Yep, she was certainly torn.

"Yes, yes, I agree," she said slowly, nodding. It was hard.

"But you know what?" Mark asked, as if mind reading, "We could go round and round, but there's no point arguing, pointless really. It's not that hard. We just choose to trust each other, right? I trust you going to work every day and you trust me every day. We just make a choice, yes?" he said, looking askingly.

She did feel that the situation had been unclear, that she'd jumped to conclusions. She really should trust him. So she did, "Yes, darling, I do trust you and I will trust you." Her brows were furrowed, indicating confusion, but her mind was made up. It remained that way, all the way home. She was glad.

*

In Sydney, Lauren was laughing and laughing at Derren Brown re-runs. She'd just got done watching an episode where Derren, a magician and hypnotist from the UK, had helped a punter take home winnings from a losing ticket at the greyhound races. She marvelled at the power words had on people's perceptions. YouTube automatically loaded the next video which, although only three minutes long, was to have a profound impact on the group. It again demonstrated the effect of words on people's actions and decisions. Derren Brown hopped into a London Cab, and with three sentences confused the poor driver so much he couldn't find the London Eye: a massive structure on the South Bank of the Thames. Lauren clicked the share button and wrote an email to her mum, dad, and Monique, asking, "How is it that words alone (and a little body language) change behaviour so profoundly?" She hit send, hoping they would watch the video.

*

The next day, Monique showed Karen her electronic journal page on the iPad and explained the work they had done on the weekend learning about neuroplasticity. Clearly it was going to take weeks, or months to adapt and create lasting change, but she was prepared to work on it consistently. She told Karen about rushing home to the missing kids in panic. Once that was out, she told her about the incident with Jane's dad (who was still in a coma).

"So what do you want to work on today, Monique?" Karen asked, moving to the therapist space.

"Well, my state, my condition; and my mood, my feelings; and my memory, the deep pool of hard things I've been avoiding," Monique said, ending softly as she realized how large that list potentially was.

"Hmm," said Karen. "That sounds like a bit of work, more than we have time for today, so what's the most useful place to start?"

"I, I don't really know," Monique said, chewing her bottom lip. "The issue with memory, which I guess is sort of driving all this, seems like it should be the place to start, but it all feels so unsafe for me right now. It's like a cave full of monsters. I think it's better if we just leave it all alone. It's too risky."

"Hmm, monsters, a cave, a deep pool, and we're certainly not going in there until you're ready, okay?" Karen said reassuringly, "But I just want to make sure of one thing. Have you analysed all the risks?"

"Whatdaya mean?" Monique said incredulously.

Karen continued, "Well, you're a facilitator; you understand finance and defence risk. You say it feels unsafe; I just want to know if you're looking at all the risks, or only half of them. Right now you're saying, 'Looking at my past feels unsafe; it's too risky,' and I guess the corollary in your mind is that staying as you are is safe… so not investigating is safe, right?"

"Yes, I guess that's what I'm saying—it's too risky," Monique agreed.

"Right, but here's the thing, your decision is based on only counting half the cost, examining half the risk. What's the risk of staying as you are, staying 'safe'? What price are you paying right now and into the future by ignoring it?" Karen asked kindly but firmly.

Monique paused long and hard to think about it. Put that way, Karen was absolutely right. Now that she mentioned it, living on without dealing with the past was also quite risky. The car trip home on that day she had a meltdown showed that. Her sanity was hanging by a thread. She was running a high risk. Her behaviour on the weekend, and Jane's dad, and the dissociation, freaked her out. Like a good therapist, Karen stayed present to her client, but stayed silent.

"On balance, Karen, I think the higher risk sits with doing nothing. It's much better to examine why I dissociated on the weekend. Let's examine what's so scary to my unconscious that it had to derail my conscious mind and take over?" Monique said.

"I have a suggestion," Karen said. "It's a fairly gentle process that stays content-free, meaning you don't have to tell me anything about your story, or what's going on in detail. Wanna have a go at it? You kind of have to move around a bit." Monique agreed. "Firstly, I want you to get clear about what we are hunting for here." Rightly or wrongly, Karen chose those words on purpose because of the word "monsters" used before. Internally Karen was referencing all the models and alternatives she had to hand. Her mind settled on the "time line" she had read about in *Trust Me, I'm the Patient,* by Philip Harland. Then, to be sure she and Monique were clear about what they were working on, she asked, "What's the outcome here? What would you like to have happen?" Monique opened her mouth to speak. Karen beat her to it, saying, "Before you tell me, please understand, I don't actually need to know. As long as you're clear in your mind what issue we are dealing with here."

Monique thought a moment, then nodded.

"Can you get a feeling for what that's like?" Karen asked, and again Monique nodded and said, "Like a darkness, a pool of filth and trouble." Karen frowned because a) she didn't need to know that information and b) that wasn't an outcome. She suspended content-free for a moment and said, "So there's a pool of filth and trouble. And when there's a pool of filth and trouble, what would you like to have happen?"

"Well, I want to get rid of it, to move past it," Monique offered. Not wanting something was not the same thing as wanting something. "Get rid of" was still not going anywhere; it wasn't an outcome.

"And when you get rid of it, and move past it, then what happens?" Karen asked.

"I can live in freedom; I can move on," Monique said, and Karen smiled. That was a lot of moving language. She decided to proceed with the time line idea, but make it physical instead of a conversational exercise. This kind of time line process (called re-imprinting) had been proposed by therapist Robert Dilts.

Karen had two offices, linked by a corridor and shut off from the main office area by a door. She took Monique out into the corridor and said, "Monique, I'd like you to find where past and where future is in this corridor, please."

Monique pointed to the right and said, "That's future, and this way is past," she said, pointing to the left.

"Great, thanks. So I want to you find a place in this corridor that represents today." Monique walked halfway down the corridor and stopped.

Karen continued, "Okay, put your past behind you." Karen had moved to the end where Monique's time line started, at her birth. She opened the door so she wasn't standing in Monique's 'life-line.' Then she said, "So start moving backward down the corridor, slowly. I want you to feel for the moment when this darkness, this pool, this trouble goes away."

Monique shuffled backward with her eyes closed and viscerally felt it go away (the imprint, as Dilts had postulated). Karen had Monique mark the ground with chalk then asked her to continue moving backward, and to her surprise it went away again, like a second phase, or a second garment coming off (an earlier imprint). She stopped again and they marked it again. Then she shuffled all the way back to the end of the corridor, where Karen stood.

"Can I tell you something weird?" Monique asked. "I'm controlling this process, you know, being in charge. But we're hunting for this emotional experience, which right now I feel so separate from. And when I moved past it, bam, it was so physical! Like it was falling off." Karen checked in that this was okay, that Monique wasn't distressed, and all she could say was, "It's like someone's split my brain." But that was okay.

Karen had her walk slowly toward the nearest mark on the floor, but not stand on it. "Now remember the second- and third-person exercise your friend had you do? I want you to look at the memory, the situation, dispassionately. Can you do that from here?" Monique nodded so Karen continued, "I don't need to know how many people are there, but I assume it's more than you?" Monique nodded and said, "Yeah, it was just me and him. We were fifteen." Again, too much information!

"Okay, step off the line and step into second position… I want you to be that person. Give them all the resources they need to make this a positive experience for both of you," Karen instructed.

Unexpectedly, big tears rolled down Monique's cheeks in rolling droplets. She stood for a long time until finally she nodded, smiling just a little. Usually the first impression is the lightest, but in her case it might have been the strongest. "Come back and stand on the time line, just before the chalk mark again and see if we can move forward across that first chalk mark." Monique did, and smiled broadly.

"It's not gone, but it feels more like a bump in the road, or like sandpaper," Monique said, jubilant.

Monique expressed a desire to move onto the second event instead of working at completely removing the first one. So they repeated the process for the second imprint; this also only involved one other person, her husband, at the age of twenty-six. This one faded away more quickly, partly because she had done the exercise once before. Taking all these changes with her, Karen had Monique walk to the "today" spot and experience the change in "now." Monique was very pleased. She was able to bring all those changes into today and really experience them. Their time was spent, and Monique thanked her for the session. As they walked back into Karen's office, her screen saver read:

"Creative activity is a type of learning process where the teacher and pupil are located in the same individual."
Arthur Koestler

The next day, Karen had the opportunity to suspend her normal work and attend a seminar on communication. It was being run by Mark Goulston, an articulate and intuitive neuropsychiatrist, coach, and communicator who had authored (amongst others) the book *Just Listen*. Karen's boss had interacted with Mark on a hostage situation, during his time on secondment with the Californian police. He felt the model Mark had developed would be useful to all. The sixty-seven-year-old (who frankly looked more like he was in his early fifties, according to Karen) was doing a tour in Australia.

After sharing some anecdotes from the field—from tough sales negotiations to parental situations, emotional confrontations and high-stakes hostage crisis work—Mark shared the model which lay at the heart of *Just Listen*. While the book laid out nine core rules and a pathway with twelve ways to obtain buy-in from others, Dr. Goulston only had time to cover the rules section. He focused quite strongly on the very first one. Karen journaled notes for preparing a summary later.

The multi-layered brain. Our brains have several layers. The top layer is the thinking part, which scientists call the cognitive layer. This is what makes us human. The next layer is where memory, learning and emotions are. Scientists call this the emotional layer, or the monkey mind for fun, because it is so social. The bottom layer is watching out for threat and focussing on survival all the time. Scientists call this the biological layer because it controls the body and the vital organs. It is also called reptilian or 'croc' brain because it's so primitive.

Move from 'oh crap' to 'okay'. Under stress, people drop to the 'croc' brain (oh crap) and there's no way they can communicate properly (neither can we for that matter). Move up from that, through realising you're in stress mode, through re-centering (how am I, where are my emotions?), up through re-focussing (cognition and looking outward) to re-engage (I'm okay).

Rewire yourself to listen. First impressions are a jumbled mess of assumptions and thoughts. Put them aside and make a determination to find the real person. Otherwise it will be your fictitious idea of yourself talking to your fictitious idea of them (and remember they're doing the same thing to you)! That's four muppets trying to talk. Ain't gonna work.

Make the other feel 'felt'. Try to 'get' the other person. Real empathy is being able to put yourself in their shoes. As soon as you understand where they are coming from, and they actually feel you've made the effort, and understand, antipathy can switch to collaboration.

Be more interested than interesting. Conversations are not a game of ping pong, smashing the topic back and forth. Practise being interested in the other person, and be sincere. Play detective, be curious and ask real questions.

Make people feel valuable. People that complain, obstruct, resist and whine usually do so because they don't feel valuable. They deserve to feel that they matter. Do this and you will find the passive-aggressive behaviour starts to dry up.

Help people exhale. Some people walk around with pent up emotions and a fury of thoughts running around their brain. This is because their stress has accumulated into distress. Make a place for them to vent safely, in a non-judgmental environment.

Check your dissonance at the door. Dissonance means there's a gap between seeing and perceiving, or between how you expect something to be and how it is. We create this dissonance with people when they perceive and receive us one way, and it's different to our experience of ourselves. The best way to short circuit it, is to ask our friends and family how they perceive us. It is two way, so check in with them about themselves too. [Note to self, you've heard great versions of this: "The story I'm telling myself right now is… " or "My fantasy/illusion/hallucination about what you're saying is… "]

When all is lost, be vulnerable. Remember that croc brain? When you're feeling threatened, attacked or cornered dig deep… feel your fear, face your deficiencies and try a bit of vulnerability [Note to self, go watch that Brené Brown TED talk again].

Stay away from toxic people. If you never say no, you might be codependent. If you struggle to say no, you might be needy or neurotic. If you're terrified to say no, you're probably dealing with a toxic person (con-artist, bully, self-absorbed narcissist, tyrant, psychopath). The best thing you can do is stay away from them. We're not talking about establishing a boundary here, we're saying run!

Karen wrote other notes through the seminar, as her brain fired off connections from the content to link with issues her clients faced. For example, this idea of going down through the layers of the brain as you became more stressed was useful in combat. If stress naturally pressured the conscious mind into the basement, then resilient soldiers would need to learn "oh crap to okay" as a rapid-fire drill to get rational again (Karen noted to write to Mark about this. Maybe her boss would give her Mark's email). Many veterans were struggling with family relationships. Parents could push children into the basement of their croc brain, and as they both got heated and argumentative they would fall further away from rationally resolving their discussion. Kids could get time out to cool off, and the parent too in order to get rational. She'd told many a client, "Don't discipline when you're angry." They were probably in the emotional limbic system and not thinking rationally.

Once the seminar was over, and she had gone back to the office, Karen did a little research on the Internet. She found the original theory of mind first proposed by Paul D. McLean in the 1970s. Paul was a neuroanatomist who observed that the brain had three main layers or systems and combined that observation with what neuroscience then knew about the roles and functions of each region. His biological, emotional, and rational were not very exact separations… and McLean had got into trouble for proposing they were an evolutionary progression. That idea was later debunked, but the layers were there, and they did what he said they did. It appeared that this way of viewing the brain was eminently useful in the field too, as Mark Goulston showed with his various examples from hostage negotiations and marriage counselling to international peace accords.

Karen sat down to write a quick email to Monique about it, knowing her interest in brain science and its application to self-transformation. In it she included links to the works of Mark Goulston, Brené Brown, Paul McLean and another fellow involved in neuromarketing named Oren Klaff. Oren had applied Mark's model of "oh crap to okay" to sales and marketing: you need to address the target's croc brain before you can ever move on to a sale (i.e., do they feel safe and do they trust you?).

Monique received the missive, wrote a quick thank-you in reply, and grabbed a summary off the Internet to review later.

Monique left work with her conscious mind in a "run down" state. She was kind of zoned out, kind of daydreaming, and certainly not concentrating. The drive home was arduous, with traffic heavy, a construction zone, congested movement, and slow progress. She could literally feel her mind sinking quietly down. It was hungry, it was lonely, and it was getting ticked off, frustrated, and emotional. By the end of the drive she was edgy.

She parked the car, honked the horn to let her kids know she was home and went in the front door. Most days Monique was a patient parent, but not today. The energy for her thinking and decision-making was… sub-optimal. She was firing from the emotional hip and the kids were going to cop it. There were toys on the floor, the back door was open and the remains of afternoon tea were left on the benchtop. Unsurprisingly Monique screamed at them. But they didn't come.

A cold kind of intelligence grabbed control of her behaviour and Monique growled. "Get inside… N O W," she yelled. "Clean the bench! Pick up those bloody toys or so help me, God, I'll jam them down your greedy little gobs!" she howled, red-faced and panting.

They got up, and her daughter, somewhat unwisely, thought it was time to tell Mum a bit of home truth.

"You can be such a cow sometimes! You come home from work without so much as a 'hi kids' and you… " That's as far as she got.

Monique grabbed her by the collar and she gave a squeak. "How DARE you! You little weasel-faced rat! Go to your room!" Monique said, incensed.

Her daughter knew a beautiful mistake when she saw one. She seized the opportunity and took off.

As she ran to her room, Monique yelled, "Young lady, you come back here! You need to clean up!" completely illogically.

In retrospect, Monique felt embarrassed at her behaviour. It wasn't rational, it wasn't reasonable and nor was it logical. It was not intuitive, loving or principled. But some part of her felt self-satisfied that she had won. She'd cowered her enemies! Monique apologized to her kids, who in turn apologized her. She made no excuse, but simply got on with preparing dinner, a chore left to her (along with shopping, cleaning, washing, and providing).

She read the material from Karen's workshop, along with the information from McLean, and then the penny dropped. At work today she was in her neocortex, the human brain. On the way home, she'd descended into her limbic system… gone monkey mode… all feelings and emotions… flee from work, fight with the traffic, and desire a mate. At home she'd dropped into croc brain, and so had her daughter. From there, everything was safety and protection. Of course nothing was that simple, her whole brain operated all the time, but still… the metaphor helped.

Monique watched Lauren's video on Derren Brown and laughed hard at the poor cabbie's confusion. Having first put his croc brain at ease ("Would it be okay if we set our equipment up? You'd be okay if we… "), Derren had managed to speak directly to the monkey mind which, when in control of the steering wheel, had no access to memory or logical thought. It was getting late, but she decided to take Karen's email and turn it into a lesson and action plan for the group. The next time they met, they'd have two sets of homework to talk about!

Monique looked back across their journey of self-discovery and self-development. Wistfully she thought of the early days, in deep winter, the frost and dead-looking trees reflecting much of her soul. Weeks of quiet learning and deep struggle, her insanity, and aching depression constantly undermined her sense of progress and a constant state of not enough.

How could she see the improved relationships with her kids, especially in sight of today's debacle? How could she see her workmate's admiration, or the feelings she had provoked in Mark? She couldn't. Far from recognising her amazing potential, or the limitless nature of her human spirit, she felt like she was, in fact, backsliding. Today was a day of failure, not victory (from her perspective). If she were able to stand outside herself, Monique would see great growth, amazing progress, but in a somewhat subterranean aspect.

She was tired, bone-tired, and decided to turn in at last. Sleep swept her into its embrace and no sooner had her breathing become even than she started to dream. She was in a very bizarre building, working and toiling away at her laptop on the top floor. Everything was painted bright cobalt blue. The atmosphere buzzed and hummed with rapid thought, powerful electrical jolts and noise. Suddenly she received email notification to go down two floors to thirteen.

She had an omniscient sense that the top six levels would be painted this blue colour, all buzzing with alpha- and beta-wave electricity. Everything was executive and action-oriented, calculated, linguistic, formulaic, and determined. Quite the place to be. Monique panned around for a name and found it on the elevator button wall. She was in the "neocortex." Was this building a brain? A company brain?

Something demanded she enter that elevator and descend a few more floors, so she punched "9" and went town to an amazing mustard-coloured level. Everything was connected, cables and wires running, crossing, buzzing everywhere. Through a porthole in the floor she could see five more floors full of emotional equipment, memory, learning and environmental response units. The noise here was different, and her "knower" told her it was gamma wave bursts, all very high-energy and creative. Going back to the elevator, she punched "4." Monique wanted to leave what was labelled (as a warning?) the "limbic system."

The final decent took her through four floors decked out in magenta, all the gross and fine-motor control, safety and protection systems, wake-sleep cycle modulation, and sensory-somatic interfaces hummed quietly away, powered by theta-wave sleep and delta-wave power. In the elevator, these layers were called the "brain stem." Monique had a growing sense of danger and panic, like this giant building was somehow alive, sentient, somehow knew her intimately. She woke suddenly, sweating and breathing hard. An image slowly formed in her mind.

She quickly sketched it then jotted some notes and breathed quietly. It was time to sleep, properly.

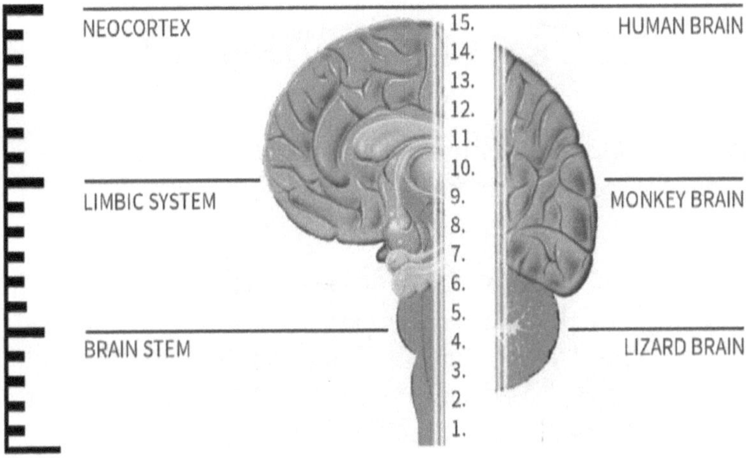

Action list

- Move from 'oh Crap' to 'okay'. This week become aware of dropping into croc brain or m mind and work on moving back to Okay.
- Rewire yourself to listen. When you meet a new person for the first time, put aside your impressions and decide to find the real person.
- Make the other feel 'felt'. Choose one person this week and try to 'get' the other person. Really put yourself in their shoes.
- Be more interested than interesting. In one conversation this week practise being interes the other person and be sincere. Play detective, be curious and ask real questions.
- Make people feel valuable. Choose one irritating person in your life and work to make su they feel that they matter to you, your cause or business.
- Help people exhale. This cannot be staged, but should an occasion arise, serve someor making a place for them to vent safely, in a non-judgmental environment.
- Check your dissonance at the door. Ask a friend or family member how they perceive yc after an interaction.
- In conversation when you hear someone's story say, "The story I'm telling myself right n is... " or "My fantasy/illusion/hallucination about what you're saying is... "
- When all is lost, be vulnerable. When you're feeling threatened, attacked, cornered dig deep... feel your fear, face your deficiencies and try a bit of vulnerability.
- Stay away from toxic people. If you're terrified to say no to someone, stay away from the We're not talking about establishing a boundary here, we're saying run!

CHAPTER ELEVEN: THE MIND BODY SPLIT

"If you would be a real seeker after truth, it is necessary that at least once in your life you doubt, as far as possible, all things."
René Descartes

Gyan was pleased to join the book club started in his honour, as he got back into the swing of life at uni. It might have been something to do with the uni, or the group of people involved, but finding a "common" book seemed really difficult. Each chosen tome pleased one or two and gave the rest a headache. A guy from the science department had suggested the 1994 classic *Descartes' Error* by António Damásio, thinking it was a book on philosophy. Two new members had joined as a result. It turned out that Damásio was a neurologist. His book was basically arguing against the mind-body split.

Today was meeting day and Gyan did not have a headache. He could well follow the discussion as he'd read John Sarno's weighty work, *The Divided Mind*, on psychosomatic illness. That book (which frankly he'd have preferred) explored the way the body created mental illness and the mind created physical pain. He let the layers of conversation wash over him, as he hovered beneath the surface like a large-mouth bass waiting for a tasty morsel to snap at. With his eyes closed and his head in the sun, he felt the intermingling currents surround him…

Gyan was sitting in a cluster of four. They were sticking to topic. Descartes believed in an inseparable divide between body and soul. He acknowledged that these two organs were joined in the brain, but practically he separated body from brain. This is the error Damásio railed against, saying somatic, or body experience, is absolutely central to the formation of ideas of self in the mind, and that the mind would indeed be devoid or deficient without the signals from the body.

Gyan could also hear a group to his left: Clarity, Ming, Lauren, and others talking about a lecture by cognitive scientist Noam Chomsky (a fan of Descartes). This discussion was on language and the structure of ideas… the way mind, body, and brain interact, and a touch of politics. The problem started a long time ago with Plato, they said, who created the mind-body split (someone used the phrase "ontological dualism"). Impressive. Gyan nodded.

But I'm not buying in.

To his right, Jeremy, Paul, and the guy from the philosophy department were discussing René Descartes, the sixteenth century, and the phrase "I think therefore I am." One of them dragged out Eckhart Tolle's 2005 book, *A New Earth*. The reason Descartes' formulation was inherently problematic… was that the "I" that thinks about the "I think" must be a second person. Impressive again, thought Gyan. Furthermore, who is the second "I" at the end in the "I am"? There have to be two intelligences, perhaps even three. But Gyan swam past that very tasty morsel. He had some things to add, but not to philosophy, only to hard science.

Although Lauren was bright, she struggled when the discussion got medical or philosophical. After book club, she quietly asked Gyan if he'd debrief with her. He agreed keenly, always enjoying her company. They went to a local restaurant to talk.

"Pardon my being obtuse, but what exactly is the point? Who cares if Descartes divided the mind and body; who cares if he was wrong?" Lauren asked, rather exasperated.

"Well, there are a large number of applications, Lauren," Gyan said, taking on a bit of a lecturer style. "For example, you know there's plans afoot for a head transplant in Italy in 2017?" Lauren nodded; it had been in the news a lot recently. "Well, setting aside ethical and religious issues for a moment, just consider… if your idea of "self" is only produced in the head, then good for Descartes. But if self is defined by your relationship with the whole nervous system, then that sucks for the Russian guy getting the transplant, because he won't know who he is anymore."

Lauren had heard at least one urban myth about people getting a heart or lung transplant and waking up with someone else's memories. So why not your entire identity?

"Okay, identity is head and body… and I've heard you talk about psychosomatic illness, and brain-body interactions before… that guy who studied phantom limb syndrome and stuff," she added.

"Yep, yes, that's right, but there are more applications," Gyan said. "Damásio says that without the body there is no ground state for the mind. He says that without somatic markers we have no reference for risk, or feelings, or a sense of 'now.' People who know but do not feel are poor at all these tasks." Lauren shivered at hearing him call feelings a task. "The body provides the brain with practical correlates for time, space, and movement," he concluded, with obvious enthusiasm.

Honestly, Lauren thought, *talking to Gyan sometimes feels like talking to Sherlock Holmes. Can he just use normal words for once?*

"Why do I feel like there's more?" Lauren asked.

"Oh because there is!" he said. *Scrub that,* thought Lauren, *I'm talking to Sheldon from Big Bang Theory!* "So I mentioned feelings before; well, somatic markers make emotions felt—afferent. You cannot feel feelings without the body. Descartes was wrong, so wrong, about it. You can't separate or split the mind and the body." He paused thoughtfully for a moment, oblivious to others in the room, then continued, "In fact, medicine is now finally learning about integration, inclusion, cross-checking with other disciplines. In fact, we are discovering more and more about the nervous system. Your body has intelligences of its own."

Before Gyan could go any further however, Ming and Clarity burst in on their covert meeting. Lauren welcomed them openly, Gyan less so.

Meals and drinks were ordered, then Gyan returned to their discussion. "It would seem Damásio stops short of calling the body intelligent. But that book was written in 1994 after all, and since then Michael Gershon, esteemed neuroscientist that he is, has published *The Second Brain*. Gershon laid out the scientific basis of the gut instinct. The gut has a neural network the size of a cat or dog's brain and it acts independently. He argues that it's far too intelligent to just be for accepting or spitting out food," he said. Others in the restaurant were leaning to listen. Professor Gyan was really enjoying this. "The enteric nervous system produces more than thirty neurotransmitters including eighty-five percent of the serotonin—which we use for goal-directed behaviour and happiness, dopamine (for reward), glutamate, norepinephrine and almost all of the painkiller benzodiazepine comes from there. Perhaps here we have the second 'I,' but wait… there's more!" he said.

"There's more?" Ming asked. "You just told me I have a second brain! How do I get to use it?"

"Like I said, a lot of it is about food, safety, motivation, and pain management. But some of it is about intuition, hunches and feelings. Anyway, this is where the HeartMath Institute come in. They have completely mapped a third brain in the heart brain. It has an independent, co-linear cluster of neurons the size of a mouse brain. It produces adrenalin, oxytocin (the chemical of love and connection) and acetylcholine. Here, folks, we may have the third 'I,' and Descartes never knew it. Two other brains and they're down in the body!" Gyan grinned like a cat who'd eaten a mouse.

Lauren responded first. "Well that, and what we learned from Arden and Klaff and McLean about having three layers or systems in our head brain! What a marvellous and complex system!" she enthused.

Ming and Clarity looked on curiously, and asked what on earth she was talking about.

Lauren told them about the lizard, monkey, and human brains, and Gyan couldn't help but correct her ontology and the spurious conclusions that the systems had come from evolution. "Better we call them physical, emotional, and mental systems, I think," Gyan said.

Lauren felt chagrined, embarrassed that being correct about grammar seemed to matter to Gyan more than hearing the actual content of her idea.

*

Since the coastal weekend, Lauren and Monique had exchanged emails a couple of times. Their missives were rarely light and chatty, preferring instead to remain solid and pithy. Monique asked Lauren about her study, anxiety, friends, and Gyan. Lauren asked Monique about her kids, work, homework, and generally sharing about their state of mind. This had been a long-forming bond that had somehow formed between them.

Neither of them told anyone else and thus created a harbour of quiet and trust in which to rest and off-load their cargo.

Lauren shared with Monique what she had just learned about the heart and gut brains, leaving aside almost all of the mind-body philosophy. Monique shared with Lauren about her going postal with the kids, and the way she had descended through her emotional brain to something cold and sinister. They asked each other about homework and progress with neuroplasticity.

*

Meanwhile, next door, it had taken until now for Jane to check her daughter's email. She watched the YouTube video of Derren Brown confusing the London cabbie. When she'd watched it, something growled in her throat, low and ominous. In the lower parts of her brain a defensive system awoke and started tracking back through memory, looking for the suspicious behaviour of others. Eventually it served up the conversation she had with Mark in the car, and the way she had come to agree with him. Then, instead of head fury, she switched to heart curiosity, which was surprisingly seamless. Could Mark have done that to her? If so, what would the conditions have to be?

She did a few searches around the subject of hypnotism at first, and found Derren himself at his page, The Core, saying he did not really believe in hypnotism (in spite of being trained in it, and making a living using it). He felt hypnotism was the subject allowing him or herself to become highly responsive to the hypnotist. They had to be suggestible. Individuals might be highly susceptible to one person and not to another. Work at Harvard had shown that you would not do anything under hypnosis that you did not want to do. But suggestion played a huge role in influencing others, she read.

Moments later Jane picked up the phone and called her friend Maryanne, with whom she had studied at UQ. Maryanne had gone on to study the Program in Placebo Studies at the Harvard Medical School. There she had explored pain-free surgery, almost pain-free childbirth, trance states, and brain waves using QEEG and ECG technology.

Maryanne answered the phone almost immediately, and they caught up for a few minutes before Jane asked about the current state of her research. Maryanne gave her a brief update and asked Jane about herself. Jane shared her concerns that "someone" might have tried manipulating her using persuasion, then asked, "So Maryanne, as a doctor, do you believe in hypnotism?"

"Well, yes and no, Jane. I guess you and I have never really talked about it, but the phenomena is certainly real. The problem is that most of the tests and scales and scores we've used in the past haven't really been testing hypnotism; they've been testing suggestibility," Maryanne said empathetically. "In my field, there were some early trials in the 1970s on the power of suggestion by people in authority. They managed to create a placebo effect on patients preparing for surgery," she concluded.

"Oh yeah, I've heard about those; no, wait, weren't there anaesthetic-free surgeries in the war?" Jane asked.

"Yes, that's where we started to get curious. You'll also recall a fair number of court cases around psychologists and children before testimonials. Suggestion is powerful in creating false memory in children; it's still a hotly debated topic and quite inconclusive," Maryanne said.

Jane probed further, saying that the person who had tried it on her (successfully, as it turns out) was not an authority figure to her (poor Mark).

Maryanne tried to expand on her explanation, "Well, neither are most hypnotists to their audience. But as the show goes on, people are wowed.

Other cognitive variables can contribute to susceptibility like cognitive load (having a lot going on in the background), tiredness, having a great imagination, your level of expectancy, and how motivated you are to believe."

Jane thought, *Oh, okay, that's me.* Her stomach churned and she felt a tension there, kind of like anxiety or guilt.

They chatted a little further, exchanging information about websites and research and then, after promising to stay in touch, they said goodbye.

Jane sat at the desk, wondering. This kind of influence goes unseen almost everywhere. She'd been at a cosmetics party at the house of a friend once and noticed the "script" her friend ran on those present. It was laced with phrases like, "By now you should have seen" [buy now!] and "most people don't fulfil their day… just dream of the day when… " [fulfil your dreams!] and "we're looking for a miracle cure that… we all need a healer… this cream works wonders" [miracle healer cream!]. She was revolted by it.

Jane filed this away and resolved to be on the lookout for manipulation. That's how she saw "influence" and "suggestion.".

Once Mark got home, Jane rather guardedly shared a little about her day and her conversation with Maryanne, watching Mark's face the whole time to see if there was any trace of guilt or shame. There wasn't.

For his part, he had been stewing on Art's feedback. Jane had forgotten the detail of Mark's trouble at work. Exasperated, he reminded her: "Art reckons I need to learn to take negative feedback better, less defensively. Actually, if you discount for niceness and overcareful delivery, he actually said I never take any negative feedback well," he said.

His response both surprised and disarmed her, and she forgot all about her accusation of manipulation. "I don't know," she replied, "you've always done that pretty well with me, I think. What else did he say?"

"He also reckons I manage information with him, only tell him the good stuff, and keep the bad news in my head. Like I don't know how to confront and just tell it like it is. What do you think?"

"What do I think? Yeah, I think you manage the news; who doesn't? We do that all the time," Jane said. "What else?"

"Well okay, but he wanted me to confront and tell it like it is," Mark said expectantly.

Yeah, confrontation isn't a strong suit for either of us. Only some people really get off on that. It might be a problem in business, I mean, when you're on your own, she said, in her head adding, *Or not so on your own because you've invited five others along*.

"What else?" she asked.

"Well, he said I think tactically and not strategically," Mark said finally.

"I'm, err, I… what's the difference?" Jane said unsurely.

"Oh, okay, sorry, Jane, well… " Mark tried to think of an example she might be familiar with. "Think of Rugby League or Union. Yeah? The guys out on the field are practical thinkers, doing the stuff. The coaches are the tactical thinkers: game plans, offensive and defensive plays, training regimes and so forth. The team owners are the strategic thinkers. They are operating at whole-of-game level. Money, supply, stadium, crowds, culture, everything."

"Sounds like war. The soldier, the field commander, and the general back at the Pentagon," Jane said.

"Exactly!"

"Well that's the worst news of all, Mark. You can't run your own consulting firm if you aren't able to do that!" Jane said with just a little too much attack, pushed by a small edge of fear.

He gulped, sitting down, the weight of those words heavy on his shoulders, and paradoxically the truth of them setting him free in his heart at the same time. Some part of him knew this all along. His doubts came to a head, doubts about his ability, preparedness, and the business plan all coming into sharp doubt because of Art's truthful words. Hard-edged, loving, and honest. What was he supposed to do now? His gut reaction was to throw in the towel and ask Art if he would have him back. After all, Art had taken a huge risk at dinner that night, and bothered to take him out to training too. Maybe, just maybe…

Both their phones sounded an appointment alert. They both reached for their phones, almost bumping heads as they checked what it said: "Cooking School, Belconnen Markets."

"Oops. I forgot; did you?" Jane said, and Mark nodded. If it was possible to smile mournfully, that's what he did. He was happy-sad about the outcome of their conversation and about the cooking school. He wanted to sulk at home with a glass of wine. But out they went.

*

Mark and Jane were booked to do three weeks of cooking classes at a cooking school at the Belconnen Markets. It was based out of a restaurant in

Civic. The objective of the school was to teach people how to cook healthy food for themselves. Mark and Jane pulled into the car park at the Belconnen Markets, a car park surrounded on four sides by single-story buildings that housed restaurants, seafood, meat, and vegetable wholesalers and other stores. They looked around and found the white marquee, where trestle tables had been set up with barstools. Two chefs were standing at the front and there was a very respectable mix of people their age who had come to learn. Over the door was a sign that read,

"Listen to your intuition. It will tell you everything you need to know."
Anthony J. D'Angelo

One of the things the chefs were passionate about was the obesity epidemic. This night was going to be a little longer than Mark and Jane thought—three hours actually. The chefs would be taking them through ingredient selection, flavour matching, nutrition, food preparation, and cooking.

They kicked off by presenting the student chefs with a long row of ingredients and asked them to come and select the elements of a salad. There were five different kinds of lettuces, four kinds of tomato, tuna, hard-boiled eggs, Niçoise olives, kalamata olives, anchovies, beans, boiled baby potatoes, asparagus and purple onion. Everyone got a serving of vinaigrette dressing. The only rule: it had to look good, and for that there had to be diversity and colour.

One chef was all about the food. The other was all about the science. They enthused about all sorts of interesting information. Mark and Jane learned that the body naturally desires to be healthy. But in the hunter-gatherer phase of our history, we learned to look for and eat foods which were high in natural sugar, salt and fat. These elements were terribly rare back then, but are plentiful now, in virtually every food. Our "software" hasn't caught up with the environment change and now we're getting obese.

Science Chef said, "The French say *L'appétit vient en mangeant;* the Italians sound a bit sexier, L*'appetito viene mangiando.* It means the appetite comes in the eating… French and Italian cooking is high in fat. More fat is enough to make for more food intake!" He giggled.

One person, struggling with their Niçoise salad, asked, "How do we get back to the 'crave health' state if we've so far gone as a society? And there's so much fat, salt, and sugar in our foods? I mean, it's everywhere, right, hidden away in almost all of our foods! We don't stand a chance!"

Science Chef answered, "That's a great question. We must first get free of our addictions. A diet high in these three ingredients—and all Western diets are—is as addictive as cocaine. So it's going to take time to go through rehab. We start with fresh ingredients: raw and whole foods, and we start with homemade instead of bought!"

Mark and Jane then learned that whatever you eat slowly changes your brain and your gut. If you consistently eat one set of things, the "striatum" in your brain changes and resets the appetite (or the seeking mechanism). This takes about six weeks to switch and six months to cement the change.

"Slow everything down, relish the meal. Don't rush to get through it! Allocate more time to your meals!" Food Chef preached. "Slow change makes deep change."

Now that the salad was made, Food Chef had them come to the front and grab a circular tray with tiny plastic cups, each with a single ingredient in it. They were told to hold an ingredient, like a cranberry, peanut, sultana, popping candy, popcorn, or sweetcorn. After they had touched it, they were to smell it, and after that to rub it on their lips, and only then to pop it in and let it melt. No chewing! It was a wonderful experience.

"Changing diet from Western to healthy also changes your gut, or more specifically the bacteria in it," Science Chef said. "Scientists used to believe that cravings were the body's way of telling us what to eat. They learned that this is a myth and has been debunked. Instead, it is the microbiota, the gut bacteria, that give us cravings. These are demands of food for them, not us. If it is bad bacteria craving a victory over good bacteria, don't give in!"

"By contrast," Food Chef said, "we should check in with somatic signalling. This is what people call 'gut instinct' or intuition. We're not looking to obey cravings at all; we're checking in with the wisdom of our gut brain. That's why I had you come and select the salad ingredients, and you selected the tasty morsel to enjoy. That's more likely to be instinct than craving because you're choosing from this prepared menu, not from 'desire.'"

Science Chef nodded his agreement. Then he brought out a range of meats: chicken, veal, venison, lamb, beef, king prawn and pork. He instructed them to put aside their prejudice or preference and ask their "somatic intelligence" about, which meat to BBQ. He wanted them to explore a healthy intuition and once choices had been made, he had them BBQ the meat to his exact specification. While they cooked, he brought out a range of sauces: Smokey BBQ, Peri Peri, Fruit Chutney, Garlic Onion, Salsa-Verde Yoghurt,

Moroccan Dukkha, Port-Wine Jus and Creamy Pepper. Again he asked them to instinctively match the sauce with the meat and together they enjoyed the salad, meat, and water for the meal.

The education was way more than Jane or Mark had bargained for. Honestly, they had expected to learn some good cooking, but in addition they learned about obesity, taste buds, a bit of brain science, microbiota, instinct, and intuition. The wife of Science Chef got chatting to them afterward. They showed an above-normal interest so she suggested they look up a book by Grant Soosalu and Marvin Oka called *mBraining*. They thanked her and travelled home with full bellies and fuller minds. They were exhausted, so they turned in, leaving any "braining" research to the weekend.

*

The next day dawned as beautiful as a song. Both Mark and Jane decided to take a flexi-day. Mark just wasn't ready to talk to Art or ask for his job back. Jane had done more overtime than anyone else in her section. So here was Friday, warm and inviting. They seized the moment, opening the day up for whatever they might create. First thing was a swim in the heated pool, then a light breakfast together and a walk for the dog.

The day soon warmed up properly, and the two of them basked in the sunshine and each other's company. Mark sat with his laptop and Jane with her iPad. She was speed-reading a Kindle version of *mBraining*. She learned that the body, or the nervous system, had three brains: the head (cephalic), the heart (cardiac) and the gut (enteric). She had written down:

- The head brain controls cognitive processes, perception, thinking and logic; making and assigning meaning; the chemistry of emotions and protective instincts.
- The heart brain controls the process of emoting, feeling, and affect; relational attraction (oxytocin), bonding and connecting with others; our values system and what's important
- The gut brain controls acceptance and rejection, disgust and contempt; personal identity preservation/safety; mobilization, motility and the chemistry of courage.
- Head, heart and gut are connected via the vagus nerve. The Autonomic Nervous Syster (ANS) has two branches: the sympathetic and parasympathetic. One is an accelerator, t other is a brake. They get out of whack and need resetting from time to time. The most effective way to do that is through breathing exercises. (I wonder if that's why yoga is he to Monique?)

Mark was working his way through the Jamie Oliver website, looking for lunch and dinner recipes. That dinner last night was simply amazing and he wanted more.

Jane had put down *mBraining* to focus on an idea from last night. How to distinguish "good" desire—for raw, natural, healthy, nutritious food, and "bad" desire—produced by the microbiome of bad gut bacteria trying to sustain itself. She realised that this was futile because the colony actually assisted its host (her) to digest food. So she went on the Internet to find out about discerning between cravings and gut instinct. She came across something called "Damasio's somatic markers" and explored the literature for that. She came across some research from the psychology community working with the three brains among eating-disorder sufferers.

It grabbed her interest so she called out to Mark, who was in the middle of downloading a gâteau recipe, "Hey Mark, this German researcher is looking at rational and intuitive decision-making about food... she says that eighty percent of your decisions should be self-regulated—gut brain, instinct, and twenty percent self-controlled—head brain, reason overriding craving... Hey, what's that you're looking at?"

Mark looked a bit guilty. Chocolate cake? Okay, that was fat, salt, sugar, and probably not what his body really needed... but still! "I guess it's in the self-control category?" He smiled weakly.

Jane frowned and continued, "People whose eating has gone into addiction land, like the morbidly obese, and those suffering anorexia or bulimia, spend ninety-nine percent of their mental energy on suppressing gut instinct, ignoring their 'knowing' what the right thing to do is. Shocking, don't you think?"

He demurred. He still liked chocolate cake. He typed in a search for "fat-free, sugar-free, salt-free dessert" and up came brownies, oatmeal pies, banana bread and almond milk ice-cream recipes on Pinterest (he gave the spicy roasted chickpeas and the cream of broccoli ice cream a miss).

"I wonder how to make a useful exploration of gut instinct and heart intuition?" Jane thought aloud. But Mark had gone inside.

Something inside him was weeping. Twice this week he had journaled about weight loss. The images had turned his mind to weight loss now. He was standing naked on the bathroom scales. Mark weighed in at 91 kg. For a man his age and height, that put him in the overweight category, one step from obese. He resolved to do something about it. But what?

Previously Mark had been off to see a nutritionist, who had given him the revised Australian food pyramid. It clearly showed more vegetables than he ate, and a lot of vegetables he didn't like. Mark simply loved meat and wasn't about to apologise for that. He and Jane, who by contrast really did like veggies, worked at their menu plan and he'd lost a few kilos. But the weight just came back. He had been told to move away from carbs, and this was backed up when they read Tim Ferriss' *4-Hour Body*. So they opted for a low-carb diet, avoided potato, watched their alcohol intake and again his kilos shed. But they came back. On another occasion he and Jane started juicing for all the micronutrients to boost the immune system and GI tract. On this occasion Mark felt amazing, but lost no weight.

Still Mark stood there on the scales wondering, *What else?*

Jane was also struggling with her weight. Although you'd never know it to look at her, Jane also felt she was overweight. And maybe she was, by a kilo or two. That was why she was so keen to explore the gut brain, somatic wisdom and her enteric intuition. She knew her body craved health, and she wanted to give it a path toward that. She opened her email browser and was surprised to find an email from Monique and Lauren, bringing her in on their conversations about *Descartes' Error*. She was fascinated to learn that for centuries, and even still in medical schools today, people would consider physical symptoms separate from thought life and mental illness separate from biological causes. Those days, she hoped, were coming to an end, as integrative medicine took hold.

She flicked them a copy of her notes from this week, which included her learning from *mBraining*, the cooking class, and her research today, and copied Gyan and Mark. At the bottom of her missive, she included an action list:

Action list

- Explore eating this week. If you make your own breakfast or lunch pause to see what yo like having, what you are hungry for may be different to what you need to eat.
- Explore food this week. Slow the whole eating process down. Smell, touch and slowly ta your food.
- Discerning the difference between a craving and a genuine somatic intuition. The bacter within, the brain is without.
- Reset your ANS using the heart neuron through a breathing exercise. Breathe in for six seconds, hold then breathe out for six seconds. Then try ten in and ten out.
- Grab a hot water bottle (full of hot water from the tap of course), and hug it for a few min Then put your feet on it, then your hands. Lay down and put it on your tummy (stomach) Journal your thoughts and feelings.
- This week be on the lookout for sudden or strong and compelling "feelings" or a judgmei something is right or wrong. Notice your intuitions, and where they arise from (heart or g and decide whether to follow them or not.

CHAPTER TWELVE: HEALTHY MOTIVATION

"Intuition is always right… it is always in response to something and it always has your best interest at heart."
Gavin de Becker

So there he lay, perhaps through no fault of his own, completely helpless and also completely oblivious to the world around him. So far as the doctors, nurses, palliative-care staff, and night cleaners were concerned, Jane's dad was blissfully unaware. Had any of them cared to attach a deep-cycle QEEG machine to his head, they'd notice consistent delta and theta waves pulsing away. But when Jane visited, he would emit alpha waves from time to time, like a submerged log attempting to surface, only to be driven down again and sink. Occasionally, the readings would tell them, he would hear and even understand. But only occasionally.

Perhaps this was the way with all coma patients, or perhaps only those who have strong emotional (positive or negative) feelings and attachments to their visitors. Such was certainly the case for Jane's father, who carried his fair share of guilt, though little shame, and strong love, though little affection, for his daughter. She stood over him, her feelings mirroring his own. She felt ashamed of him and little guilt about her suffering at his absence. She felt affection, as one does for a lost puppy or a trinket, but little love. So, why are you here? she asked herself. Yes, why indeed. Because she felt she needed to. That was enough.

Jane wandered the ancillary corridor, attempting to self-analyse. It was as though she were trying to peer into places without words, places that had only feelings, instincts, guttural, and visceral motivations. What lay at the back of her "need to"? *Is it guilt? No. Obligation? Yes. But why? Because of… pain. I feel ashamed of my father's behaviour, and I am trying to honour Monique. Ridiculous,* she countered herself. *Neither dad nor Monique know I've come. It's not for them; it's for me. Pain. Hmm. There's also something else. Maybe Monique will find out and then… she'll be grateful. Miracle of miracles, maybe dad will find out and he'll be grateful… or punished by the burden he's been to me.*

All her reasons so far sounded fairly… base, kind of beneath her, but she lacked any "higher" purpose or drive. *Visiting him certainly does nothing for my self-coaching or brain hacking, does it?* she reasoned quietly. *I'm coming because I choose to come; nobody has a gun to my head; Mum isn't here to guilt trip me. Nope, just me, so why am I here?* The trail went cold and she found no bigger-picture motivation. And so she left.

*

Mark was grateful that Art tended not to be arrogant, proud, or one to say "I told you so" because otherwise this meeting would have been really hard to take. Art gestured toward a pair of wingbacks by the windows. All the scene needed was a wood fire and a throw rug and they'd be having one of "those" conversations he'd had with his father. He did feel a bit schoolboyish, his pant legs riding up his shins as they were.

"Art, thanks for seeing me," he started awkwardly. "I guess you know what this is about?"

"I can guess," Art said.

Mark was grateful again. No playing dumb and forcing him to draw it out. "Right, well then, what can I say?" *Come on, Mark!* he thought to himself, *Words stay in your head till you form a complete bloody sentence!* "Well, it's about my resignation and your chat with me at Figaro's. I've thought about everything you said and I've come to agree, well, mostly agree, with you. The thing that especially gets me is my inability to see strategically," Mark continued, Art smiling encouragingly. "It means I'm not really very able to go out there and do this myself, and it also makes me less appealing to another firm. Sorry to make this selfish, but I'm wondering what you were going to do with me if I hadn't resigned?"

Art continued to smile, looking for all the world like a person who had a plan. "Mark, what you've done today is very courageous, and also very humble. I'm assuming you were going to get around to asking for your job back?" Mark looked at the floor, smarting at the fact that Art got there before he did, "But before we talk about that, I'll answer your question. The plan was to pair you up with Smythe and Johnson, send you out on assignment with them, rub shoulders with the big boys, and absorb the way it's done. But first I was going to have the three-point chat with you, and you beat me to the punch," Art said, nodding.

"Oh, fair enough then, so I hurried things along?" Mark looked surprised, given the review he'd just had. "Smythe and Johnson, they're gonna make partner soon, aren't they," he finished without the rise in tone required of a

question.
They sat in silence until Art asked, "So what now?"
"What now indeed. The main driving force behind my stupidity was being upset with you because we always saw my reviews differently, and I felt like you were punishing me. But I can see now that was my own blindness, and the way I was framing everything you did. Man alive, look how much evidence I deleted from the equation! The creativity training, then the goal-setting training, the team-development days, the action-learning coaching, and your talk at Figaro's. You were grooming me all along," Mark said, grateful and sad at the same time.
"And I still can," Art started, "if you can convince the partners. I only have so much sway, but at the end of the day the rest of them have to believe you're worth it. I want you to draft a letter, but forget the apology and the self-deprecation. Mark, you need to fight for your life! Tell us what you've learned, tell us what our investment has done for you; tell us what your aspirations are now, and how that will help the partnership. Tell us how you're going to address your shortcomings. You'll have me at your back, and who knows, you might even get a promotion for it."
Mark could scarcely believe it. He was terrified and excited at the same time, and he thanked Art.
Art jumped up from his chair and Mark joined him on his feet more slowly. Art said, "Don't thank me; this was the whole board's idea. You were, that is to say, you are, a rising star. You just gotta pitch it." And the meeting closed.
Rising star? thought Mark. *What do they see in me?* Mark didn't know whether to return to his office, which he officially had for another week before his resignation date, or to go home because there was no work for his post. He stayed and wrote and wrote and rewrote until his fingers hurt. It sent a powerful message to both his workmates and his supervisors.

*

Monique was brooding over the way she had gone postal at her kids last week. In the course of any parenting, she imagined, parents lost it. Kids did too. Only yesterday her son told her of a kid in the park who just snapped and "totally lost it." The phenomena wasn't new for her, but the self-awareness was. She had literally felt herself going from highly emotional to cold hard punisher, while at another level a part of her stood watching calmly, wondering why she was being such a brutal and emotional person. Since that moment however, the three had collapsed back together and she only had one consciousness again. Even during meditation and yoga, this separation did not occur. But Monique remained curious.

She penned an email asking Lauren what she had learned about going postal, losing your temper or mind. Had she experienced such a thing, not being a mother yet and all? Some hours later, after study break, Lauren found the email and wrote back describing her "four levels" experience, and Gyan being able to track seven layers of thinking. Lauren suggested having an IM conversation and an hour later, once Monique found the email, they got started.

M: hey babe

L: hey yourself

M: so I'm curious to see if we're saying the same thing

L: me too

M: my 'three' were three kinds of consciousness

L: mine were four layers of consciousness

M: mine were like persons, three positions, being split up

L: mine were like four places of attention, streams

M: could you feel them, in different places inside yourself?

L: nope, I could sense them, in four places outside myself

M: right so they might be something different. Mind or body?

L: oh, I don't know. Probs mind though. I'll watch next time

M: I don't know what mine woz either

L: Gyan gets seven streams of thought, internal, but they're not people/persons

M: looking 'outside' including mind, heart and gut might give him even more streams

L: feeling inside might do the same. I'll talk to G

M: cheers

L: bye

*

Gyan was tall and lanky and looked straggly in any lounging furniture. His arm span was wider than his height and his calf length was longer than most seating. So he always looked hunched, or squashed. In an attempt to look more casual and less uncomfortable, he lay stretched out on one of Lauren's single-seaters. It was absurd.

Lauren finished texting. "I hate Facebook IM. I don't know why. I guess I just got used to texting," she said.

“I hate phones. They’ve become massive, multistream communication devices. I mean, just look at this stupid thing”—Gyan said, pulling out his phone—“Just start with the fact that I can’t reach the top of the screen with my thumb, it’s so long! I get notifications on Facebook, Facebook messenger, LinkedIn, the uni group on LinkedIn, text messages, missed calls, and Pinterest. It goes off all the time!” As if to underscore the truth of this, his phone dinged.

Picking up on a useful metaphor, she said, “Hey, Gyan, Monique and I were talking about her meltdown last weekend; the lizard-, monkey-, human-brain stuff; the head-, heart-, gut-brain stuff… ”

“Oh yes,” he said, sitting up, curious.

She continued, “Well, she had an experience where there were kind of three of her, three places of watching and experiencing behaviour. Is that what it’s like for you with those seven layers of thinking, or is it more like that phone of yours, with seven streams of data coming in?”

“The phone? Yes, much more like the phone,” he concluded. “But there are days when I feel highly motivated, where I can find multiple sources of motivation inside me. That’s not exactly like being three people, but it is like different sources inside.”

Fair enough, Lauren thought, already drifting to the problem of ontology: he said this and meant that; she said that and he thought it meant this. Were they talking about separate things? *Probably*. For a start, streams and people and layers and places were very different metaphors. Each word also carried diverse meaning. This could also be true of a single event, with three witnesses seeing it from different vantage points. It seemed to also be true of self—*my experience of myself can often be very different to the way others experience me*, Lauren thought.

*

Jane felt the same way standing in front of her gym instructor at the AIS. He held up a chart in front of her, saying, “Jane, look, the ABSI isn’t the most accurate measure of your health, even though it includes your waist size, which is fine by the way. I’d rather stick you in the DEX machine to get accurate BMI, but just look at the diagram,” and he held up a graph with diagonal lines and yellow-, orange- and red-coloured areas on it. “For a woman your age and height, you’re in the normal range, right in the middle of it. You’re normal,” he concluded.

Then she stopped, thought, and returned to being combative. “All right, then why do I feel so fat?"

He was smart enough not to jibe her, or attack, but instead went for placating. "I'm no psychologist, Jane, and I can't say why you feel fat. You don't appear to have a mental illness." *An unfortunate choice of words*, he thought later.

"Mental illness! Look at me, I'm not anorexic, for God's sake!" Jane said, raising her voice.

"No, no, obviously no, sorry. What I meant… " he said, holding up his hands with open palms face up, "What I meant is that you might feel larger or heavier than you are, or at least larger than we perceive you to be; you might feel bloated but not be heavy, right? You might be a certain weight but be carrying water. Or you might feel great but have internal-organ fat. It's so hard to get that right." He smiled hopefully at her and Jane was calming down a bit. So he continued, "What really matters here is how you feel. I'm encouraging you to aim for being healthy rather than for a target weight. Instead we aim for good exercise and good diet."

Jane nodded in agreement. *Okay*, she thought, h*ealthy as a target*. Then her unconscious served up a hundred ways she had started eating or exercising right before and failed. This prompted a question.

Her face must have adopted a questioning look, because he jumped in with, "Why do I feel like you have a question? I hope it's that and not something else!" He smiled benignly.

"Sure it's a question; it's not indigestion. You know this isn't the first time I've gone on a gym binge," she started.

He chimed in over the top, "Not a binge—a program—something to stick to," he said.

"Yeah, but before they were all on-again, off-again. How do I stick at it? How do I make this one last? I want to go the distance and really become healthy," she said.

"Well, it's interesting you ask because we're holding a seminar tomorrow night about motivation, health, and food," he said.

"Oh, okay, tomorrow night. I'll see if I can make it," she promised. He handed her the timetable for exercise and on the flip side a simple diagram of a clock with "23 and a half" written next to it, and a picture of a smiling doctor beside that. "What's this?" she asked.

"Oh, I'm so glad you asked! That's Dr. Mike Evans. He did a whole bunch of research and found that the most effective treatment for depression, and knee-injury recovery, and a whole bunch of other metrics, was half an hour of exercise a day. That leaves twenty-three and a half hours for the rest of your life, right? Brilliant idea, brilliant. We put that there to remind you that even if you choose not to stick to this timetable, just do half an hour of anything: walk the dog, get off the bus a few stops early and walk, garden, swim, anything!" His enthusiasm was hard to deny.

"I'm training for the triple triathlon, for God's sake! I'm not going to just walk two stops off the bus!" she was going to say. But as soon as she thought of it, some other part of her realised that fact contradicted her "I look fat in these jeans" head space. So she didn't.

*

Still in her gym gear, Jane headed for home; she had a clear run at this time of night. She and Mark were due at their second cooking class later that evening. Arriving home, she gave Mark a quick peck on the cheek, took a five-minute shower, and they were off. It was much easier the second time round: they knew the rigmarole and expected the flow of the evening. Some food would be pre-done whole, some would be partly prepared, and some would be ingredients for them to cook from scratch.

As they worked their way through the entrée, Food Chef reiterated the idea that sugar, fat and salt were addictive chemicals that changed the actual structure of the brain. He asked them to share their own attempts and struggles to shift to raw, whole foods, and Jane had to repress her superiority (and laughter) when the woman next to her spoke of buying kin-oh-ah for the first time. She learned over to Mark and whispered, "It's 'keen-wah.' Please!"

Food Chef spoke of needing to take time to "clear your addictions" and change your tastes before your body would crave health again and gave testimony to the fact that it took him three struggled-filled, mentally stressed, coming-off-addiction weeks to quit sugar, then his taste buds became really sensitive to it.

Mark was pleasantly shocked at the combination of tastes they were given in their servings. Once again there was a palette of options: whole roasted garlic in rosemary sauce, eggs devilled in white wine and paprika, strawberry paste on celery sticks, cherry tomatoes dipped in chocolate, citrus-and-wasabi-soaked prawn toast, beetroot in green peppercorn sauce, and balsamic vinegar on figs.

Food Chef had them prepare and cook dinner, which carried on the strangeness. They made choko and strawberry jam, pork crackling and sour plums, crocodile in white chocolate, emu with passionfruit and lavender, or chicken with camembert and lemon basil. The Chefs gave full credit to Carl and Kelie Kenzler from Ritual Restaurant in Nelson Bay for their degustation menu and their focus on "molecular gastronomy."

Dessert included Besan cake and mild curry sauce, kumquats in sage, apricots in harissa yoghurt, palm-cane sugar coffee sorbet, and ginger-soaked yuzu. As they were brought out, and the participants shown what to do, Science Chef told them about the importance of using seasonal foods, especially foraged foods or, at the very least, Australian foods.

"What do you think the big deal is about foods like these?" Science Chef asked.

"They're certainly different, but surprisingly yummy!" one student called.

"Yep, and what's the big benefit of different? By the way, every combination tonight has been chemically matched; they really go together!" Science Chef said. "Your body knows how to do this naturally, but we've been swamped with fat, sugar, and salt."

Food Chef called out before any student had a chance, "It surprises the brain and it starts to pull together disparate ideas and thoughts. That's gamma-wave activity: divergent, collective, creative!"

The students drew a blank look.

"Yep, that and if you take a careful look at what we've served you tonight," Science Chef enthused, "you'll find a cornucopia of neuropeptides! In these dishes we aimed for the emotional ingredients that change your mood. You should find the buzz very similar to endorphins. Your food literally becomes your mood—trust us."

One earnest, middle-aged student put his hand up and asked, "Sorry for being simple, but what's a peptide?"

Science Chef humbled and replied, "Ah yes, sorry. A neuropeptide is a molecule that neurons use to communicate with one another, kind of like the semaphore, the flags ships use to speak to one another. But these bad boys influence the brain in really specific ways. How can I put this, um, one set of peptides is involved in modulating your immune system, another set manages blood pressure, another for insulin, another for sexual attraction, and another set for emotions. They all come to us through food!"

Satisfied, the man put his hand down.

The evening finished on a high as Food Chef "poured" them all a glass of

Irish cream and peppermint ice cream through liquid nitrogen, which beaded instantly. None of them had ever seen it done before. Mark and Jane already felt like their investment had been worth it and they had one more week to go. Tired and full, they hardly talked on the way home.

*

The next morning, Jane told Mark about the motivational seminar at the AIS gym. He hesitated at the idea of a "motivational" seminar, but Jane assured him that it wasn't "that" sort of motivational… she meant to call it a seminar about staying motivated. But that didn't make it sound any more appealing. He said he'd think about it.

Something had really been snagging at Jane since the group had discussed state management. She knew that changing state changed outcomes, and she'd even had a brief discussion with her "self" about the resistance she'd had to running the Sri Chinmoy. The net result of that discussion was Jane B's complaint that she wasn't listening. But Jane B had refused to give any specific signalling or permissioning during her training since then. Jane had promised to "be more aware… and watch for you pulling me back." Instead though, there had only been very non-specific resistance to the training regime as a whole and Jane had done a lukewarm preparation for her upcoming event.

She texted Ian Snape, asking if he had five minutes to answer a question about unconscious resistance. He did. She fired up Skype on her iPad and dialed him.

"Hey Jane, what's up?" Ian gazed intently at her and smiled briefly.

"Hey Ian," Jane said, knowing she needed to get straight to the point. Ian was a highly intentional individual: direct and purposeful. "You know I've been prepping for a race, and I've been trying to work with my unconscious on signalling around permission. Well, I'm kind of stuck. I've dealt with internal beliefs, I've built a Circle of Excellence, I've respected unconscious boundaries, but she still seems to be resisting me."

"Hmm, okay," Ian intoned curiously. "What was the first thing your unconscious said to you?"

Jane blushed for a second, looked down, then said, "She said, 'I don't trust you.'"

"I don't trust you, I see, and what was the last thing she said to you?" Ian asked.

"She said, 'Some respect wouldn't hurt either,'" Jane replied, still unsure where this line of conversation was taking them.

"It seems to me," Ian said, "that your unconscious is unwilling to co-operate because she feels threatened, she doesn't trust you because you've overdone it before and done damage to yourself. Or at least she senses you don't respect her and you're trying to control the outcome instead of cooperating. So you're in a stand-off."

"Yes, yes," Jane agreed slowly, "she said we would achieve more together than just me on my own."

Ian nodded. "And that's absolutely true, Jane. You need to build rapport with self, and resolve this inner conflict. You don't trust each other. The path to that is for you to treat her with respect. You have different motivations. She is driven to avoid pain, to protect you, to keep you safe, and is watching your environment all the time. To get your goals, you really can't be pulling her into harm's way. Why don't you start there, with respect instead of control?"

After they'd said goodbye, Jane was startled by Mark as she turned around.

"Do you think that'll work with weight loss too?" he asked.

"Oh, honey, hi! I didn't see you standing there," she said. He smiled unsurely, and she answered, "I don't see why not. I mean apart from some other diet or idea, and we haven't tried sugar-, salt-, fat-free yet, this could be part of the yo-yo we're on."

Mark was about to protest that she looked as fabulous today as she did when he married her, when he bit his lip. They'd had that argument before and his opinion never seemed to weigh in on her self-perception. He let it go through to the keeper.

That evening Mark conceded and they went to the seminar being held at the AIS aquatic and fitness centre. Once the body beautiful had cleared out after Super Circuit class, a couple of the instructors put a bunch of chairs around on the main floor. It was set to start at 7:30 p.m. and people trickled in, all dressed casually. There were over fifty by now and the coordinator stood to open the session. She introduced herself as Brooke. They had been trying for a few years to get a guy called Dan Pink out to speak to coaches and trainers, but Dan hardly ever left the US. Perhaps the best-known work Dan had written was Drive, a work about human motivation.

"What we're going to give you tonight," said Brooke, "is an interactive experience. We've got permission to show you footage from a recent seminar Dan ran on motivation, a beautiful whiteboard video summary of the book, then we're going to work our way through worksheets." With that, they began. Mark and Jane had fun writing notes together during the seminar, each getting a different idea or angle on the point being made:

> Motivation can be external (extrinsic) or internal (intrinsic).
>
> Mark: Motivation 1.0 – driven by very basic need – avoiding painful things like hunger and thirst; pursuing pleasurable things like shelter and reproduction. Dan used the example of people living in caves.
> Jane: Motivation 1.0 connects directly with McLean's three brain model... Pleasure and pain are very physiologically based, probably lizard brain. Stay away from harm, get close to nice, warm things.
>
> Mark: Motivation 2.0 – driven by slightly higher needs – desiring to obtain rewards on offer in the environment and avoid punishment, usually social and which may manipulate behaviour. [Simple logic, must be 'if this, then that']. This is the extrinsic carrot and stick approach.
> Jane: Motivation 2.0 connects with the way the social brain, the emotional and connected brain, the monkey brain would respond to reward and punishment. Of course it had to be simple, if this then that, just like a rat in a maze or a monkey clicking a lever for a food pellet. Limbic system had to work on this level.
>
> Mark: Motivation 3.0 – as soon as a task becomes complex, esoteric, multifaceted and requires logic then 2.0 fails to motivate. At the highest level we need to access autonomy (self-direction), mastery (self-improvement), and purpose (higher or transcendent) to stay motivated. In the arts, music, engineering, coaching and a range of other situations people will be most creative when motivated by things they are interest in, enjoy, receive personal satisfaction from, are intellectually challenged by or which serve a higher purpose.
> Jane: Motivation 3.0 jumps to the neocortex. Level three in the brain, the cognitive part needed self-direction (I'm in charge), self-improvement (this is making me better) and transcendent purpose (I'm really going to make a difference!)...

It was clear, as part of Pink's thesis, that 1.0 was outdated motivation; rewarding and punishing activity was clearly unproductive. 2.0 was now also faulty because most people's basic needs are now met through their salary, and their jobs are "heuristic," not algorithmic; complex, not simple. On both counts he was right. The best forms of motivation were now (at least in the prosperous West) intrinsic 3.0 kinds. Autonomy could be found in a results-oriented workplace (ROWE), mastery injected through Goldilocks' "just right" tasks (enough challenge, enough reward) and work would be more enjoyable if it had meaning.

Still, Jane couldn't help but feel that 1.0 was still with us. This kind of motivation works well for very young children, or when the circumstances are unclear or dangerous (e.g., a prison), she thought. We still have a lizard brain and it still wants to flee pain and move toward pleasure. She also felt that 2.0 was still with us too. Plenty of tasks were simple or routine like commission-based sales, housecleaning, or going to the gym. Of course 3.0 was also with us in the ways outlined.

Brooke brought the group back together after the video presentations flowed into group discussion and in some cases heated debate. Before they went further she said, "Ladies and gentlemen, the reason we ran this seminar, and the reason we thought Dan's model was of interest to you, is because we have been road testing it in our personal-trainer programs, in our athletic-coaching sessions, and personally, I've been using 3.0 in my weight-loss work outside the AIS. So before we move to the next and final section, I'd really like you to write down actions you could take to apply this for yourself."

Brooke gave them all fifteen minutes to do so and carefully set up her laptop as they did. She wore a Bluetooth headphone and had connected the computer to the room's screen, microphone, and speaker system. When the scratching and typing had died down, she approached the stage with aplomb and announced, "Ladies and gentlemen, given our recent shift into summer time, and it now being 9 p.m., I can announce that we have the honour of meeting Dan Pink himself," and as she spoke she switched the main screen to Skype, which showed Dan's smiling face. Brooke greeted him afresh and thanked him for joining them at 8 a.m. his time as a special favour. He greeted the group and told them he was ready to field questions from the floor for half an hour. Everyone was gobsmacked.

People had questions about application not only at work, but also in parenting, teaching, and health. Another person, a fan of Tony Robbins, asked about 1.0 again, telling them all how Robbins teaches that pleasure and pain are fundamental sustaining change and personal-change work. "It's important to anchor it to massive change," he said. Dan didn't dismiss the question, acknowledging the long-term usefulness of 1.0 in man's history, but pointed out that 1.0 had serious drawbacks too. He used the example of getting children to comply with parental wishes by using food forcing and love withdrawal, both having long-term psychological consequences.

Jane shared her freshly minted motivational strategy (the 1.0, 2.0, and 3.0 lining up with the three layers of the brain, providing all seven forms to help achieve your goals). Dan conceded that in some religious contexts people relied on 1.0 motivation and in lower socio-economic situations people relied on 2.0 whenever a task was simple that still worked. But even in India or Africa, 3.0 was a better choice for keeping people's hearts in the task. Jane compiled her notes, applying motivation from the weekend:

Action list

- Check in with internal rapport again. Are you treating your unconscious with respect, like elder? Are you checking on and listening to signalling?
- If you have a Mexican Standoff, strike a parlay, lay down your weapons and ask uncons for help.
- Watch Dan Pink's fifty minute seminar talk at https://youtu.be/LFlvor6ZHdY
- Watch the ten minute Drive talk at https://youtu.be/u6XAPnuFjJc
- Pick something you need to be motivated about and lay out all seven forms of motivatio toward of your goal:

1. Pleasure - how it getting this goal pleasurable? Can your physiological brain 'see' your
2. Pain - how does it hurt to not have this goal? Add loss to your goal like a fine.
3. Reward - measure your movement toward the goal, celebrate change! Monkey likes a reward.
4. Punishment - connect with social comparison, be accountable to someone else for you
5. Self-Improvement - keep it up for at least five times as you track changes and progress
6. Self-direction - find the least number of steps toward your goal and find ways you can c goal without someone else (coaching).
7. Transcendent purpose - if you don't have a reason, find one. Remember Simon Sinek. with 'why?'

CHAPTER THIRTEEN: THE MAGIC EFFECTS OF SLEEP

"People say, 'I'm going to sleep now,' as if it were nothing. But it's really a bizarre activity. 'For the next several hours, while the sun is gone, I'm going to become unconscious, temporarily losing command over everything I know and understand. When the sun returns, I will resume my life'."
George Carlin

To Lauren it felt like an age since Gyan had returned from India and another age since they had surprised her parents with their visit to the coast. The semester had wound on, slowly progressing toward the end-of-year exam period. They had reached the class-free period, the lull before the storm when students either studied in earnest or took the opportunity to party. As the weekend approached, she and Gyan decided to take time out from their heavy study schedule and head for Canberra.

Lauren was a bit of a worrywart when it came to driving. If she had to straddle Canberra to Sydney by herself, she would break it into three sections and two stops: one at Goulburn (86 km) and the second at Mittagong (86 km) leaving 108 km to Sydney. People ridiculed her when they found out, but Lauren had reason to take care. She had, at the age of nineteen, fallen asleep at the wheel and driven off the road, narrowly missing a power pole. She'd been coming home at 5 a.m. after a party. Then last year she had a micro-sleep on the freeway and drifted into the side of a semitrailer. The car had, by some miracle, bounced off, missing the rear wheels and she had careened off into the central grass island and stopped, unharmed.

Both she and Gyan were tired after several late nights of study and, true to form, she cautioned him to let her take over the driving when he was tired which, she informed him (again), was twelve hours after they got up. He wasn't frustrated. He appreciated her care. They headed off in the morning, as traffic was always nasty on a Friday afternoon. Even then they faced a snag at Parramatta Road and again near Bankstown as they hit the M5 Motorway.

Gyan had been listening to Kevin Geary on the Rebooted Body podcast. He'd somehow found his way there in his search and study of healthy foods.

This search had begun not because of Jane and Mark's culinary adventures in cooking class, nor because of a need to lose weight. He had an increasing conviction that he might need to add "Fermentable Oligo-, Di-, Mono-saccharides And Polyols" (FODMAPs) intolerance to his seafood intolerance (it gave him a rash). Lauren had never heard of it before, but Gyan's family were quite into naturopathy and discovered the "Fermentable Oligosaccharides, Disaccharides, Monosaccharides and Polyols" intolerance recently. He had rather scientifically explained to her that FODMAPs are small carbohydrates, not properly absorbed in the GI tract, which cause pain. Gyan had been testing food items one by one by subtracting them, then adding them back in. His "most-suspect list" for pain in the gut now included apple, pear, mango, and watermelon; milk, cheese, and ice cream; breads; kale, broccoli and canola oil. Gyan's nutritionist pointed out that this same list could also point to a fructose/lactose/gluten-fructan/cruciferous intolerance. Lauren felt but did not say out loud that he had missed all the emotional reasons one might experience pain in the gut, such as anxiety, stress, worry, or even a pang of guilty conscience.

This audio journey which had led to Kevin Geary now brought a new podcast to light which covered food, diet, and Paleo. When Geary had finished, Gyan and Lauren earnestly discussed why food intolerance seemed to be on the rise and how the gut brain might be being affected by processed foods. Lauren, who was otherwise quite open-minded, felt that Paleo was a marketing fad and a clever campaign to eat more meat (though she wasn't much of a vegetarian herself) and saw little scientific backing in it. Gyan initially defended it as being a sound low-carb, high-protein alternative, but slowly began to agree.

Lauren, in full flight against Paleo said, "How on earth can they prognosticate about what people did and didn't eat so long ago? Sure we have Aboriginal middens, but the only thing that survives are clam shells. How can they include some things and randomly exclude other things? Like dairy, God! Cows, buffalo, llamas, and alpacas were domesticated ten to fourteen thousand years ago. And legumes… caveman probably ate nuts, especially peanuts, which don't need cooking! And potatoes (I love those things) and grains! Come on, wheat's been around 10,000+ years; since Egypt, right?" She glanced over to see Gyan looking a bit defensive.

"I concede… quinoa from Peru and rice in China are more like fourteen thousand years ago," Gyan said. "If you're going for criticism, I don't think

Paleo really imagines our Aborigines, whose diet changed radically from one season to another, or the Inuit with high-fat and high-protein meat diets, or PNG highlanders who ate exclusively root vegetables, berries, fruit, and fish." He shook his head, then said, "You're right, but I like the way the food choices line up with helping me out on my food intolerances. As far as I'm concerned my gut issues are real, and I need to find some answers."

Lauren found that hard to argue with and besides, she liked the low-carb diet Mum had introduced her to after reading *4-Hour Body*. The program which Gyan was playing on Swell (a kind of Pandora for podcasts) suggested they might like to hear Evan Brand. He was speaking on the Notjustpaleo podcast about adapting to stress (and forest bathing, whatever that was). They started into it, but fairly quickly decided to skip ahead and find another one. The app found Evan talking about "Hacking Your Brain and Your Sleep" on the Justinhealth podcast. They were hooked.

Evan discussed adaptogenic foods, brain-hacking supplements, grounding and earthing, and something called the "REM Rehab" program. As Gyan drove, Lauren jotted down notes on adaptogenic foods which, from a pharmacological perspective, resulted in stabilisation of physiological processes (metabolism, adrenal adoption, melatonin uptake) that promoted homeostasis (being constant or standing still). She also wrote about sleep and its effects on the brain, blood hormones, and various tips on sleeping. Before they knew it, they were pulling into the driveway at her family home and had arrived just before her parents.

*

Jane had spent the day working with EEG readings and playing with her athletes on finding flow state, specially signified by alpha wave (at rest) with gamma wave (divergent thinking) spikes. She was interested in which athletes could get into alpha wave while being physically active. The marathon runners and the swimmers (she imagined) did it best. The ability to switch "off," to relax and enjoy the activity was, anecdotally, experienced by surfers, skateboarders and skiers too. Such was the flow of thought running through her mind as she, in flow state herself, pulled into the driveway, almost running up the back of Gyan's car. Jane stopped suddenly, skidding the tires with a chirping sound.

Nonplussed, she wandered inside calling out to Lauren, but could not find her anywhere. Eventually, as she put the kettle on, she glanced outside and saw them in the spa. "There you are!" she called out and Lauren and Gyan waved to Jane enthusiastically. With a cup of tea in hand and with the end of a long week at her back, Jane joined them on the verandah and they caught up about the semester.

*

About an hour later, Mark left work and turned for home. As he drove along, he reflected on the meetings he'd just had. The first was with the selection committee from the partnership. To his great delight they had accepted his proposal to re-join the team and join the new initiative with Defence. Smythe and Johnson had already been embedded for a few weeks, but it was time for Mark to tail them. As he ran the gauntlet up Northbourne Avenue, past the Rex and onto the Barton Highway, he considered the week ahead.

This new position demanded a new attitude, a new focus, and a new energy. He had listened to the audio book *Lords of Strategy*, which taught him about the management-consulting industry, and he read *Strategic Thinking* by Bill Birnbaum. For future study he had ordered *Essentials of Strategic Management* to help him along (and wow, wasn't that expensive). *Strategic Thinking: Today's Business Imperative* was recommended reading by a local university but it looked too… well, he didn't know… academic? He figured strategic thinking in the business and government marketplace couldn't be academic anyway. Suddenly he found himself pulling into his driveway and stopping. There wasn't room! Of course! Lauren was… *Wait a minute*, he thought, *that's not her car… Oh, it is Gyan.*

As Jane and Mark relaxed in the spa, Gyan and Lauren headed to the kitchen to prepare a meal for the four of them.

Even though the clock had only just nudged five o'clock, Monique was hoping they'd allow an interloper. She knocked on the door and Lauren, wiping her hands on her apron, went to answer it. There stood Monique with a steaming tray of mild chicken curry, Ryan trailed behind with papadums, and Rylie had a bowl of wild rice ready to cook.

Lauren's mind raced. On the one hand this was a breathtaking presumption and she felt offended. On the other hand, she loved seeing Monique and her kids, and especially this weekend, as it afforded them the opportunity to catch up as a group. Not sure what to think, Lauren simply laughed and welcomed them all into the kitchen. And so the weekend arrived and was welcomed, with hearty food, heady conversation, and full, satisfied bellies.

Mark's instinct was to have a group coaching catch-up after dinner and Jane concurred. It didn't take much to prevail upon Gyan and Lauren, so once the meal was done they all wandered out onto the verandah to chat over hot drinks. Mark took the group all the way back to neuroplasticity at the coast: states (become traits), mood control (by labelling emotions), memory (practice improves it), learning (something new), eating (affects everything), exercise (every day), education (for your work), environmental issues (don't isolate), and sleep. Gyan asked if they were going to hold one another accountable. Lauren reminded him that it wasn't part of their coaching agreement. Gyan conceded the point and asked them if they had set goals, deadlines, and measurements. They all looked a bit sheepish, Monique, Gyan, and Lauren all admitting they'd done little about that.

Monique shared her experience on the time line, dealing with past issues, and how she felt freer now. Then she reminded them all of the "oh crap to okay" model—the three layers of the brain (lizard, monkey, and human) and even told them about her meltdown and yelling at the kids and subsequent dream. Jane and Mark smiled but said nothing. They had heard everything. The houses weren't that far apart. They had all practiced the ten-item checklist from Mark Goulston and grown tremendously in communication and self-management.

Lauren went next, reminding them all about book club and the learnings she and Gyan had about the way people try to separate brain and body. Gyan prompted her about the head, heart, and gut brains, and the exploration they had around accessing the other sources of intelligence, especially intuition. That was an opportunity for everyone to discuss how they'd gone. Monique had found it easy, and noted most of her communication upward from the heart and gut were non-verbal: feelings, impressions, ideas, with no words. Gyan proposed that was because the vagus nerve and enteric nerve came up through lamina one, in the spine. He tried to explain: "These body-neural 'thoughts' make their way to the brain stem, the croc brain, right. The thalamus, at the top, distributes information to the right hypothalamus. Some information goes to the right anterior cingulate and some of it goes to the right anterior insulate." He smiled to himself in a satisfied way. "The information is all in your right brain… your non-linear, creative side." He looked around. They stared back at him blankly.

Nobody understood, so he explained that generally (in ninety-seven percent of people) verbal, that is speech-related or word-related, issues were processed by the left hemisphere. Intuition (non-conscious intelligence) has no words; it's all somatic impression, and it's going to a part of the brain without words. Sure parts of it have language processing (semantics, metaphor, synonyms), so you might "hear" words, but it was unlikely. That explanation made vague sense to them, and they pretended to understand.

Jane jumped in with her experiences at the cooking school with Mark, sharing the amazing combinations they had tried and how they had learned to trust their nose, mouth, and somatic intelligence better. They'd learned about foraging, raw and whole foods, and the problems with the food pyramid. This gave Gyan cause to share his own exploration with allergies and intolerances. Guiding the conversation gently toward motivation, Jane told everyone about her revelations from the seminar held at the gym. Humans had seven kinds of motivation, she surmised: seeking pleasure and avoiding pain, which struck her as very "basic" drives; pursuit of reward and evasion of punishment, quite social or limbic-system drives; self-direction, self-improvement, and serving a transcendent purpose, which were very noble, and "higher," drives. She apologized for not sending them out to everyone, and did so there and then.

They all discussed this and the way the three layers of the brain segued into the three kinds of motivation, not to mention the three brains and coherence between head, heart, and gut. Before time had completely got away from them, Jane also told them about her conversation with Ian about rapport with self. She asked them how they'd been going with treating their unconscious with respect, as an elder or even just listening to their "gut reaction" or somatic signalling. They all admitted this was an area to keep working on.

"If I had to pick an area that I think comes to mind a lot, it would be sleep. I really don't do sleep well," Gyan admitted.

"Yeah, me neither," Lauren chimed in. They'd already told each other that coming down. "It's like the more stressed I get the less sleep I get, and I know I need it."

"I reckon I'm running on five, or maybe six hours on a good night," Monique said.

Jane was sitting there Googling "sleep doctor" and "sleep lab" and finally "sleep quotes." She read:

"Sleep is the single most important behavioural experience we have.In an average life you will sleep for 32 years."

Russell Foster

"Jeez Louise," Jane said and read the Foster quote to everyone else. "I guess it's time for bed then." And it was, so off they went.

*

Canberra in late spring has to be seen to be believed. Once the winter has stopped trying to convert summer and fled for the north in earnest, the grass becomes verdant, the trees resplendent in new growth, and flowers of every kind come to life. Many of the wattle trees, which begin flowering in late winter, continue to flower through spring.

To celebrate, Canberra puts on a festival called Floriade. Acres of flower-filled garden beds are prepared beside the lake. Today was certainly the day to go and enjoy them. Mark and Jane headed off after breakfast in the temperate sunshine and warm breeze. They spent a wonderful morning meandering through a million bulbs and annuals. Tulips, poppies, daisies, and a hundred other species made for remarkable photography for Monique, who was on the other side of Commonwealth Park. She had just gone past the agricultural display where vegetable gardens and herb gardens hummed with bees and insects.

After grabbing lunch and not running into Monique, Mark and Jane left before she did, to clean the house and do some gardening. They were lost in their labour when alarms went off on their phones. Cooking school.

For once they were not the last ones to arrive; in fact, there appeared to be a couple of people missing. Jane asked Food Chef where they were, and learned that two couples were away this week. She asked if her daughter and her boyfriend come along for one week? He supposed they could. So Jane called Lauren and in short order she and Gyan were standing behind their bench under the white marquee looking quite enchanted. Well Gyan actually looked bewildered and Lauren more bewitched.

This week the two chefs were helping attendees tell the difference between the main macronutrients: carbohydrates, protein and fat. Food Chef mentioned a few other elements like fibre, sugars, and lipids. Science Chef walked down the trail a little further, explaining amino acids (which make up proteins), peptides (the precursors for neuropeptides), enzymes (that help chemical processes), probiotics (bacteria and yeast), and micronutrients (vitamins and minerals).

They said all this while preparing the entrée and asking everyone to come up and try something new. Tonight would be based on a fusion of two things: bush tucker/foraged food mixed with foods people would hardly ever have tried. They had balanced the range of macronutrients, micronutrients, and amino acids. The platter before them had a fascinating mix of options: snails in garlic; frog legs in ginger butter and parsley; slow-cooked python ribbons in chilli and pepper sauce; Belgian buffalo worms in basil and tomato salsa; steamed cumbungi (bulrush) slivers and green beans with caraway seed; and kurrajong seed mini-muffins. Lauren's stomach churned a bit. What is this? she wondered.

Gyan engaged both chefs in a discussion on the Paleo diet and found that Food Chef took the low-carb, no-starch approach (not Paleo strictly). Science Chef had all the reservations Gyan might have expected, including the issue of starving the system of carbohydrates, driving it into ketosis (consuming reserves). As this discussion raged, the participants were asked to select mains from some non-usual choices: Indian buffalo tail with red wine chorizo in Warrigal greens (native spinach); Mongolian BBQ emu with roasted murnong (yam daisy); Peruvian alpaca skewers and okra in cinnamon, anise, and chilli; Australian camel, cumin and apricot burgers; chargrilled eel in lemongrass and turmeric; balsamic, fetta, and pistachio goat tenderloins; or peppadew, pindo (palm-tree fruit), banana on fufu (cassava mash). *Again*, thought Lauren, *not a lot for vegetarians*. She was adventurous, tried a few things, and decided to wait for dessert.

Mark and Jane said a lot less on this occasion. They were trying to think of the salt/sugar/fat addiction they were trying to overcome (nothing here fed that appetite) and the three-brains learning from last week. Choices about food seemed much more intuitive now. As they cleared mains and prepared dessert, Science Chef informed them of recent research that a glass of room-temperature water assisted digestion but that a piece of fruit did just as well. Research also showed, he said, that a warm drink and a light carbohydrate hit just before bed assisted sleep. The amino acid tryptophan causes sleepiness. As participants asked about the effects of caffeine (which had a half-life of 5.7 hours, he informed them) and which drinks to have to avoid getting up in the middle of the night, he brought them toward dessert and a selection of drinks.

Hot chocolate, a range of teas like chai, pu-erh, jasmine, green, peppermint, chamomile, and other herbals were laid out to be taken with dessert, which again proved to be unusual. Black wattle seed vanilla ice cream; wild rosella cheesecake with dark chocolate; bunya nut and leatherwood honey bavarois; lilly pilly and nectarine cobbler; glossy nightshade and pecan flan; and finally wild lime, lemon myrtle, and ginger tart.

“When we went hunting, we found manna gum trees and collected some, but not enough. We found sugarbag—the comb of the native bees, which is wonderfully bittersweet but again not enough. The glossy nightshade is a member of the tomato family. Don’t go hunting for this without an expert because its cousin is deadly nightshade! One is glossy, the other dull,” Food Chef said.

The evening finally drew to a close. Mark and Jane had absolutely loved it. Gyan was curious but indifferent, as this was his first time. While Lauren didn’t count herself a vegetarian, she didn’t really love meat and had found her options limited and her heart closed toward the process. She didn’t love it. They chatted in muted tones on the short journey home.

*

Sunday morning came in as slow as the tide, and when the family had emerged from their slumber they found “Professor Tillman” waiting for them. Gyan was in “I’ve researched and now I want to lecture” mode. Jane told him nobody was lecturing anybody until they sorted out breakfast, or at the very least coffee. A trip to the bakery and four cappuccinos sorted that out and they gathered in the living room, slouched down on couches, sipping warm caffeine and nibbling croissants.

“Okay amigos,” Gyan started, “I heard you all complaining on Friday night about sleep, and it was a theme yesterday, as well as the chef mentioning it, so I went back to find the quote by Russell Foster. Turns out the guy is a circadian neuroscientist,” and as he drew breath Lauren asked, “Woah, big guy, circ-what?” She stared at him for a moment.

“That’s a chrono-biologist, who studies how you act and move and feel, in rhythm with light and dark.” Her blank face cued him to make it simpler. “Your body clock!” he said and finally saw understanding in their eyes. “Your brain does not sleep when you do; in fact, many areas become more active at night.” He’d taken the trouble of reading Dr. Foster’s research, watched his TED Talk, and had summarised the pertinent details in a document (typed up and printed out already) for them to examine.

Before they read it he said, “Please have an open mind just now. I know sleep doesn’t seem like a high-powered thing to focus on, or even be able to self-coach. But I think you’ll come to see that it has such a profound impact on performance that it cannot be ignored. Well, it can be ignored—we’ve all been doing that—but I propose this is our next and maybe most important subject!” Gyan said and looked around the room. They all agreed to suspend

disbelief for now. He read from the notes he'd printed out:
"Why do we sleep? There are two main theories…

- Restoration: certain genes only get turned on when we sleep, and these ar almost all associated with cellular restoration and absorption of destructi chemicals.
- Brain function: processing and memory consolidation. We come up with novel solutions to complex problems during sleep. One experiment show three-fold advantage in the well-rested."

Taking a breath, Gyan decided to interrupt himself, going off-notes. "So this 'down cycle,' or turning off consciousness, is really important to getting healthy, learning and memory, as well as to problem-solving. Foster talked about a recent study he'd done that showed that the neural system which is active from the last thing you learned before sleeping is reignited after sleep, which indicates memory consolidation. This machine," he said tapping his head, "is so smart. Sleep also seems to weaken synaptic connections created during learning that the system deems non-essential to functioning! I read another report that said metaphor construction took place at night too, based on dream studies." He read on…

"What happens when we don't sleep? Lack of sleep—five hours or less—is highly correlated with: poor memory, increased impulsiveness, poor judgment, and impaired attention. If you have a tired brain, it is a brain that craves stimulants: drugs, cigarettes, caffeine to switch on, and alcohol to downregulate and sedate itself."

Lauren loved the boy, but he really was like Sheldon. Downregulate? Sedate? C*ome on, speak English*, she thought. They continued again… this time she took up the reading,

"Reduced sleep creates a fifty-percent likelihood of becoming obese because of the increased excretion of the hormone grelin. You feel thirty percent more hunger and when you wake up, you crave heavy carbohydrates. You are twenty percent less able to feel full and, in addition, sleep affects metabolism rates. The rate of integration and consumption of the food we eat drops by twenty-five percent. In addition, blood levels of insulin start to rise."

"Well that's good news," said Mark.

Jane looked kind of angry. "Good? That's terrible news, Mark, we're screwed," she barked.

"Well you can look at it that way, or, glass half full, say we have a chance to turn it around if we can get our sleep sorted out," he said without defensiveness. Gyan tapped the paper as if to say, just wait till you see what comes next!

Lauren read on…

"If you live a stressful life and produce increased levels of cortisol and adrenalin during the day,"

She took a breath and Gyan interrupted, "Which over fifty percent of us do, by the way," and he smiled benignly.

"Which over fifty of us do," Lauren agreed, reading on,

"The only mechanism you have to reduce it is during sleep. Prolonged increased levels of blood cortisol and adrenalin (stress hormones) mixed with higher insulin levels signal fat cells to hold onto their energy."

Lauren laughed nervously and summarized this last part. "So we're hungrier, less able to feel full, our metabolism slows down, and now our fat cells want us to stay fat?" she asked. Gyan nodded solemnly. Then he nodded at the paper.

"Lack of sleep causes sustained stress to the endocrine system. Hormones play a major role in energy balance, as the secretion of hormones is directly affected by sleep. Metabolism changes, obesity and stress hormones ultimately cause immune-system compromise, with a higher likelihood of infection. Changes in melatonin and cortisol directly affect your risk of cancer too," she said, reading from the page.

"By the same amount as smoking," Gyan said enthusiastically. "Get that: lack of sleep is as bad for us as smoking!"

Mark groaned. "I quit for nothing!" he said, half meaning it. Jane giggled and Lauren read on… "Oh, here comes insulin again. Lack of sleep reduces insulin sensitivity by forty percent, drastically increasing the likelihood of type 2 diabetes." Lauren paused, considering those two horrible facts… cancer and diabetes.

Gyan took over talking. "But wait, that's not all! You also get severe mental illness!" he said, smiling, and perhaps not recognising his joke was in very poor taste. Their family had a history of bipolar and affective disorders. He wasn't to know. Without picking up on the social signals, he continued, "Lack of sleep is closely related to and highly correlated with the incidence of bipolar, depression, and schizophrenia. The neural networks that give you normal sleep and those that give you normal mental health overlap one another. It turns out that lunacy really is a thing!" The room was quiet. He didn't get it.

This was a lot to take in on a Sunday morning and they agreed to pause, get more coffee and carbohydrates, then continue. They picked up at the "good news" section of Gyan's notes from Dr. Foster's research:

What happens when we get enough?
When you get enough sleep, good sleep (8 hours +) you get:

- Better concentration
- Sustained attention
- Improved learning
- Sharper decision making
- Higher levels of creativity
- Better memory
- Improved academic performance
- Reduction of stress hormones
- Lower appetite
- Increased metabolism
- Better weight loss
- Improved endocrine function
- Stronger immune system function
- Increased energy levels
- Reduced mood changes
- Lower risk of mental health problems
- Lower stress and anger response
- Better impulse control
- Lower risk of micro sleeps and accidents

"Oh my God," said Lauren, "That list is huge! Who knew? Everyone's banging on about equality and anti-discrimination and the immigration issue and gay rights, but who's fighting for sleep?"

They resolved right there and then to improve their sleep.

"Well, as it so happens, I have prepared a sleep hygiene check list for each of us. Oh Monique isn't here. Perhaps you can bring her up to speed? We have to go after lunch," said Gyan. Lauren admired his preparedness. This was Gyan's sleep hygiene list:

Action list
Get a baseline first. Take the Pittsburgh Sleep Quality Index:
http://www.neurocoachingaustralia.com/resources/neurocoaching/pittsburgh-psqi.pdf

1. Daytime

- Get outside during the day and absorb some melatonin.
- Eat melatonin rich foods like oats, corn, rice, barley, ginger, tomatoes and bananas. Cal and magnesium supplements can help too.
- Maintain a regular eating and meal schedule, try to keep them within 30 minutes of 'norr
- The half-life of caffeine is 5.7 hours. No caffeine after lunch. Watch energy drinks, tea ar herbal tisanes too.

2. Self-awareness

- If you need an afternoon nap, do not exceed 20 minutes. To ensure this, have a cup of t coffee or energy drink just before you nap. It will kick you awake in good time.
- The half-life of endorphins is 1-2 hours, so no exercise after dinner.
- Keep a diary and write down (notice) when you get tired. It comes in waves 90 minutes a

3. Sleeping area

- Remove all blue light. Blue light is known to activate the SCN (especially laptops, cell ph led lights).
- Black out the light. Get good curtains to block out street lights and under your door.
- Make it the bedroom. Only. Remove everything that does not involve bed and bedtime – desk or chair, no couch or lamp. A dress mirror, a place to apply makeup perhaps but nc else. Remove all electricals, including the TV.

4. The run up to sleep

- Dial down all excitement in the 'run down' hour. No adrenalin. Choose reading, calm mu relaxation technique, journaling and mindfulness breathing.
- Drinking warm non-caffeinated beverage (chai, herbal tea, milk) and a light carbohydrate snack helps: a small bowl of cereal and milk, a few cookies, toast, or a small muffin.
- Sleep cool, not hot. Adjust your bed, blankets, doona, window, thermostat to find the bes temperature for you. It is likely to be above 18°C (65°F) and below 24°C (75°F).

5. Sleep time

- Make bedtime predictable, go to bed within 30 minutes of that same time. Catch the circ 'wave' to bed.
- Turn off all devices which can make sounds. Get ear plugs if you have to.
- Falling asleep to music, a podcast or the TV activates the learning networks in the brain will wake you in a few hours as it switches to memory processing.

6. What if it doesn't work?

- If you can't fall asleep after 15 minutes, get up and rest somewhere else, then come bac not somatically associate the bed with tossing, turning and frustration.
- Try a muscle relaxation technique, progressive tightening and loosening.
- Try an imagery or visualisation technique.

CHAPTER FOURTEEN: REFRAMING PERCEPTION

"Human beings are, above all, meaning makers."
Don Carter

Monique sat at home removing her profile from site after site. While they had provided her some entertainment with people who looked like losers asking her to chat, and others with weird profile names and only one photo up. *How am I supposed to know who you are?* she thought, she was getting out. Online dating had also thrust nearly a thousand nuisance texts, app contact requests, and inquiries upon her. Her finger hovered over the right mouse button, the cursor hanging over the delete button for her profile at Zoosk. This was the end of her Internet dating fling. Twenty-three people had made it through the "connect and chat" barrier, nine had made it to a face-to-face encounter, and absolutely none of them were for her. Well, they were "for" her in the sense that they wanted her. Despite Monique's low self-esteem and because of the healing she had received from past abuse and pain, she was simply not willing to be someone's trophy, their one-night stand-up comedy, their conquered victory. *Then why*, she thought, *am I hesitating*?

Several reasons presented themselves to her. Like the semi-transparent computer screens hanging in midair before Tom Cruise in the movie *Minority Report*, the reasons arrayed themselves in a semicircle of monitors before her mind's eye, cursor blinking… brain typing "because it feels like I am admitting defeat"… and "because I'm taking myself off the market"… and "because it means nobody loves me." At this last comment she said "rubbish" out loud and in her mind she erased it, willing herself to say goodbye to Zoosk. Her mind eventually offered… "because I haven't found the one who loves me." That was better.

"Go on, delete it and move on," said a voice behind her. She jumped, startled, her finger on the mouse.

Monique immediately relaxed when she heard Jane's gentle giggle. She turned and said, "What on earth are you doing here?" Jane had her hands on her beautifully curving hips, wearing a black dress and heels. Behind her Mark was carrying his laptop through the front door. "And what are you doing here?" Monique exclaimed. Instead of answering her, Jane simply said, "Get your glad rags on, lover girl, we're going speed dating!" Jane smiled when she said that; she'd been wanting to do it for Monique for ages. Monique's face lit up like a lake's surface at dawn, shining and wet with tears. She deleted Zoosk that instant and shot out of the room to get changed. Ryan and Rylie were in their rooms finishing their homework before bed, and Mark was going to babysit. This was going to be sweet.

In short order she was in the bathroom applying makeup, teasing her hair, and spraying a little perfume. Jane waited, checking the time of the speed-dating trials again, the address, and the current time. She had this down to the finest details. The girls laughed together at the absurdity of it all and left. Mark watched them go and settled down to play sitter for the night.

Downtown they went to a bar first and did some shots of tequila. In Jane's mind, she had dressed down, so that Monique looked better. Monique's head stood just above Jane's shoulder, so Jane decided she would have to be sure and sit when the game was on. She wasn't here to date; she was here to make sure Monique got a date, and moved away from the danger of being attracted to her husband.

From Monique's perspective, Jane was taller, making her skirt comparatively shorter, her legs longer, and with a bright smile, long hair, and confidence, Jane outdid her. Monique thought at first that Jane was out for some fun. What the truth was is anyone's guess. At the bar they both got propositioned. For Jane it was deliciously affirming, and just a tiny bit wicked. She gave the guy the flick.

Soon Jane progressed them down a long tree-lined avenue, across a street and one block to the location of the speed-dating event. Muddle Bar, in the Melbourne Building, was a library-style cocktail bar with rich, dark timber floors, throw rugs, pot plants, and deep, plush furniture. It was unlike anything the two of them had been in before. The host, from Jump Dating, ushered them into the throng of thirty-to-fifty-somethings, all trying not to give off an "I'm desperate" signal, and most of them failing.

In fact, it seemed to Jane the room was full of needy women who seemed willing to do almost anything for company. She silently hoped Monique was not a member of their club. Statistics showed that neediness was a huge turn-off, even when they were wearing red, had done their hair, and were all trying to be "unique." It reminded Jane of the *Monty Python* sketch where everyone cried "We're all individual," which ironically made them all the same. Jane and Monique mingled superficially until the last paying contestant arrived, a slick-looking Italian with too much "I'm the hottie" written on his Rudolph Valentino face. T*oo much baggage*, thought Jane as she wished Monique luck. She went to grab a drink from the bar and join the wing-women who had to sit to one side when the games began.

The host explained the rules to the participants. Basically the ladies were in charge, and the men were trying out. The ladies had the choice to give certain men their contact details at the end. The men then had the power to follow them up, or leave them alone if they didn't like the person for whatever reason.

Since Jane hatched the idea of speed dating for Monique, she had read background articles and done research. In the *Atlantic,* she'd read an article by a man who hosted dating parties in the UK. He said speed dating was "slow by comparison to Tinder." An analogue speed-dating event gave the ladies "ten potential matches on any given night" and those same precious people "probably wouldn't survive an app flick fest." Jane might never belong to the group gathered here, but she easily could have. Many of her friends were divorced and some had just never been lucky in love. She felt compassion, or affinity, for them.

Jane sipped her drink, watching intently as round one began. It lasted three minutes and the men moved tables to meet a new woman. Over and over the bell rang and the men moved. It was a circus. Everyone trying to be someone else, trying to run their scripts, trying to put on a show, or be cheeky because some dating site said that was good advice. *Idiots*, Jane thought. *Be yourself, or get out of the room!* Jane could see the classic error at least three of the men made—taking too long talking about themselves, and not enough interest in the lady. Several of the women took down numerous names and phone numbers and shared their own. Jane thought them desperate. Monique was either a shy catch (burned by her online experience) or a very sharp judge of character. The men she met were shallow, self-indulgent, self-possessed, self-made, or uninteresting. She wondered quietly whether her standards were too high… but against what would she compare these men… her ex? Certainly not far to rise to get above him. No most of this lot were not for her. By the end of the evening, Monique really only felt like she had any interest in two of them.

As they wandered out of the bar, Jane noticed that Monique was clearly wrestling with something. Jane broached the subject, asking if tonight was okay. Monique's face lit up. "Oh yes, it was a wonderful idea, Jane—thank you. Pity I only liked two of them but still, that's more than none!"

"Then what's troubling you?" Jane asked kindly.

"Well, did you notice one of the older men looked a lot like your father? It reminded me of what happened, what I did… and of my ex, and why I was even in the dating game. It's just that your dad is still in hospital, and we haven't visited in ages, and I thought since we were so close, we could just… " Monique trailed off. Now the idea was out of her mind and out of her mouth, it sounded precocious and silly. She scanned Jane's face for a reaction, but saw nothing but perplexed, deep thought.

They walked along in silence, heading back to the car park. Eventually Jane said, "Look, Monique, I know the studies say talking to a coma patient is a good thing, but it would take years of neglect and years of silence to even begin to balance the debt he has with me… being absent for so long, I don't even feel sad anymore. Maybe my heart's just calloused… or maybe I should forgive him… but he doesn't deserve it. The dad I deserve, well I never had him and the one that I have is dead to me."

"Sounds like him lying there in a physical coma, unwelcome and unvisited is just like what's going on inside you," Monique said. "He's in your soul, lying still, in a coma, and nothing's been resolved."

Those words hit Jane like a rocket, exploding in her consciousness. Profound. True. Hard. Kind. She'd never forget it.

*

Mark and Jane each had a very different experience of the Derren Brown video. He thought it was wonderful; she thought it was horrible. He admired Derren's influence; she called him manipulative. He said it was just good, directive talking. She said it was tantamount to hypnotism. It really got Mark thinking about their marriage, especially their differences of perspective and opinion.

Mark and Jane had been married just over twenty years. He had found the last twelve months, or perhaps progressively the last six years, frustrating. Once Lauren had grown up, in fact before that, when she was about fifteen, the two of them had plunged themselves into their careers with renewed conviction. In his mind he made a list:

Recreation: she ran and he played racquetball; she swam and he rode the motorbike. Occasionally they read the same books, but he loved fiction and she read nonfiction. He loved his sports car; she hated it.

Employment: He worked in management consulting and she in biomechanics and

psychology.
Nature: He was rough and tumble; she was a neat freak. He was outgoing and she was more of an introvert.
Point of view: He tended to be present-hedonistic, enjoying the now, taking pleasure in his work and family and recreation, she tended to be a kind of glass-half-empty, always-looking-backward and remembering-how-it-used-to-be type of person. She steeled herself against eventual disappointment by not hoping for too much, which drove Mark mad. She, the pessimist, and he, the optimist, found many causes for argument or disagreement.
Desire: He wanted attention, affection, sexual pleasure, and fun; she was cool-headed, never needed a hug (but would give one when asked). He was intrinsically motivated and self-oriented, she was task-oriented, rule-oriented, and frustrated when things didn't work out like they planned.

His dissatisfaction ran deeper than mere difference of perspective though. It wasn't the money; they had plenty. It wasn't the home, yard, pool, or anything they owned. It wasn't the sharing of domestic duty; they cooked and did the yard work equally. Not food, or music, or interests either. It was… their common life. With the exception of the recent cooking school, they didn't even watch the same movies. As the weeks passed, he pondered the emptiness of their relationship, his sadness slowly pooling into misery. He carried a hundred offenses, slights, and infractions like the misunderstanding at the beach with Monique. Though truth be told, Monique raised his heartbeat in the way Jane used to. She was… attractive and willing. It wasn't that Jane was any less physically beautiful; Jane just didn't take care of herself: the small things, makeup and so forth. As a result of all of this, his heart had become injured over time.

There was an inequality in their experiences of their marriage. If you had asked Jane, she was quite happy. She had a man who earned well, loved her daughter, carried his fair share of domestic duties, remained faithful to her, was a great companion, and a willing conversationalist. Not that they had ever drafted a list, but if a list were drawn, her top five needs were being met. His weren't. She needed safety and security, financial stability, family commitment, conversation, and honesty from him (and a long list of other things below that). By contrast he needed sex and physical affection, affirmation and admiration, physical attractiveness (or at least paying attention to self-management), companionship, and shared common interests.

As the years progressed, her needs were met and his were not. This was not because of callousness on her part, nor intention. It was also not due to his attention to her list either. It's just how the balance of personalities went. By nature and by circumstance, her needs were met. She was simply not very interested in sex anymore, nor very inclined to praise him, or her staff, or anybody else. Besides, in the vacuum she left, he was quite capable of boasting about his accomplishments. Despite his attempts to encourage her to take care of herself, she found makeup unnecessary at work and they had few occasions for which to dress up. She chose not to do it just for him, and more's the pity.

To Mark's searching, agonizing mind it didn't seem fair that her needs could be met inside and outside the marriage: security systems, her own work earning money, marrying a man with family commitment, conversation at the office and home—when his main need could not be met anywhere but with her. Well, it could, but his moral compass, his conscience, wouldn't allow it.

Today he found himself driving to work wondering just what he'd gotten himself into and what was a marriage anyway? It had to be more than just being friends because friends weren't sexually intimate (usually, in his experience). It wasn't just having a friend with benefits because they didn't raise children or own property together. It had to be about more than sex because many older couples stop having it and yet remain deeply committed. So what is it that is irritating me? he wondered. Could it be something as simple as affection? When was the last time she had kissed him, really kissed him? Or snuggled up beside him on the couch? Or prompted or started anything really? Maybe it was a lack of respect, he seeing and admiring (and saying so)… It seemed to him that either love had run cold or priorities had switched. Mark mentally drafted a list of essentials for his marriage:

- It was based on a covenant not a contract, a promise not a legal obligation, backed by o word and our honour not by threat of court.
- It was founded upon friendship and common interests. This had grown into passion and magnetic draw. He recalled a time when they just couldn't wait to be in each other's pres
- We had each other's heart, we fell in love and we gave each other our bodies. So marria does, at least during the attempt at child rearing stage, have intimacy and sex.
- We shed two houses to purchase and live in one, so it involves a common life, a shared and an invasion of each other's space. There is a certain forcing and acceptance of worl on our selfishness.

Any relationship might have one or more elements of that, but in his opinion their marriage had to have all of those things. He pulled into a multi-story car park beside the client's offices. It was a bit like the relationship between his company and this Defence client. At the entry stood a sandwich board in yellow and red which read "Rooftop Car Park Full". So he took his ticket and proceeded up to the fourth level, just below the rooftop. There, at the entrance to the rooftop, was another sandwich-board sign saying, "Rooftop Car Park

Full." Begrudgingly he found a park on the fourth level, all the while bemoaning the fact that he had to pay top dollar for parking.

He walked across the air bridge to the client building, signed in through security and found Smythe and Johnson, who had been here for several weeks already, in the corridor near the information desk. The three of them chatted about the day's work and headed off to a day full of client meetings and negotiations.

The day went fast and by four o'clock they were winding down. Defence people seemed to clock on at seven and leave at three or four, so the corridors in this area were fast becoming empty. Seeing no reason to stay, the three of them agreed to come early the next morning. Signing out, Mark returned across the bridge, found the car and then remembered his ticket. Proceeding to the ticket machine he saw a lady, having paid her ticket, getting in the elevator to go up to the top floor. He was curious, so he jumped in behind her and asked, "So, you're parked on the top floor?" She nodded. "If you don't mind me asking, what time did you get here because I arrived at nine a.m.!"

Assessing him and her own risk, she said, "Nine a.m., like you, why?"

"Nine a.m.? That can't be right; there were signs out saying the rooftop car park was full," he said, surprised at the facts as she presented them.

"Oh, those, they've been around for weeks. They were doing construction and repair work up here, but that finished ages ago." She smiled, walking away to her car.

He stood there feeling cold in the pit of his stomach, then rage, then disappointment and finally humour. "Those clever, plotting so-and-so's! They're probably trying to spike revenue!" he declared out loud.

His analytical brain immediately kicked into gear and started a review of what had happened, noting the way he automatically believed the signs because of their colour and official-looking nature. He caught the lift back down to the fourth floor, and paid for his ticket. As he walked back to his car, he noted there was no chain across the entrance to the level above. There never had been. He brooded on this event all the way home, his earlier thoughts about his relationship with Jane far behind him.

*

He told Jane the car park story, with an appropriate amount of self-deprecating humour, and she laughed. As they prepared the evening meal together, she thought about his story and shared something with him she recalled from her early studies in human behaviour. Scientists had done neurological research into the way people make mistakes like Mark had. One of them, as she recalled, was a psychologist for the Israeli Defence Force (IDF). He had observed that the performance and leadership rankings of officers in training his department produced failed miserably in predicting their future performance. But the IDF kept using them. This made him curious about the way the brain gathered and ignored information.

"If you change the way you look at things, the things you look at change."
Wayne Dyer

After dinner she went to the bookshelf and scanned for the book, finally pulling out the work of Daniel Kahneman and Amos Tversky, *Judgement Under Uncertainty: Heuristic Biases.* Flicking through the index, she showed Mark three pertinent kinds of failures:

The representativeness heuristic: The brain's tendency to look for similarities between what we are seeing and things we have experienced before. If it seems to generally match an existing "parent group" of experiences, it automatically places it in that group, frequently excluding reference to the finer points of difference.

The availability heuristic: Our brain's tendency to remember things that seem important, or at least more important than alternative solutions which are not as readily recalled. As a result, we tend to heavily weigh recent information, or information that we are most familiar with and jumps to mind more readily.

The anchoring and adjustment heuristic: This comes into play when we are uncertain, then we tend to anchor on information that we know or are confident about and adjust it until we come up with a plausible estimate. The adjustments are rarely sufficient because they are not based on research or on careful thinking.

Mark scratched his chin, saying, "The signs I saw this morning were very similar to the 'parent population' of authority signs I had seen before and my heuristic, my rule of thumb, jumped to the wrong conclusion. It also assumed that this sign had been placed by someone with actual authority instead of a car park attendant after more money," Mark said forlornly.

"Oh honey, don't be down on yourself," she said, giggling at his Eeyore face. "I'll bet you weren't the only one fooled, and it'll be different tomorrow, right?"

"Damn straight it'll be different! I'm going straight to the top floor," he said confidently.

*

The closer the exams came, the harder Lauren studied; the harder Lauren studied, the more tired she became; the more tired she became, the more anxious she was; the more anxious she was, the harder she studied. It had been this way for as long as she could remember. It was as if her self-estimation dropped slowly and imperceptibly driving her effort up to compensate, to make sure she passed. Her effort however would almost always produce high distinctions and that seemed to surprise her.

It was late and it began slowly. She noticed a slight hand tremor. Her focus narrowed as if focusing on the road ahead of her, like fog rising from a river below, a bridge cutting off her view. Lauren felt a churning sickness in her tummy. Then some dark and shadowy unnamed fear crept from the underbelly of her brain, tickling her conscious thought like feathers brushing past her mind. This primal, monstrous feeling came shameless into the open: a danger unspoken that caused her to freeze in fear. There was no secondary version of Lauren or disconnected part to her experience, but rather, as she would later explain to Gyan, it was all-consuming.

She groaned involuntarily, attempting to rise and perhaps flee, but dizziness set in and she nearly threw up. Her chest tightened, her heart pounded, and her cheeks flushed as she held her head, yelling, "I feel like I'm losing it, I'm losing it… Gyan… heeeeellp." But the words did not form correctly, and besides, Gyan wasn't in the room. Her neighbour heard something through the thin, shared wall but could not make out what it was. Lauren collapsed to her knees, near the wall. She thought of knocking, but couldn't. "Heeeellp, please, someone, it's coming, I need you to… to get me, I'm not going to make it," she yelled at the top of her lungs. To her it felt that way, but her neighbour only heard something more like squawking and someone being sick.

This time it was loud enough and strange enough that her neighbour knocked on the wall, calling out to see if she was okay. But there was no answer. Lauren had slumped under her chair and curled up into a ball. Her neighbour came to the door, knocked and knocked, then went to get the warden.

The first Gyan heard of it was when Lauren called him the next morning from the Royal Prince Alfred Hospital. She had been sedated and taken to the mental health facility there. Since moving to Sydney, Lauren had initially used the Sydney University Counselling Service when she had anxiety and stress. Recently though, she had seen a psychologist. In her opinion, this was an escalation, a full-blown panic attack, perhaps even psychosis Lauren told Gyan later.

Gyan made his way immediately down to the hospital, despite having an exam in an hour. Lauren's psychologist had recommended she watch A TED Talk by Kelly McGonigal on the way we perceive stress, and Lauren had, after all what else was there to do now the panic had passed? Lauren tried to explain the video to Gyan, sharing how McGonigal argued that the way we perceive stress, or the way we frame it, has an incredible impact on our experience of it. She used to believe that stress was bad. But research from 2012 and 2013 caused her to rethink that position. "It turns out," Lauren said, "that stress is only bad if you believe it to be bad for you". In fact, people who believe stress is good for you are the healthiest, strongest and longest-living people of all! Gyan found it all very hard to believe so she logged in and they watched it together.

Gyan jotted notes down as they watched, in his usual style, as they waited for the paperwork to be done so Lauren could be released.

There are physiological signs that stress is coming. Become aware that it's happening and do not ignore it. Stress comes for a reason, and that reason matters. Realise that there are a variety of reactions you can take like freezing, fleeing and fighting; or alternatively you could rise and be excited. Stress is a natural part of life and drives most of the things that are meaningful to us.

This one fact – how you think about stress, might save your life. In a survey of 35,000 people, who were asked to measure if they were a) a little stressed or b) moderately stressed or c) very stressed were also asked if they believed stress was a good or a bad thing. They found two interesting outcomes. Firstly those most stressed who believed it was bad had a 43% higher chance of mortality (dying) than the others. But those who were most stressed but believed it was a good thing were the least likely to suffer health problems. The big deal here is cardiovascular constriction, or blood vessel diameter.

Gyan doodled a process and titled it 'Change Your Mindset':
1. Acknowledge the stress as we experience it coming.
2. Welcome the stress; it is normal and it's there because you care.
3. Make use of the wonderful energy stress brings you.

Another study of 1,000 individuals found that those who were stressed and were hit by a large life event like the death of a loved one or major loss were 33% more likely to die. But those who had spent time caring for others and serving in their community had absolutely zero change to their baseline mortality rates. Caring is living, when you're under stress!

Furthermore, this is not easy believism (just change your mind), or trying to just cast a positive spin on every event. Some things suck, like the death of a loved one, or having a heart attack. Those are also very stressful.

Finally, the nurse arrived and got Lauren to sign the forms. Thankfully Lauren's next exam wasn't until tomorrow, so she was able to return to her dorm room and rest. Gyan apologised for leaving, but had to get to his exam. He promised to come visit her in the evening. She felt at once both excited and disappointed. She had new information which could be potentially life-saving, and yet she had also now had her first "breakdown" and the psych had said it was unlikely to be her last. She hung her head as she walked across campus to the dormitory.

She fired up her computer and the kettle, with no heart to study for her exam. She had to get to the bottom of the stress thing because it was killing her. As the kettle boiled, she wondered whether she should tell her parents or not. They'd just worry themselves sick, so she decided against it until the exam period was over and she could give them all the relevant information.

Tea made, she fingered a printout of one of McGonigal's references, a study at Brock University. Before the studies Kelly had mentioned, the scientific community had found that stress itself was served up in two forms. Eustress was good and motivated you to work, provided incentives to get things done, set you up for pressing through. Bad stress was when things were too much, when tension builds, all work loses its joy, there is no relief and the fall starts toward depression. Who knew the line between the two was simply perception? There was an unholy quaternity that cajoles us to experience stress as negative. When:

1. You feel inadequate to the task,
2. The task isolates you from others,
3. The work feels meaningless, and
4. You have to do it against your will.

She read with interest the advice on how to get it right, to become stress-resistant, and wrote the advice down for Gyan, with her own ideas next to each:

- Stop feeling guilty about your reactions, they just are (mindfulness).
- Be decisive about your strategy (goals and attention).
- Avoid being a perfectionist (yep been there already).
- Set priorities for yourself (decide what's important, do journaling).
- Stop procrastinating (get motivated).
- Live an optimal lifestyle (keep self-coaching).

*

Gyan came over after his exam to see how Lauren was. His concern, to an outsider, would have seemed rather robotic, as though he were going through a list in his head, or checking off a medical report. But Lauren read his concern and his care in his barrage of questions about her symptoms. Satisfied at last that she was all right, he settled down on the couch with her, holding her hand as she explained what she'd found so far. Reading her notes, and reviewing the papers, he seemed quite critical of Brock, as though their work hadn't been academic enough.

"I mean, at least McGonigal had 35,000 in her sample; these guys are running a student population and have less than a thousand," he complained. She wasn't an expert in statistics but thought anything more than a couple hundred was a "large" enough sample.

"Anyway," she said, releasing his hand, a little exasperated, "just before you came I was tracking the phrase 'stress resistance' because it seemed like something we should really be, or have, or whatever you're supposed to say." Uncertain of their connection, he laughed uneasily, rose, and poured them both a glass of wine.

That phrase brought them to another TED Talk, this time by Elizabeth Stanley from Georgetown University. Evidently she had been asked by the army to prepare stress inoculation pre-deployment for the troops and that work had grown to become the Mind Fitness Training Institute. Straight away Lauren liked her because she asked attendees to stop and check in with their bodies, to hear any somatic signalling or unconscious instructions. Elizabeth talked of body-based self-regulation skills which Lauren and Gyan took to mean self-awareness and listening to somatic intuition with bio-feedback.

They paused the video to consider her analogy that the brain behaves much like a muscle: just as you train for strength and endurance, you must train the brain for correct response to stressors. They thought about making an action list for her content and just how much repetition she'd needed to get her results. They discussed the fight or flight system in the croc brain again and marvelled at the amount of energy, focus, and physical change we can muster in a heartbeat using the stress response. Returning to the video, they laughed because Elizabeth addressed the triune brain theory and the way the three layers react to stress. Been there, done that, thought Lauren.

"The only way through stress appears to be if we consciously reframe our experience and tell ourselves a different story," said Lauren. "Then the other parts of the brain listen."

"Well, yes, that and if we consciously listen in to our physical signals, if we pay attention to those layers of communication and awareness coming to us like the phone signals," Gyan said, agreeing and disagreeing at the same time. The only way he got away with it was by shaking his nodding head, India, style. "Now this is where our Dr Elizabeth disagrees with Dr Kelly, because she is saying stress plus effective recovery and rest equals resilience. But Kelly says reframing plus stress equals no ill effects," he finished.

"Does 'no ill effects' equal resilience?" Lauren asked, getting a little confused.

"Yes, I think these are analogue," Gyan replied flatly. But it turned out he was wrong. At the end of her lecture, Elizabeth said, "The stress-response system which deploys attention and all the resources we need for rapid response can do either one of two things… it can anticipate: be future-oriented, or it can be resilient: present-oriented."

"Yes, yes, I see it now," Lauren said, like a person waking up from a dream, "on the one hand there are two ways of framing or perceiving stress—good or bad, and that changes our experience of it, and on the other hand there are two ways of deploying stress. Using it to predict, which in the long run makes me anxious and have a panic attack, or using it to be present and respond to or solve my problems, be mindful."

"Yes, Lauren, I too see that's right now. Don't discount the incredible value of prediction: to grow we need to be challenged and stress pushes us forward. But we must come back from there to the present, to mindfulness. I also see the value of unwinding, coming down, sleep and rest, hanging out with friends like now," Gyan said. Then he rumbled through his backpack, looking for a book. He pulled out an orange-and-black-covered book with a bookmark in it and he read her a story.

It was the story of two brothers. One had died in a car accident and the other was mourning that tragedy, and was still depressed a year later. A friend came and asked the brother why he was still depressed, and the brother gave all the usual self-sorry reasons a person would be sad that his best friend and brother had died. The friend asked him, "Do you think your brother, if he could talk now, would be pleased with you?" and the brother said, "I don't know, why?" The friend replied, "Well, I think he'd be disappointed, and maybe even angry with you." This shocked the man and he became quite defensive. The friend asked the brother to imagine he had been in a horrible car accident and lost both his legs. The friend went on to say, "In sympathy for your condition, I'm now going to take off both my legs. How would you feel about that?" The remaining brother replied, "You'd be a fool, an idiot, why?" the friend said, "Because I've now wasted my legs, and in no way does that bring back yours. It's the same with your depression—what would your brother think of you losing your life, as well as him his?"

It was a profound moment for both of them, and they sat in silence a moment considering the implications of this story. They had a lot to be grateful for, a lot to reframe and get on with. With his exam over and the stress of Lauren's hospitalization behind them, Gyan's blood cortisol and DHEA levels were steadily dropping and oxytocin came flooding in with his appreciation for Lauren. He leant over and once again they kissed.

Action list

- Check in with your body right now. Ask it if there's any action, movement or change you to make to be better or more comfortable.
- Check in with yourself about your attitude to stress. Do you see it as a good thing or a b thing?
- Write a list of eustress activity – stressful but good things and a list if distress activity – stressful but bad things.
- How engaged are you with the things that occupy your day? How engaged are you with that make you laugh or learn or love or grow?
- Try paying attention, deploying attention today and notice the people, the road condition lawns and trees, the car park signs, your workmates. Be present to them and see, really
- Think about a past experience that was very painful, difficult and which you've been avo ruminating on. Now bring that event up and think about it as an opportunity to grow, to le and be stronger. Let the event educate, arm and equip you for now.
- Frame and reframe people's opinions of you. "Everything can be reframed, because it h been framed in the first place" e.g. today's problems in light of this week, this year, this decade.
- Watch for ways in which you distract yourself from task; for example, talking on the phor while you're walking the dog or watching a screen while you wash up. You're not being present.
- Stop feeling guilty about your reactions, they just are. How is your mindfulness?
- Make a strategy about dealing with stress. Set goals and pay attention.
- Do you have a standard for the task you're stressed about? Remember that perfectionis the lack of a standard.
- Set priorities for yourself, decide what's important by using journaling. Do the most impo things today first.

EPILOGUE: SECTION TWO

"Habit, if not resisted, soon becomes necessity."
St Augustine

Well there's the second third of ideas to be presented in this book, the journey of discovering the brain and its environment. Mark, Jane, Monique and Lauren have been fairly solidly joined by Gyan on the journey. Another twelve weeks have passed and it is now the end of spring. We have seen great blooming in their lives and each of them wrestle with the tough issues of life: Mark has resigned and then returned to work, and in the process, experienced his boss Art from a totally new perspective; Jane has wrestled with weight loss and suspicion of Mark; Monique has been to see her therapist friend Karen; Lauren faced her anxiety and catastrophizing. Gyan has rejected his overseas bride and turned toward Lauren.

The group have examined learning, neuroplasticity, the three layers of the head brain, the existence of a heart and gut brain, seven forms of motivation, the incredible benefit of getting a good night's sleep and learned about reframing and stress. So let's dig down into the research that sits behind this.

8. Learning about learning. Monique's attempts at online dating fail, and she remains desperate for affection. Lauren picks Gyan up from the airport, and they both realise that it's time to get serious about a relationship. Mark quits his job, much to Art's consternation and Jane explores the effect of belief on performance. Art takes Mark off to the Hotel Kurrajong where he learns Action Learning and the quad loop learning model.

Primary: The idea that learning looped back on itself to create iterative learning was initially proposed in the field of Action Research by Argyris, C., & Schon, D. (1974). Theory in practice: Increasing professional effectiveness.

Triple loop learning advanced the idea to include organisational development and change when it was applied from the engineering field to consulting in, Field Guide to Consulting and Organizational Development: A Collaborative and Systems Approach to Performance, Change and Learning, (2006) by Carter McNamara.

I came across the fourth loop in Action Learning from trainer Pieter Kopacek's paper, Advanced Control Strategies for Social and Economic Systems, delivered at the IFAC multitrack conference (2004).

Secondary: *1. Unconscious:* The concept of 97% unconscious comes from David Eagleman's book Incognito (2012), supported by Conscious and Unconscious Programs in the Brain: perspectives in social psychology (2013) by Benjamin Kissin who proposed that there must be at least 10,000 programs in the brain.

2. Metaphor: The observation that metaphor mediates between the conscious and unconscious was a David Grove quote captured by Phillip Harland in his book, How the Brain Feels: working with emotion and cognition, (2012), pg 37.

Tertiary: *1. Belief and performance:* The article Jane was reading Weger, U.W. & Loughnan, S., (2013). "Mobilizing unused resources: Using the placebo concept to enhance cognitive performance," Quarterly Journal of Experimental Psychology, 66(1):23-28.

2. Perceptual positions: John Grinder and Richard Bandler, the founders of NLP, gave us perceptual positions in their 1990 classic Frogs into Princes: Introduction to Neurolinguistic Programming. The format we see being played with here though, did not derive directly from them but from John Sautelle himself.

9. Being flexible about neuroplasticity. Mark and Jane go down to the coast for a well-earned rest. They are joined by Lauren, who they were expecting, and Gyan who they were not. Monique confronts Jane's father in her home and he has a fall, which puts him in hospital, where he falls again, putting himself in a coma. Devastated, Monique comes down and receives therapy from Jane in the form of perceptual positioning. She also gets a bit touchy feely with Mark, eliciting a jealous reaction from Jane. They all discover neuroplasticity and the ability of the brain to learn and change. Gyan points out that they really need to have some accountability, goals and deadlines to see if they are accomplishing change.

Primary: This chapter relies exclusively on John Arden's work on brain plasticity in both Rewire Your Brain (2010), and The Brain Bible (2014).

Secondary: The family all watch and are inspired by Todd Sampson's TV series Redesign My Brain. Series I has three episodes (2013) & Series

II has three episodes (2015).

Tertiary: *1. Brain Plasticity:* neuroscientist Adam Gazzaley was interviewed on the Tim Ferriss podcast, titled "The Maverick of Brain Optimization" (2015).

In the chapter various statistics are thrown around such as the minimum time for neurogenesis which, according to a study of terminal cancer patients in Japan, is three days: Tatsunori, S., Kazunobu, S., Parent, J.M., Alvarez-Buylla, A. (eds) (2011). Neurogenesis in the Adult Brain II: clinical implications.

The minimum time for neuroplasticity, that is for creating a stable loop or steady pathway, is two weeks: Vance, D.E., Kaur, J., Fazeli, P.L., et al. (2012). Neuroplasticity and Successful Cognitive Aging, The Journal of Neuroscience Nursing, 44(4):10.

The minimum time for lasting neural change, according to the studies at UQ, is six to eight weeks. Rossouw, P.J. (2013). The Neuroscience of Talking Therapies: implications for therapeutic practises, Journal of Neuropsychotherapy in Australia, Vol. 24: see p6.

2. Leadership: The Arbinger Institute published the business parable Leadership and Self-Deception (2000) which forms the basis of Art's conversation with Mark.

10. Who split my brain? Monique takes herself off to her friend Karen at work to discuss the darkness which tugs at her soul. Karen walks her through a time line exercise and she confronts old issues in her past. Mark and Jane have a discussion in the car in an attempt to resolve the tension over his interactions with Monique on the beach. Lauren discovers a Derren Brown video and shares it with everyone. In this chapter it is Karen who brings the content about moving from 'Oh Crap to Okay' and listening to others. In making that discovery the group also learn about the theory about the three layers of the brain and its implications for the way we decide. Monique has a melt-down, taking the elevator down to croc brain.

Primary: Karen has the pleasure of attending a seminar by Mark Goulston based on his book *Just Listen: discover the secret to getting through to absolutely anyone* (2011).

Secondary: Dr. Goulston's model of communication and limbic respond rests implicitly on the model by Paul D. MacLean, as presented in, *The Triune Brain in Evolution: role in paleocerebral functions* (1990).

MacLean's model was criticised from an anthropological point of view (we do not have a lizard brain inside a monkey brain inside a neocortex) and reptiles do not have a brain stem assembly like ours. That aside, his model is remarkably resilient because it is structurally, neuroanatomically sound.

Tertiary: 1. Neuroscience: Oren Klaff wrote about neuromarketing in his book Pitch Anything (2013). Klaff describes the need for marketers to first get past the gate keeper, or croc brain and then pitch 'hot' to the limbic system or monkey brain.

2. Psychology: Karen's adjustments to the Timeline come from observations made in *Trust Me I'm the Patient*, by Philip Harland (2012, chapter 15, footnote 2). The reimprinting timeline process itself is taken from Robert Dilts, which was refined by Jules Collingwood.

3. Hypnotism: Derren Brown deceives a cabbie http://www.youtube.com/watch?v=XLmf_hD-LQk

11. The mind body split. Gyan, Lauren, Ming and Clarity all participate in a book club at Sydney University and they discuss *Descartes' Error*. During the discussion Gyan shares with them a new model or understanding from *mBraining* – that we have a heart and a gut brain. Jane finally watches the Derren brown video and becomes highly suspicious that Mark might have forcefully influenced her. She calls her friend Maryanne who studied the Program in Placebo Studies at Harvard. Mark realises that Art's observations are absolutely right and that he needs to humble himself and go back to work. They go to Cooking School and learn about the unholy sugar/salt/fat trinity, obesity, addiction and brain change through eating.

Primary: The thesis of coaching the whole nervous system and all its multiple intelligences comes from *mBraining* (2012), by Grant Soosalu and Marvin Oka.

This book in turn relies on the work of Michael Gershon, *The Second Brain* (1998), and Doc Lew Childre who wrote *The Heart Math Solution* (2011), along with Rollin McCraty who relied on the work of J Andrew Armour who wrote *Basic and Clinical Neurocardiology* (1991).

Secondary: The students in book club are studying *Descartes' Error* (1994), by António Damásio. I hope by now you figured out what his error was.

Splitting mind and body. *The Divided Mind* (2009), by John Sarno plays a cameo role, but it is by no means a lightweight player, examining psychosomatic illness.

As Jane sits reading about cravings and control she examines the work of German Psychologist Maja Storch and *Embodied Communication* (2014).

Tertiary: *1. On Hypnosis:* Here it is again, go watch it! Derren Brown deceives a Cabbie: http://www.youtube.com/watch?v=XLmf_hD-LQk

If you're game, and you find 'The Core' it will lead you to Kirsch, I., Cardeña, E., Derbyshire, S., Dienes, Z., Heap, M., Kallio, S., Mazzoni, G.,Naish, N., Oakley, D., Potter, C., Walters, V., Whalley, M., 2011. Definitions of Hypnosis and Hypnotic Ability and their Relation to Suggestion and Suggestibility: A Consensus Statement. *Contemporary Hypnosis and Integrative Therapy*, 28(2):107–115.

2. On food: The body craves health. When a body is put on a healthy diet it changes the brain in the striatum region, according to scientists at the Jean Mayer USDA Human Nutrition Research Center on Aging (USDA HNRCA) at Tufts University and Massachusetts General Hospital.

A diet high in sugar, fat and salt is as addictive as cocaine. So said Nicole Avena in her research at Princeton University. 'Addicted to Fat: Overeating May Alter the Brain as Much as Hard Drugs.' http://www.scientificamerican.com/article/addicted-to-fat-eating/

The quote in French and Italian, raving about fat is a brilliant observation by Gary J. Schwartz, professor of neuroscience and endocrinology at Albert Einstein College of Medicine in New York. He was quoted in "Your Backup Brain: by Dan Hurley, *Psychology Today*, November 1, 2011.

The Low Carb Diet referred to by Mark comes from *The 4-Hour Body* (2010) or look it up: https://en.wikipedia.org/wiki/The_4Hour_Body

Cravings for food are not signals about what we should eat. Pelchat, M.L. & Schaefer, S., (2000). Dietary monotony and food cravings in young and elderly adults, *The Journal of Physiological Behaviour*, 68(3):353-9.

However there is a growing body of evidence that the microbiota or gut bacteria does affect taste receptors, highjacking the vagus nerve and use toxins to affect mood. Alcock, J., Maley C.C., Aktipis, C.A.,

2014. Is eating behaviour manipulated by the gastrointestinal microbiota? Evolutionary pressures and potential mechanisms. *Bioessays*, 36(10):940-949.

The distinction between intuition and instinct, and trusting your gut, or somatic markers, is further explored by good old António Damásio in *The Feeling of What Happens* (1999).

3. On philosophy: Descartes' statement 'I think therefore I am,' was examined by Eckhart Tolle's 2005 book *A Whole New Earth* who observed that there had to be two people in the statement.

12. Healthy motivation. Jane goes to visit her dad, who still lays in a coma in hospital. She searches her heart for her motivation for visiting. Was it want, need or preference? Obligation, ritual or guilt? Mark visits Art and is told he is welcome back, but has to prove himself to the partners. Monique attempts to make sense of her descent into croc brain, where consciousness is centred and whether it is the same as the streams of awareness that Gyan and Lauren talk about (which it is not). Jane discovers that ABSI has replaced the BMI and explores weight loss at the gym. Mark and Jane enjoy night #2 at the Cooking School where they learn about chemical combinations in food, pulling together disparate ideas and neuropeptides. Mark and Jane go to the AIS gym seminar and learn about seven forms of motivation.

Primary: The three layers of motivation are presented by Daniel Pink in *Drive: the surprising truth about what motivates us* (2010). It has to be said that Pink sees the three layers as hierarchical, each replacing the one below. I believe the model maps perfectly to the three layers of the brain (MacLean) and give us seven simultaneous forms of motivation.

Secondary: *1. 23 and a half hours:* Mike Evans came up with this as an aim to get us to exercise 30 minutes a day. He works to get people to find what the single most important things we can do for our health is. See http://www.youtube.com/watch?v=aUaInS6HIGo and if you want more information http://www.evanshealthlab.com/23-and-12-hours/

2. Neuropeptides: your food has been heavily studied by many labs. Richard Wurtman from MIT Department of Brain and Cognitive Sciences has closely examined how foods provide precursors to neurotransmitters. His work has since examined serotonin, carbohydrate cravings and obesity.

Tertiary: *1. ABSI:* stands for A Body Shape Index and was developed by

Jason Buberel from New York City College. It measures age, gender, height, weight and waist circumference. It has effectively replaced the BMI.

2. Degustation: Carl and Kelie Kenzler ran Ritual Restaurant in Nelson Bay, NSW as a degustation restaurant. Degustation means a careful, appreciative tasting of various foods and focusing on the sensory, culinary art and great company. They focussed on molecular gastronomy, or the application of scientific principles to food preparation, taste combination and food service.

13. The magic effects of sleep. Lauren and Gyan drive down to visit her parents and discuss allergies, the Paleo diet and FODMAPs. Kevin Geary leads them to Evan Brand and hacking their brain for sleep. Mark is trying to get into Strategic thinking as he prepares to work in Defence with Smythe and Johnson. The whole team gather for a catch up and accountability and the next day go to Floriade to enjoy the sunshine. The evening finds Mark, Jane, Lauren and Gyan going to the final evening of Cooking School. There they learn about Bush Tucker and expanding their culinary tastes to expand their minds. Gyan delivers a well-timed lecture on sleep and the incredible benefits of getting enough.

Primary: Russell Foster, a circadian neuroscientist who has committed 20+ years of research into sleep and the brain, has written an instructive book with Leon Kreitzman, *The Rhythms of Life: the biological clocks that control the daily lives of every living thing* (2011). For a brief version of his findings see his TED talk: http://www.ted.com/talks/russell_foster_why_do_we_sleep?. For a more complete and up to date version listen to his full University of Western Australia 2019 lecture at http://www.ias.uwa.edu.au/lectures/russellfoster

Secondary: *1. Stress:* Evan Brand spoke on "Stress and Forest Bathing," episode 133 of the Not Just Paleo podcast. In case you're curious, forest bathing, or Shinrin-yoku means taking a short, leisurely visit to a forest. He also spoke on the Just in Health podcast "Hack Your Brain and Your Sleep," episode 29.

2. Metaphor: When Gyan mentions the construction of metaphor in sleep he relies on 1969 "Dreaming as a Metaphor in Motion," by Montague Ullman from the Archives of General Psychiatry, 21(6):696-703. The Sleep Hygiene Check List provided at the end of this chapter is a blended list taken from: 'Checklist for Better Sleep,' Psych. Tools (2015), 'Depression Tool Kit – sleeping better,' from the University of Michigan (2014) and 'When Sleep Becomes a Nightmare,' by Scholastic (2013).

3. Cancer: The material about sleep and cancer is the result of Stanford University psychiatrist David Spiegel and Sandra Sephton who say that sleep problems alter the balance of at least two hormones that influence cancer cells. Sephton, S. & Spiegel, D., (2013). Circadian disruption in cancer: a neuroendocrine-immune pathway from stress to disease?, Journal of Brain, Behaviour, and Immunity, 17(5):321-328.

Tertiary: *1. Wild Food Harvesting:* In the cooking class the chefs use a range of unusual food stuffs. I have wild harvested in the way described here and provided you with actual locations of where I found these food items. Black wattle seed comes from the eastern side of Mt. Ainsle; wild rosella is a flower from Lake Burley Griffin but can be found in many gardens; Bunya pine are a huge pine whose cones are the size of a football. The nut can be found in season at the Botanic Gardens; the Creek Lilly Pilly (*acmena smithii*) grows beside Lake Ginnindera and in many back yards. The fruit of most of the syzygium family is also edible; glossy nightshade (*solanum americanum*) can be found just about anywhere. Do not confuse it with deadly nightshade (*atropha belladonna*). Wild lime & lemon myrtle would both have been ordered in.

2. Recipes: Many of the recipes they use in Cooking School come from Wild Lime, (1996) by chef Juleigh Robins who now runs Outback Spirit, suppliers of bush tucker. For more recipes see Tukka: real Australian food, (1996) by Jean-Paul Bruneteau. The meats can be ordered as follows. The buffalo, camel, emu and goat can be ordered from https://www.mcd.com.au (with pigeon, ostrich and crocodile too). The buffalo worm is a grub from http://www.ediblebugshop.com.au The alpaca can be ordered from http://www.primealpaca.com.au

3. Digestion: The information about water and digestion comes from nutrition specialist P. Kendall at Colorado State University Extension who did a study with the Mayo Clinic. This can be read at http://www.livestrong.com/article/429906-does-drinking-water-affect-food-digestion/ The research on the effects of carbohydrates on sleep came from the National Sleep Foundation.

https://www.sleepfoundation.org/bedroom-environment/taste/food-and-sleep

14. Reframing stress. In this chapter Jane helps Monique reframe her experience of dating by changing mode and taking her speed dating. Mark learns to reframe his assumptions about parent populations and board signs being representative of the whole. He parks on the rooftop the next day! Lauren has a panic attack as a result of her mounting anxiety from the stress of exams. During her sojourn in the RPA hospital she discovers Kelly McGonigal's work on reframing stress and the power this has to enable a completely different experience. She also learns of stress resilience and eustress. So here's what we relied on for this chapter.

Primary: Kelly McGonigal on the way we perceive stress in TED http://www.ted.com/talks/kelly_mcgonigal_how_to_make_stress_your When Gyan comes to write about the quaternity of issues that make stress impossible to convert, he relies at first on Kelly McGonigal's book The Upside of Stress: Why stress is good for you, and how to get good at it (2015). We then go on to use Sir Michael Marmot's 20 years of research on stress in the workplace and things that make it hard (called the Whitehall I & II series).

Secondary: *1. Perceiving stress:* The sources that Kelly McGonigal relies upon are: Abiola Keller et al., (2012). Does the perception that stress affects health matter? The association with health and mortality, Health Psychology, Vol 5:677-684. Jeremy P. Jamieson et al., (2012). Mind over matter. Reappraising arousal improves cardiovascular and cognitive responses to stress, Journal of Experimental Psychology, 141(3):417-422. Lastly I read Michael J. Poulin et al., (2013). Giving to others and the association between stress and mortality, American Journal of Public Health, 103(9):1649-1655.

2. Reframing: A secondary underlying principle explored in reframing is heuristic failure. In her wonderful book Criminal Investigative Failures, (2008) D. Kim Russo follows many examples of police and FBI failure because of heuristic failure similar to those displayed in this chapter. She in turn relies on the work of Daniel Kahneman and Amos Tversky (1974). Judgement Under Uncertainty: heuristic biases, Science, 185:1124–1130.

Tertiary: *1. Stress:* McGonigal also relies on Gloster, A.T., et. al., (2013).

Long-term stability of cognitive behavioural therapy effects for panic disorder with agoraphobia: a two-year follow-up study, Behavioural Research and Therapy, 51(12):830-839.

In doing her research Lauren comes across Brock University, https://www.gulfbend.org/poc/view_doc.php?type=doc&id=15644&cn=

Elizabeth Stanley Georgetown University preps army for stress predeployment using inoculation, which largely relies on using mindfulness. Stanley, E.A., et al., (2011). Mindfulness-based Mind Fitness Training: A Case Study of a High-Stress Predeployment Military Cohort, Cognitive and Behavioural Practise, Vol 18:566-576.

If you want to watch the TED talk Gyan and Lauren watched see https://youtu.be/e0AMlf-mwY4. In 2014 the Islamic Azad University ran a parallel study showing that MMFT produced similar results in a civilian cohort.

2. Compatibility: When considering their compatibility and needs Mark relies upon Willard Harley, His Needs, Her Needs, (1986). Their different time preferences are based upon the research of Stanford psychologist Philip Zimbardo in The Time Paradox, (2008) which he co-wrote with John Boyd.

3. Dating: The article Jane read, that lead to her sojourn into speed dating was "Speed Dating in the Time of Tinder," by Georgina Parfitt (2014) in the Atlantic.

Summer break is upon Lauren and Gyan as they complete their exams. Like all Australians, Mark, Jane, and Monique have to balance a long summer holiday break with the need to work and provide. The next six weeks give them adequate time to embed their learning, work on the exercises, catch up on the reading some of them had pretended to do and meet a few times to discuss their journey.

Monique will see both men from the speed-dating event, but find that the presence of a person's unchecked history is too hard to trust. Lauren continues to work at reframing anxiety and stress, being triggered by all sorts of seemingly unrelated stimuli. Jane and Mark both wish that the cooking school ran a summer program; she for the cooking and he for the company it provides. He has not yet worked up the courage to share with her the rest of what he thinks about their relationship.

Jane continues to carry her dad in her heart, undealt with, and he continues to lie in a coma in the hospital. Mark, now aware of his own limitations at work, is working with a new team in Defence. Their work begins in one section and progressively makes its way across to the same area Monique works in. Mark and Monique work in the same building, park in the same car park, and eat at the same cafeteria for four weeks before running into each other.

Each of them have journeyed in their learning and practice of neuroscience self-coaching. Whilst Gyan's suggestion of accountability and measuring progress toward goals was sound, it took them many weeks before they adopted it properly. They have learned that change work, for each item, takes weeks to embed.

In some respects, they have also learned that the journey to being limitless means going backwards at first. Lauren ending up in the psych ward to re-examine her beliefs, Monique being driven to despair and opening old wounds to get past her fear of men and Mark right now examining what he believes about marriage.

This will be a pattern that develops and continues, because unlike progress in the human race's terms, personal development is not cumulative in the sense that you can make discovery on the shoulders of others. Each change must be personally integrated, and for every floor we wish to rise, we must dig our foundations another layer deeper. The growth is limitless in theory, but is often limited by our personal brokenness, dysfunction, and poor choices. Those willing to keep at the game, keep driving personal growth, and keep examining their behaviour and changing it ultimately end up at the head of every venture. This is not because they are better, faster, stronger, brighter or even have more self-control. It is because they kept going when others stopped. They view it as an eternal process, as the Japanese like to call it: Kiyosei… continuous, incremental improvement.

"The world is run by those who show up."
Robert B. Johnson

So let's return to their story as they approach the end of the holidays. Thanksgiving, Christmas and New Year are all past and the early part of January is giving way to the end of summer break.

SECTION THREE: THE BRAIN AND ITS RELATIONSHIPS

CHAPTER FIFTEEN: ENIGMATIC PERSONALITY

"We have, each of us a life story, an inner narrative whose continuity, whose sense is our lives... this narrative is us, our identity."
Oliver Sacks

Gyan felt just awful. His sinuses were congested, he felt like a spear was being driven between his temples, his nose ran, his throat was sore, and his sleep was broken. None of this would have caused Gyan to be overly concerned in winter, but this was the silly season in the Southern Hemisphere. Christmas, beach parties, family vacations, and sizzling 35°C heat should have all contributed to having fun in the sun. Instead, Gyan languished inside the house with some kind of viral infection.

His parents had grudgingly acknowledged Lauren as his "special friend," but would not concede the battle to find him a "real wife" from home: a Brahmin Hindu. Lauren sat in their house, feeding him. They seemed to have an idea that food would heal him, which perplexed her a little. Inwardly Lauren was saying, *Right, here's some Goan-style chicken... so protein in coconut gravy is going to give him strength? Oh no, wait, maybe it's the cloves, cinnamon, or star anise? Okay, the tamarind is good for your skin, but really? Yellow dal to dip deep-fried rotis in; well, apart from the fact that Gyan rejected it, being too difficult to swallow, they're not even healthy, for God's sake. And sour hung curds in cardamom? Yuck! I think cardamom might actually have some health benefits, like ginger, mainly for heartburn—which you're gonna get from eating Indian.*

So went her unheard conversation while he drifted in and out of sleep. When he was resting, she pulled out some reading. She was halfway through a Jodi Picoult novel on the supernatural behaviour of a child. It was hard-going. She was more taken with Kelly McGonigal's book on reframing stress. Initially it had seemed absurd to her that change could be as simple as thinking about or perceiving stress differently, but she had read it, and she had tried it, and she had gone back to her psychologist for more.

Lauren had continued to be plagued by anxiety-inducing attacks. Her psych had once again explained the "ABCs" of mental recovery to her. As if to attempt firmly cementing the theory, Lauren looked it up online and found that it was originally called Rational Emotive Behavioural Therapy (REBT). Sitting on the couch, she flicked through her notes, which now seemed less potent than when she first learned it:

A = the activating event. What am I really getting stressed about here? I usually think about (worry about) the future, the alternate scenarios, the 'what if's' and I'm usually highly self-condemning. What I think about the event, and what I say to myself about the event often blows it out of all proportion.
B = what is my belief system? What do I believe about this event, its consequences and the real probability that things might happen? Have these been examined? Are they counter-productive? Am I being catastrophic? I tend to reduce everything to its worst possible outcome and believe the chances of succeeding are slim to none. This is irrational.
C = what are the consequences of holding these irrational beliefs? I am creating a self-fulfilling prophecy (I'm going to burn out, see I burned out) and cycles of negative thoughts which go round and round (ruminating). Choose to make these thoughts visible to Gyan, and listen to his estimation of a more reasonable (rational?) approach.
D = dispute irrational thoughts and beliefs. This can be hard on my own so let others be my bouncing board. It's important to agree to experiment with, to play with changing the meaning of events, to be willing to try something out. Make a one percent change, a very small fraction that does not demand 'the world' from me.
E = the emotional effects of revised beliefs will change, must change so that distress, anxiety and panic can evaporate. If they don't, then the reframing has not worked, and the cognitive process will continue to produce the same old outcomes. Am I aware of the emotions, where they are and why I have them? Can I track change?

Lauren checked on Gyan, who was sleeping fitfully after lunch, then she opened her laptop. The blades of the ceiling fan cut lazily though the syrupy air. It was always hot over here; they didn't seem to love air-conditioning. Lauren was curious about reframing her experience of anxiety because after her hospital visit she had been forced to examine her beliefs and the kinds of things she was telling herself. She wanted to know what else there was. After one simple search for the "A B C D E" process, she found Albert Ellis, the creator of this technique.

So she did a search on him and found many journal articles and books. Evidently his journey had taken him from sex therapy to REBT to the examination of "stream of consciousness" and self-talk to personality theory. That set of links made her curious. Was self-talk connected to personality? She strongly considered ordering the book, *Personality Theories: Critical Perspectives*. She read an extract which said, "Personality is strongly predicated on a person's style of self-talk. Of course other factors play a part… but self-talk is the defining factor," according to Ellis. "Self-talk, rational or irrational, sustains or suppresses emotional patterns and enhances or depletes motivation and is the regulating force behind most human behaviour."

Wow, she thought, *this guy really thinks self-talk is the bomb.* He wasn't the only one either, since REBT morphed into CBT, much of the industry had leaned on self-talk and working with the unconscious. A great many of the personality models integrated these ideas too, she read. Others believed that self-talk and personality had a reciprocal relationship: being made up of beliefs, emotions, perceptions, and heuristics, the personality generated self-talk; self-talk was always about beliefs, emotions, perceptions, and heuristics. *Ha!* Lauren thought. *The chicken and the egg.* At first, it seemed like a stretch to her, that core personality was predicated on our self-talk. Most people she knew didn't even believe they talked to themselves! Lauren determined to call her mum tonight to discuss it.

*

Over the summer, the Defence offices got quiet. Many of the serving military had eight weeks off; some chose to take only six. Many civilian administrative personnel only took three weeks, choosing to take this chance to catch up in a much quieter environment. Karen had been going to write to Mark Goulston ever since the seminar and now she took the chance to do so. Karen had heard Goulston mention amygdala hijack and was curious to find out more.

To her great delight, Mark answered her email immediately, asking if she would Skype. She agreed of course and once they were online they got chatting about his work as a psychiatrist, her work as a psychologist, the US and Australia, and his recent visit. She already understood that when something upsetting happens it triggers the amygdala (especially under stress or anxiety). This suppresses the ability to think before reacting. What she did not know is that this was almost a 1:1 inverse relationship. When her amygdala (emotional control) was running at 35%, her pre-frontal cortex (rational problem-solving) dropped to 65%.

It also created an overwhelming emotional response, often out of proportion to what was going on. So Karen wanted to focus on shutting down amygdala hijack in patients, not just Mark's siege and hostage-crisis situations.

"Listen Karen, it's all about awareness for the client. Have you seen my list on this?" Mark asked.

"No, sorry, but send it to me, or give me a web address so I can take this neuroscience one step further," Karen said.

"Well, you don't have to be a neuroscientist; in fact, I did an article in the

Huffington Post about this; anyone can use it, really," he laughed. He gave her the nine points of awareness and she wrote them down:

1. Be aware of what triggered you. Write down what upset you.
2. Be aware of where you feel it physically and how strongly you feel it.
3. Be aware what emotion is triggered. Give it a label, give it a name.
4. Be aware of your reaction. What do you want to do, impulsively?
5. Be aware of the consequence. What happens when you act on the impulse?
6. Be aware that you might be taking it too personally, and it wasn't meant that way.
7. Be aware of reality, is there any other explanation for what is happening?
8. Be aware of the way out. What solution is there, apart from your impulse?
9. Be aware of the benefits of choosing another way out instead of your reaction.

"The whole nature of this is to bring your client up and out of emotional lockdown," Goulston explained, "because when the amygdala is in control. Remember… "

"It shuts down cognitive thought," Karen concluded, "rational and reasonable thought is inaccessible, even if it seems rational at the time."

"Right. Go look up the work of Jeffrey Schwartz and Elliot Krane. They each give a great tool for cognitive reframing when you're having a hijack," Mark said before signing off.

Karen wrote the names straight into the search engine on two tabs of her browser. Krane offered emotional re-exposure reframing to traumatised patients. They would bring up the traumatic incident in their mind and after counting down from 100, the patient explored whichever part of the scene they felt comfortable with, exploring things that might previously have been missed. The self-dialogue around integrating those parts was profoundly self-healing. Schwartz offered response-behavioural reframing to people trying to overcome inappropriate behavioural responses (e.g., OCD). He showed them a variety of emotionally charged images and then randomly assigned the word "reappraise" to appear. The patient had to then think about it differently, talk to themselves about it differently and as a result their experience of the image changed dramatically. For example, a crash scene with an ambulance might be reframed with, "Maybe I'm the doctor." She also doodled in the side margins a quote she came across.

"The amygdala has a privileged position as the emotional sentinel, it has the power to hijack the brain."

Joseph Le Doux

Two blocks away, Monique could have done with being included on this information. Her amygdala was shutting down rational thought as she hurled her handset across the office. She needed a "reappraise" to flash up on her screen right now.

"Bastards! I can't believe those bastards!" she yelled to no one listening. Monique's department was running on skeleton crew and with one away at lunch and one down in the filing rooms, she was alone to yell at the state of love and men. The state at present was… terrible. Monique had internal standards, arbitrary as they might be, that let her get to sleep at night. Alone, as it turned out. These jackasses, as she called them, wanted sex at first date, and she just wasn't up for that. Probably not at two or three either. It wasn't so much a moral thing; she figured they would have her down as "easy" and not treat the relationship seriously. She also valued herself more than that. She had asked ten acquaintances, including men, and found they all agreed. But that didn't change how she felt right now.

"I've got freakin' standards!" she yelled, mainly feeling the strength of conviction and not the hollow emptiness of having men walk away from her. So how did she manage to attract "that" kind of man online and in speed dating? Was she putting out a signal? Could they hear her internal dialogue? Did they know she was looking for long term? Did that scare them? *Or perhaps I am damaged goods*, she thought, *well, maybe not.* But perhaps they could see the scars. *Still, many of my male friends like me; decent and strong people like Mark*, she thought.

As if by some quirk in the time-space continuum, Mark walked by at that exact moment. He was on his way to begin a consulting project in the section next to Karen. He had decided to take a shortcut through this area and familiarize himself with the buildings while the staffing levels were low and he was less likely to be stopped or questioned. He was very surprised to hear Monique's beautiful sing-song voice call out his name, with quite some emotion to it. Inwardly he thought, *Monique? How can she be here? Monique! How funny…*

For Monique, this event had two effects simultaneously. First, it took her out of amygdala hijack. She suddenly became very clear that her choices were good for her; anxiety and anger fled. Second, she experienced a completely new kind of hijack. She felt giddy, like a teenage schoolgirl seeing a guy she has a crush on. A rush of swirling doubt eddied in, like maybe he didn't like her the same way. Not one ounce of those feelings made their way to being voiced. Instead the two of them embraced, closely, and then they separated awkwardly. Each of them was calculating what it might mean to be working within close proximity. Their unheard internal dialogue proceeded:

Mk: *Freak, what are you so excited about?*

Mq: *Eeeek, I'm so happy Mark's here! I love Mark, I can really trust him.*

Mk: *I wonder if she wants to catch the occasional lunch, she's better company than the boys…*

Mq: *I really want his opinion on what's happening to me with dating.*

Mk: *Mustn't tell Jane this happened, she'll think the worst. Hey… what is the worst?*

Mq: *Mustn't tell Jane about this, she's so jealous of us. No car sharing then.*

Mk: *My God she looks good! Needy but good. Am I vulnerable to that?*

Mq: *I'll ask him about the "vibes" I put out, can he tell?*

They chatted for a bit before Mark excused himself and kept moving to his target department. Later, having finished out the day semi-productively, he took himself off to the car park and proudly clocked out from the rooftop for half price again. Walking back to his car, he was surprised for the second time that day. Monique was walking head down toward the pay machine, which was behind him. He whistled low and she looked up and smiled like someone had handed her a free dinner at a five-star restaurant.

As they passed each other, he said, "What do you think about carpooling? Makes sense, right?" Mark grinned, his heart pounding with the subtle suggestion. Monique looked perplexed, as if she couldn't figure out what he meant, then shook her head.

"Yeah right, see ya later, teaser," she called, skipping on and kicking up her leg. But he wasn't teasing, and once again he was confused by her. In the car on the way home, it got him thinking about how little he understood women, a thought which brought him to the fact that he had not yet confronted Jane about the state of their marriage. He resolved then and there to have his conversation with Jane. While that was going on upstairs in his brain, further down he was murmuring that Monique seemed happy to see him, genuinely interested in what he had to say, and…

*

It was rather unfortunate for Jane that she felt the way she did. She'd had a frustrating day, her boss had an argument with her about funding, she had a rejection letter from a research committee and she had spent twenty minutes brooding about it all while pretending to read an article. The only bright spot had been Lauren's request to Skype tonight after dinner. When Mark came home, she did not acknowledge him; in fact, she remained unaware of him until he put a glass of filtered water in front of her. She grunted.

WTF? he thought. *This is exactly what I'm freakin' talking about.*

What's your problem, hotshot? she thought. *What are you lookin' at?*

Silence ensued. Mark went outside for a swim, then sat brooding in the spa, wondering if Jane deserved him making them both dinner, or whether he should just get take-out. Inside she brooded, sensing intuitively that some larger game was afoot because Mark never lingered in the hot spa water. *What are you thinking about, boyfriend?* she thought. Then a moment later she went to the bedroom to slip into her bathers, then sidle out onto the porch.

"Got the stamina for a longer stay?" she said, still brooding but trying to connect.

He paused for a second, wondering whether to punish her and leave, or take the olive branch and stay. He chose to stay. To get around his aversion to long periods of time in hot water, Mark had turned the thermostat down.

He didn't exactly broach the subject of their marriage straight-up choosing instead to ask, "How are things going with you?" and "Oh I understand that work can be a challenge, and anything else?" With Jane not rising to the bait he even tried, "How do you think people like us match up?" Afterward felt like a coward, inwardly berating himself. They burned up their dinner preparation time discussing how diametrically opposed they were in so many ways. They debated whether this difference was a positive or a negative and concluded that it really depended. If they were leaning into the relationship, it was incredibly attractive and interesting, but when they were leaning out it became repulsive and pushed them apart. Right now they hung on the watershed between both.

They chose to shower off and call for take-out and shortly after that, dinner arrived, drinks were served and Lauren called in via Skype. The three of them caught up about Gyan, Jane's dad, work and the coming semester, music and movies and how Lauren was coping with life. Lauren brought them up to speed on her learnings about the ABCDE process, her research into self-talk and the way personality either affects it or is created by it. Jane laughed and went over to the coffee table to pick up her copy of *Psychology Today*. She'd been reading, "Six Ways to Stop (Mentally) Beating Yourself Up" when Mark got home. It addressed self-talk and catastrophizing: the tendency to make way too much out of events and circumstances and to be very self-critical. They said good night and ended the call, each determined to find out more.

*

The next day Gyan was feeling much improved, but didn't want to leave the house. So Lauren rented the children's movie *Inside Out* to watch. They laughed and she cried at the portrayal of emotional intelligence in people: first one dominant emotion, then three, then five fighting against one another until the emotional characters finally learned to work together. All the time the internal structure of personality was being formed by external events, memories, core-defining relationships, and a constant internal dialogue. Lauren knew it wasn't exact, or even very real, but it served as a useful metaphor. She texted Jane and Mark: "Must see *Inside Out*, go rent it!"

So they did. But not before Jane fulfilled her part of their three-way agreement by ferreting out yet another book she had bought, been asked to read for her study, and pretty much ignored. Flicking through Shad Helmstetter's book (he was rather prolific in his field, Jane noted), she found less in *The Power of Neuroplasticity* about self-talk than she recalled. It must have been another book she owned, but surveying her shelves, she couldn't find any titles that struck a chord.

Frustrated that she might have to buy a book twice, Jane marched over to the laptop and hunted down a Kindle version (she didn't like e-books much); an Audible version wasn't available. Grumpy and grumbling to herself, she wandered into the kitchen to make chai tea and out of the corner of her vision, she saw movement. Mark was lying on the deck on a towel reading a book. Opening the window, she called, "Hey, honey, you want a tea?" A moment later, he nodded. "Whatcha reading?" she asked

"One of your books, but I don't like it, it's too… I dunno." He yawned.

"Which one?" she asked, curious; he rarely read the kind of books she liked.

"This one, about self-talk," he said, holding up the missing book!

"Is that *What to Say When You're Talking to Yourself?*" she asked, shaking her head and smiling now.

"Ah ha," he said.

Jane took out two cups of chai and grabbed the book off him, trying to confirm visually what her vague memories told her should be there—the levels of internal dialogue and action sheets for working on it. Sure enough, there they were.

She carefully noted the five levels as a useful model for the group to use later:

Level 1 - Negative acceptance ("I can't"). Negative self-talk is harmful and develops doubts, fears, misgivings and hesitations. These become automatic unconscious programs that spring into action to respond!
Level 2 - Recognition and need to change ("I need to… I should"). Internal rules that work against us. There is recognition of the need for change. The issue here is that there is no solution and the default circuit leads right back to level 1. The end is guilt and shame.
Level 3 - Decision to change ("I never… I no longer"). Recognise the need for change. Make a decision to do something about it. Hear yourself in present tense. Rephrase old negative 'cannots', tell your unconscious to make the change from now on.
Level 4 - The better you ("I am"). The most effective kind of self-talk paints a new picture of yourself, the way you really want to be, handing it to your subconscious and saying, "this is the 'me' I want to create!"
Level 5 - Universal affirmation ("It is"). Self-talk that speaks of a higher plane of consciousness, transcendent purpose or spirit. Rather than targeting specific problems or goals it takes a broader perspective of life.

Later that afternoon, Mark and Jane sat down to watch *Inside Out* which was, for Jane, a marvellous insight into Lauren's world. She was rather disappointed that Mark seemed not to engage with it. He sat doodling on an art pad the whole time. What she didn't realise was that he was in flow state, well and truly integrating disparate parts of their experience: the *Psychology Today* article here, the self-talk book there, a dabble of the movie there and a peppering of REBT for good measure. By the end of the movie, he presented her with a page full of ideas and a smile on his face. By the end of his explanation, she went from being angry with him to wanting to hug him.

The essence of his design was to have a conference with yourself. He imagined a meeting room, of any kind most suitable. He imagined all the different kinds of persons inside himself: the moods, reactions and personality types. Some young and some future or aspirational selves.

As an example, he had drawn a massive surfboard-shaped table, with six positions around it. The six seats in his case were labelled Debater, Dartagnon, Artiste, Sociopath (Sherlock?), Entrepreneur (Elon Musk?) and Gandalf. To him these represented the insecure kid inside him who wanted to argue the case; the gallant fighter in him who had won Jane's heart; the artistic part of him that rarely found voice; a very calculating and unemotional character he had largely kept hidden from others, who wanted to blow the world to hell; an entrepreneur who wished to do things as large as the founder of PayPal, Tesla, Space X and Solar City; and lastly, a very kind warrior and wise magician who was out to save the world for the most dignified reasons.

Down the side of the page he had written questions like "What's the name of the character?" and he'd only come up with names for half of them; "What are they like?" which he intended to be a description of the person; "What do they want?" meaning why does that character exist inside my soul?; "Decision style" when things are going well, and when things are going badly and; "Rituals for best state", meaning what sort of things did Mark need to do for this character to emerge.

Whilst it wasn't really finished, it was a thing of beauty and gave Jane enough visual information to do an exercise for herself. She was also curious about some of the specific 'Marks', such as who is Artiste? Mark explained that was fancy for an artist. Why the sociopath, Sherlock? He told her that this character was too great for him but this could be a placeholder name. Who else was he going to choose? Dexter… Hannibal Lecter… the Joker? She suggested he simply take the very best of any and all these characters and create a completely imaginary hybrid person. It was his life after all, right? He agreed. Jane wrote everything out on her laptop: a summary of the call with Lauren yesterday, her learnings from the self-talk and Mark's exercise, which she dubbed "Who's at Your Table?" This she sent to Lauren, Gyan and Monique.

Next door, Monique read Jane's email and felt strongly that she should read and work through the material herself and also forward it to her friend, confidante, and psychologist, Karen. So she forwarded it, even though it was a weekend, in the hope of stirring a conversation. In the email she included a triple invitation, saying, "Love to do lunch, and otherwise a session! Check out this stuff on self-talk and personality—It's freakin' me out! By the way, I've told you about this group; I really think you might like hanging out with us. Ciao bella."

To her great surprise, Monique received an answer an hour later, while she was loading the movie *Inside Out* to watch with her kids as per Jane's instruction. Karen enthused about Monique's group and shared with her what Dr. Goulston had told her on the amygdala hijack (really helpful for Monique's outbursts): being aware of triggers, seeing the upsetting elements, finding where you feel it, discovering what emotion is triggered, seeing your impulsive reaction, considering the consequences, finding alternative explanations, looking for a way out, and the benefits of choosing another way out instead of your impulse. This whole process seemed to serve both as a self-awareness piece and as a process to stop self-destructive cycles.

It matched neatly with the REBT process Jane had shared with everyone (thanks to Lauren): Being aware of the activating event, wondering what your belief system is about that, thinking of the consequences of holding these irrational beliefs, disputing any irrational thoughts and beliefs (they may all be irrational), and being aware of the emotional effects. This process seemed to Monique to be suited for examining limiting beliefs, especially under stress. This seemed useful to deal with any habitual non-useful pattern of thinking.

Both processes invited a person to live a more examined life. *To some extent,* thought Monique, *journaling brings out what is inside.* Now along came self-talk, which worked the other way, changing the cognitive process by listening at first to self-talk, and then by systematically changing that self-talk from Level 1—Negative acceptance to Level 2—Recognition and need to change, through Level 3—Decision to change and Level 4—The better me to finally Level 5—Universal affirmation. This last process appealed to her the most. Self-talk was easy to access… in the car, the shower, or walking alone.

Monique wrote those five levels down because that's where she was going to start. She figured self-awareness was the key here, whether she was having a "moment," or a genuine crisis through to her self-defeating inner conversations. As the movie started, she took a Texta and some paper and wrote up a sheet for her bathroom mirror and another for the children. The diagram Mark had drawn made no sense to her at this stage, but then again, she hadn't seen the movie.

To this point she had allowed for a conscious and an unconscious self, and the self-talk seemed to be adequate with only two players. Why she might need four or six or more eluded her.

Nevertheless she drafted an Action List for herself and the group and sent it around:

Action list

- Start to listen to your self-talk.
- If you find 'hearing' hard, then listen when it is absolutely silent or you are alone, e.g. in t shower, in the bathroom, exercising, driving to work etc. If you ordinarily fill this space w noise (like music, story tapes, audio books) then turn it off.
- If you're still stuck go back to journaling, only this time allocate lines of 'code' as C for conscious or U for unconscious.
- If you're still stuck try having a conversation with yourself out loud, addressing yourself b

your first name and asking questions such as, "Well Mark, what are we going to do now' you want a little fun, change voices every other reply.

- Once you have a dialogue happening, examine what level of self-talk it is.
- Repeat a dozen times and see what your preferred level is.
- Choose to try and change that level upward.
- Go weeding. Replace:

  - "I don't have a choice" with "I have chosen to"
  - "I can't" with I choose not to
  - "I'm stuck" with "I wonder what I could do next?"
  - "It's not my fault" with "I wonder what I can learn from this?"
  - "It's too hard" with this is unfamiliar to me

Download and do the 'Who's at your Table' exercise:
http://www.neurocoachingaustralia.com/resources/neurocoaching/whos-at-your-table.pdf

CHAPTER SIXTEEN: WHERE SELF-ESTEEM COMES FROM

"Self-esteem is the reputation we acquire with ourselves."
Nathaniel Branden

Why are you laying here? thought Jane starring at her father, who was still in a coma. Comas are a rare and strange thing. He had been deeply unconscious for four months now; completely unresponsive to the environment, his condition or the visitors who infrequently came. And nobody knew when he might wake up. The first neurologist had said two to four weeks. The second neurologist had said that once they were past the second month it was indefinite. They were now talking about transferring him to Jane's home, or a full time care facility. With all her heart she didn't want that. She wanted him to wake up, get up, go home and walk out of her life.

The oxygen mask quivered and the heart-rate monitor spiked for a moment as Jane's father seemed to move. The intensive care nurse came jogging in with the beeper on her waist going off. She examined the charts, examined the monitors, and then shook her head and walked out. Jane figured he wasn't coming back soon and turned to leave. She looked out the window at the dew covering the grass and steel below. The sun was gently rising over the mountains to the east and silence waited outside. She began to move to the door when a quiet voice gently startled her.

"You're a little thinner than before," he whispered, muffled through the mask.

Jane spun to look at her father, his eyes half closed and absolutely no strength in his hands as she lifted them toward herself. To her surprise, tears came unbidden to her eyes and she felt a touch of joy at his consciousness. Then, just as soon as he was back, he was gone. Behind her, the consulting doctor was standing in the doorway and had seen the end of their exchange. He assured her this was normal, and that he was actually now conscious but passed out. He had moved up from brain-stem to whole-of-brain activity.

Jane texted friends about the incident and asked Mark to do the preparations for having the group over while she dealt with the consequences of the morning's events. A coma patient's relationship with the medical equipment was the first hurdle: could he breathe on his own? Could he eat? How was his muscle condition? Could he walk? These and several other considerations now came to the fore and his recovery became paramount. He did not wake again, so Jane took leave and drove home. She didn't relish the amount of work which now lay ahead in working out what their relationship should look like, but month after month she had faced the facts as they were.

*

"You know we can't all fit in the spa now," Mark said to Monique. He wasn't being rude necessarily; just stating the obvious. He said it to her because she'd brought Karen who, all things considered, wasn't backward in stepping up and jumping into hot water with a bunch of people she hardly knew. Mark, Jane, Monique, Lauren, Gyan (who was much better now), and Karen sat in a cosy little circle in the spa in the backyard. *It might be eight*, thought Jane, who had invited Sean, knowing Mark had invited Dave from work.

It was nearing the end of the summer holidays and they had gathered to kick off the New Year and see if any new faces would like to join the group. Sean and Dave had never responded to the invitation, it being that time of the year. Karen, a recent divorcée, was free this weekend, and her kids were with her ex. Monique's ex-husband had fought for more access to their kids and, to her astonishment, the judge had seen through his charade and told him in no uncertain terms to leave the arrangements alone or she would get punitive. Monique was elated and in her heart was still celebrating all these weeks later. She smiled at both her kids lolling around in the pool.

On the deck behind the spa a whiteboard stood balanced on a tripod, with markers and paper making the area, looking for all the world like an Amway pitch meeting. On the table next to that, Mark's artwork with the surfboard-shaped boardroom table and the "Who's at Your Table" exercise stood propped up against the sliding-glass door. Whilst the others caught Karen up on the journey so far (she had a lot of catching up to do, she discovered).

Despite Mark now working only one building over, and despite them often parking in the same car park, Mark and Monique had not run into each other again. Neither had they risked doing lunch, each fearing a different potential argument with Jane. In some way, that had eroded their trust for each other a little. For the same reason they had not carpooled and this, to Mark at least, seemed absurd and wasteful. All this rose to the surface of his mind, irritating him like dirty flotsam and foam on the seashore.

Monique saw a lull in the conversation and she leaned over conspiratorially to ask Mark about the self-talk material and his model, especially why he had created so many people. Frowning, he said… "Well, for a start I don't like unipolar or even bipolar models of personality. I feel like all of them, even MBTI, as complex as it is, results in a box. I just don't think we're like that. I reckon we have dozens of contradictory elements in our personality. Think for example about the way our right brain has little sense of time and space while our left hemisphere does. Already we have a time-bound, conscious sense of now whilst at the same time a part of us carries every previous version of ourselves like they are all present."

"Wait a minute, what?" she said, incredulous.

"Sure, Jill Bolte-Taylor, the neuroscientist on TED, had a stroke (of insight) and wrote heaps about it. She said, 'the right mind visualizes existence as a superposition of states, imagining every probable state and carrying them at the same time.' Every version of you comes along as now—which is why your time line stuff worked; you can go back there now and treat it as though it were now and it has effect today, even though you're working on the past," said Mark smugly.

"Holy smokes, I never thought about why it worked before," Monique exclaimed quietly.

"Well, so why not elect a representative sample of the population inside your unconscious? Why not also allow some from the future, you know, aspirational selves? Then we, me, can agree together on what to do!" Mark said evenly. Leaning back to rearrange his swimming trunks, he sat down and continued, "You've surely heard the American Indian proverb about how to test a decision?" Monique nodded agreeably and slid toward him an inch. It made her feel tingly and guilty at the same time, drawing close and dominating Mark's time like this; it was delicious. "Well, the thought experiment of wondering what your grandfather and your grandson might think is analogous to this 'Who's at Your Table' exercise," Mark continued, enjoying her attention too.

The others round the spa were also chatting in pairs, and each conversation held the attention of its participants. Monique checked the mood of the group carefully and decided to continue her conversation with Mark, risking both Jane's ire and the group's need for a conversation. That made her feel guilty again, but she continued anyway. Ever since he'd done the "power pose", or told them about it, Mark's confidence-boosting trick before Art's door had niggled at her. It was such a bold move, such a high chance of getting caught, but Mark said it had worked a treat. So she opened their next conversation with a reminder of his shenanigans. He laughed freely and agreed that it worked well as a state changer.

"Well, so what if your stance, this power stance of yours, actually made both Superman and Lex Luther?" Monique asked teasingly. The smile faded from his face.

"How do you mean?" Mark asked, almost offended. The look must have set Jane's protective instincts off because she leaned over and asked what they were talking about.

Monique danced on. She had found a study from psychological science that said standing in a power pose for ninety seconds increased cortisol and testosterone enough that confidence flooded in; that much was true. But the science did not give her the confidence she needed to try it herself. So she kept looking.

"Well, since the self-talk stuff we started a few weeks ago, I found a follow-up study to Amy Cuddy's one. This new one found that power posing only caused feelings of self-confidence for those who had positive self-talk. For those who have negative self-talk, it decreased their self-confidence and increased the likelihood of transgression, to behave like a heartless jerk. Plus… " she smirked and couldn't help feeling a little smug this time, "if you adopt a power pose before a boardroom, you'll feel powerful, but if you adopt it whilst being searched by police, you'll feel humiliated."

"You're kidding?" Mark said. "Send that to me, would you? I mean, that's pretty amazing."

"Happens in research more than you might think. It's usually the product of smaller numbers in the study, or because of too broad a focus," Jane said, feeling a little sorry for him.

Jane got out of the spa, followed by Mark, who was overheating. Jane offered drinks around and Mark dived into the pool. Lauren and Gyan followed, leaving Monique and Karen to talk. She started awkwardly, asking Karen to tell her if conversation slipped over into therapy, and once Karen had nodded, she started to talk about her dating life. Since the outburst a few weeks ago, and the speed dating before that, and the online dating before that, Monique had been mystified by men's treatment of her. She wondered if women "put out signals," and if men picked them up.

"You mean like an ESP thing? Or a sixth sense men have? I doubt it," Jane said from behind her.

Craning her neck to look Jane in the face, Monique said, "Well, yes and no. I don't believe that it's something supernatural, but can we naturally pick up what other people are thinking, or what they are like somehow?"

Slipping into the spa to triangulate them both, Jane said, "I don't think so, well, not what we think anyway. How we feel might come through our choices, our proximity to people, our music selection and body language… but none of that would be visible, right?" Jane looked over at Karen, inviting her to engage.

"Diana Russell did studies on women who had experienced incestuous abuse as children and found that fully two-thirds of them were subsequently raped. It certainly looks like they have a sign on their backs, right?" The other two women nodded, concerned at these statistics, "but I think that's more to do with abusers looking for an easy mark than with everyone else who might be 'normal'. Perhaps closer to your question and perhaps more alarming is the way the unconscious works to allow that. The abuser is looking for nice, attractive, kind women, and we're the ones putting that out… trying to attract nice men, right? One theory is that we neurotically endeavour to rewrite our past or undo our previous mistakes, you know, kind of self-justify… " She paused, seeing Monique's face showing signs of withdrawal and sadness, but she felt her friend needed to hear this. "What we end up doing after all that is a kind of clinging to slivers of hope to avoid the dangerous truth about ourselves and others."

"So we run away from something, only to find that we are creating the very thing we are trying to avoid?" Monique asked quietly.

Karen and Jane nodded in unison and Jane said, "We often meet our destiny on the road we take to avoid it. I read that somewhere… it works the same way with dating."

Seeing her chance to conclude the point, Karen continued, "The other half of the equation, the abusers, are unfortunately very attractive personalities. We call them the "dark triad": narcissists—you know, vain, grandiose, self-attracted… psychopathic—uncaring, immoral, and selfish… and Machiavellian—duplicitous, cynical people after personal gain."

They both looked at Monique, whose jaw was hanging slack. She couldn't believe that description… the truth of it, the exact and precise nature of it… those were all of her last dates and yes, Lord, yes they were attractive. In spite of the warm water, she shivered involuntarily. *Is that why I got hurt?* she wondered.

"They kind of go together like a magnet, don't they? I suppose the solution is to find a good man instead, and from my experience on the dating scene it would appear they're all taken! So a good woman must stay alone." Monique said, a little crestfallen.

Just then the phone rang and Jane looked for Mark to answer it, but he was nowhere to be seen, so she jumped dripping out of the spa and went inside. From outside, Lauren could see her mum nodding and gesticulating, water pooling at her feet. Eventually she came back outside to grab a towel and wipe down the timber floor in the kitchen. Lauren quizzed her about the call and Jane explained that a friend of hers who worked in a local college had become ill. She needed a stand-in expert to talk about how to build self-esteem.

*

Lauren and Gyan stayed for the following week, making themselves valuable, knowing the stress Jane was under with her father coming out of a coma. Mark stayed out of it. The three of them shuttled back and forth to the hospital, bringing home at first hopeful reports then repudiations. His condition was recalcitrant to standard treatment. Having been recumbent for so long, even with regular turning, his muscles had atrophied externally and internally by the same degree. In the background to all of this, Jane worked and came home as early as practicable to start preparing her presentation.

They watched as Jane steadily compiled every bit of background material: books, texts from university and lecture notes along with online research. For Lauren it was fascinating to watch Jane lean back on her original bachelor of psychology. She picked up a book by Nathaniel Branden from her mum's pile of study materials. It was titled *What is Self Esteem?* According to the blurb on the back, Branden had been a follower and lover of Ayn Rand the Russian philosopher and founder of objectivism. Lauren knew her as the author of *Atlas Shrugged.* On the inside leaf, a quote:

"Of all the judgments we pass in life, none is more important than the judgment we pass on ourselves."

Nathaniel Branden

Jane's desk was in the nook provided by the designers of the house, halfway between the living room and kitchen. Papers were assembled in neat piles, ordered by topic in an array that, it seemed to Lauren, marked their relationship to the subject. The material from William James lay closest to the laptop, but was turned sideways from the axis it should have been on in Lauren's figuring. Her finger tapped the tome, clicking quietly in time with Jane's footsteps.

Jane observed the scene for a moment then observed, "Founder of the self-esteem movement and a complete idiot if you ask me!"

Lauren was startled more by her mother's ferocity than her company. With her hand still on the book, she wheeled around and looked askance.

"James formulates self-esteem this way: self-esteem equals success divided by pretensions. That is, we have pretensions about ourselves, what we're like and what we're good at and these make us feel good. According to his theory, we measure those expectations against how well we do at life, our actual success. Our self-esteem goes up and down according to our performance. But it's rubbish. I might call that self-worth, a very ephemeral and rather fickle scale we ride up and down, but self-esteem is much deeper and much simpler than that."

"Thus why you have put the book sideways; it's not being included in your lecture then," Lauren surmised correctly.

"No, God, no, and his messiness goes further," Jane continued. "This trait or experience James describes can be highly task-specific or trait-specific. It can also be very global, like the halo effect. I really don't think that's helpful, especially to students."

"So what are you using instead?" Lauren asked, casting her eyes across the other books arrayed variously in the fan around her mother's computer.

"In my opinion Nathaniel Branden, God rest his soul, had it right. I'm going with his model because it's also the most robust and enduring. Wanna hear some of what I've put together?" Jane asked, looking chirpy.

Lauren looked over at Gyan, who was napping drowsily in the afternoon heat, and shook her head. "For starters, Dad isn't home yet; secondly, you're not finished; and lastly, Monique will have kittens if we do content without her. Wait for the weekend?"

Jane looked a bit hangdog and went outside for a breath of fresh air. She knew Lauren was right, of course. As Mum pondered work and the upcoming lecture, Lauren started on dinner in the kitchen. Mark arrived home and while he had a brave face, it was clear to Lauren he was either hiding something or struggling about something. After saying hi, and waking Gyan up by doing so, Mark beat a retreat to the bedroom when he spotted Jane out the back door. Lauren continued her labours and finally called dinner. Mum suggested they bring it out on the deck and enjoy the fading orange and purple sunset.

"Where's your car, honey?" Jane asked when they'd finished the entrée. Jane, already being tall, had stretched and seen over the fence to the driveway. Only two cars stood there, hers and Gyan's.

Lauren smiled. While she still didn't know what was going on, she felt good that she had guessed something was out of the ordinary. "I left it at work. I had trouble starting it and looked around for a lift. I found one, so that's cool, right? It got me thinking, I wonder if carpooling might not be a good idea," Mark said with a touch of nervousness.

His face looked odd to Lauren, as she stood to serve the main course. *Might not be a good idea sounded like it should be a good idea, but was actually the negative way of saying it,* she thought. *An unconscious slip?*

Jane was unperturbed. "Carpooling, hmmm. It's a sound idea, but which staff from your company live out here? I thought maybe Roger did, but at the Christmas party he told me they'd moved," she said. "I suppose you could look up a carpooling site, it's all the rage… go with strangers if you dare!" she giggled a little at the thought.

Mark sparked up, "Well, it doesn't matter anyway. I'm not working from the office; I'm on secondment to Defence, remember?"

"Oh, well, then you could just catch a lift with whomever you came home with tonight, right? That is, if you grabbed their number or business card," Jane said forgetfully, her mind turning to the weekend and her practice presentation as she wandered inside to bring out the platters. Inside, Lauren was quite perplexed as to why the identity of his driver had not come out just then.

"Great idea, babe, I'll do that," he called after her, happy at first for playing out the deception and then, with a twinge of guilt he felt the edge come off. He struggled over telling her that the ride was Monique, and that his car never did have a problem. It was a mockup all along. Now that he avoided the truth, he felt… erosion in his soul… a tiny chipping away of his self-confidence.

All this time Gyan, neither the student of human behaviour nor an astute judge of people's character or behaviour, observed Mark's glances over the fence. At first he thought Mark must be looking for his car, then he thought maybe Mark was seeing some strange object in the hedge or fence. But standing to confirm his prognosis, he saw nothing and could only conclude, correctly, that Mark was looking for Monique. He could not fathom why, except perhaps that she and Karen were due to come over for a weekend catchup. *No, wait,* he thought, that's tomorrow. *Maybe Mark is confused.*

"Mark," Gyan said forthrightly, "are you looking for Monique?"

"What? Shhhhh!" Mark said conspiratorially.

"I'm sorry, it's just that you kept looking over the fence. Monique will be here tomorrow; you can rest assured," Gyan concluded.

"I cannot rest assured, Gyan; what the hell are you driving at?" Mark said, then, thinking again, he continued, "No, wait, forget driving at anything. Thank you, yes, she'll be here tomorrow, and with Karen," he finished. Great! Now I'm trying to deceive the human supercomputer! Mark thought. He felt terrible, but he'd done worse and could not afford for this newfound deception to get out of hand; he'd tell Jane soon, really. Dinner arrived and regular chitchat ensued. But later than night, Lauren got chatting with Gyan, who said flatly, "I think maybe your dad is dating Monique."

It was a bombshell Lauren just wasn't ready for and besides, she argued, how on earth could he say that… and Gyan in his typical flat, analytical fashion laid out an iron-clad reasoning for his conclusion. Without realising he was "in trouble," he retreated a little by saying there was only an eighty-percent probability of his correctness, and several alternative hypothesis which included…

"Shut up, Gyan!" Lauren yelled, and stormed away.

*

On the weekend, Jane had finished her draft presentation for the following week, and expressed her gratitude to the group that she could practice on them. Standing at the kitchen end of the living room, with her audience in the leather lounges arrayed in a semicircle, she gave them a little background on the self-esteem movement. Starting in 1913 with William James, she brought them through to her favourite model by Nathaniel Branden.

His model, she admitted, was a good deal more complicated than her summary. He worked his way from first principles all the way up to the conclusion of good or bad self-esteem. But in her opinion, that was all too much for college-aged students. In essence, when it comes to truth and the things life throws at us, we either face it or flee from it. Those who consistently face life, good or bad, develop great self-esteem. Those who flee and avoid life consistently erode self-esteem and end up with a trashed sense of self. That is, she explained, those who face the truth end up believing they are fit for life and any challenge, whether they win or lose… or they don't. Those who don't, end up feeling like they are just not capable of handling life, like they're not fit for it.

She had prepared the following table for the students:

	Face up	Flee
What do you do?	Exhibit and choose honesty, courage, willingness to deal with your stuff, step up, confront, take responsibility, accept the truth and be vulnerable	Exhibit and choose to hide, avoid, pretend, play games, procrastinate, lie, evade, make up fantasies, stick your head in the sand, blame, obfuscate and excuse
What do you take away?	Confidence, peace & growth	Shame, guilt & anxiety
What do you teach yourself?	You have what it takes to deal with life	You do not have what it takes to deal with life
What do you believe?	You are enough	You are not enough
What's your self-esteem like?	Good/high/strong	Broken/low/poor

By the end, the gang had plenty of questions, arising mainly from self-application of the ideas. Mark shared the story of Thom Porro, as told by Susan Scott. Thom was a mountain climber and while out with his friends Don and JJ, he fell down a crevasse. Lying in hospital, Thom exclaimed, "That crevasse came out of nowhere!" His friend Don, who had seen it all said, "You look like hell, buddy. I'm awful glad you're alive. But that crevasse didn't come out of nowhere. It was risky enough at ten in the morning… you got there four hours later under the melting sun. What were you pretending not to know?" That one question rested on the group for a long time. What were they pretending not to know? What were they ignoring on purpose? In what ways were they eroding their self-esteem?

"You know what, though," Monique said hesitantly, "I think it isn't just an external 'face the world truth' thing here; that story is as much about Thom's internal truth. Like when you were confronting your need for people to like you, Mark, you remember, with Art and the review and Dave's advice?"

He scratched his chin, struggling to see a connection but knew if he played that card it would just look defensive. So he simply said, "Go on," and waited.

She paused, thinking of the best way to put it. "Well, I might be off-track, but the need for external approval and the failure to take negative feedback both point to eroding self-esteem, don't you think? And before you get defensive, I'm not throwing stones… it took me years to face the brutal reality of Mathew's treatment of me, let alone tell him to leave!"

Mark considered her point for a moment before he said, "You know, the funny thing is the more I needed people to praise me and to see me as a good guy, the less they did. The thing about being a people pleaser is that people are actually never pleased anyway, so the whole thing is a fantasy—totally on the negative self-esteem side."

After some other discussion, Karen, who had been quiet thus far, decided to weigh in. She took umbrage with the casual discarding of William James' model. It at least spoke to the way one's self-esteem is affected by social status, failure, and the opinions of others. Still, she admitted, it didn't explain everything.

There was at least one large hole in what Jane had put up as a model and Karen asked if she could share it.

She posited, "Say for argument's sake there are sixty percent of us who have broken self-esteem, at least that number, right, and accept for a moment that there are say thirty percent of us who have great self-esteem… is it possible that some number of us, say ten percent, have too much self-esteem? Is there not a category into which narcissists, psychopaths, Machiavellians, the arrogant, the proud and the self-deceived fit?"

Jane was forced to admit that she was right, that those characters didn't really have what we would call normal and good esteem for themselves. They were… overinflated.

Jane quickly drafted some pointers for this third category. Their instinct would be to fight, dominate, and be right. Their inflated sense of self would produce arrogance, over-confidence, superiority, ego threat, defensiveness, aggressiveness and denial of any fault. As a result, the goals they set would be unrealistic and irresponsible. The kind of strategies a person like this deployed was obvious to all sitting there: fighting reality, reactivity, anger, blame, obfuscation, defensiveness, denial, and ignoring feedback.

"Gee," Mark said, "That might also be me! A bit of soul work to be done here, I think!"

Jane was so grateful for the team and had been amending her notes as they went. She agreed to email everyone a copy of her presentation when it was ready and a summary of their proposed actions.

Action list

- What specifically are you avoiding or running away from right now?
- What are you pretending not to know?
- What actions are you committing to as a way of facing up to life?
- Write six different endings to the sentences:

1. To me, self-responsibility means...
2. If I bring more awareness to my life today...
3. If I take more responsibility for my choices and actions today...
4. If pay more attention to how I deal with people today...
5. If I am self-accepting even when I make mistakes...
6. If I am self-accepting even when I feel confused and overwhelmed...

- If any of what I wrote this week in my journal is true, it might be helpful if I...

CHAPTER SEVENTEEN: DEEPENING RELATIONSHIPS

"We don't develop courage by being happy every day. We develop it by surviving difficult times and challenging adversity together."
Barbara de Angelis

Mark could hear Jane at the end of the timber-floored corridor talking to someone. He caught snippets of dialogue like, "… no, no, they were really happy," and, "it was fine, it was fun really," and "lots of questions… huh?… oh, right, well mainly about how long it takes." He was baffled. Firstly, he couldn't guess who it was on the other end of that line and secondly, he hadn't a clue what it was about. So he decided to stop eavesdropping and get on with trimming the hedges beside the house. It was a job he loved and hated. It gave him time alone to think about nothing but it was arduous, especially in the fading but still strong summer sun. With the advance of the New Year came hints that autumn was on its way. Cooler mornings, cooler water temperatures in the pool, and dew fall.

Jane got off the phone and wandered around the house looking for Mark, eventually finding him in the shed beside the pool. He was working on the chemical balance in the water. Hearing her approaching, he called out. "There's a lot to keeping a pool, more than I bargained for… more than chlorine and salt!" Leaning out of the shed, he held up a report and waved it at her, "pH, free chlorine, phosphate, boron, algae… the list goes on!" he said.

"And here you are managing all that." She glanced at the collection of eight or nine white bottles behind him on the bench. "Bet you didn't know you had to be a chemistry major to own a pool!" she said lightheartedly. "Cooking's the same though, which is why I came out. What chemistry are you hungry for tonight?"

"What are my options?" he said, brushing his hands rather ineffectively on his trousers and smearing a white stain along one side.

"Chicken, beef, or vegetable stir-fry," she said. They agreed on vegetables and as she turned to go inside he called out, "Who was that on the phone? That call just now?" He'd decided the pool could wait and followed her inside. She said it was Karen. She wanted to know how the presentation went and if Jane's friend was better yet. *Of course!* thought Mark, *why didn't I think of that?*

"Karen also told me she's super keen to continue with us this year. She's got so much out of hanging out with us, and feels she and I can really work together. It's like, it's like… a community of practice or something," Jane said enthusiastically.

"I agree," Mark said. "This group has been transformative, and it's quite unusual. But if a bunch of uni students and white-collar workers can do this, why not a whole lot more people?"

"You don't mean letting others join us? I reckon six to ten would be the maximum," Jane said, worried.

"No, no, that's not what I'm saying. I'm saying we could put all this in a document, we could start a Facebook group or a website—connect it to all the research we found, the podcasts, the recipes, the videos and TED Talks, and walk people through the journey we've been on. We could share the exercises we've done, sharpen them up a bit first maybe, and guide people into how to do groups like this… that's all," Mark said. Jane agreed that was a good idea.

*

It seemed to Mark that things were going well again between Jane and himself. Had they changed the basic chemistry of their relationship? The changes were to prove superficial because the following day Jane was to experience a big reveal on who Mark was carpooling with. In reality she should have, by rights, seen it weeks ago. Circumstance had contrived for her to be in the backyard, or coming home from the shops or work just moments after Mark had been "dropped off" and there was never a vehicle pulling away. In hindsight, Jane reprimanded herself over choosing not to see what was right there in front of her.

This day, Jane stood in the driveway absentmindedly. She was trying to figure out where she'd put her jacket and was halfway between the house and her car, stuck in a moment of indecision. Monique's car pulled into the driveway next door and Mark hopped out. The pieces just didn't go together for a moment, as Jane became twice confused. Mark, jacket, Monique, front door, car, work, Mark? Carpooling? *Carpooling*! CARPOOLING? Jane was so confused. She felt happy to have figured out the mystery, angry that Mark was… well, just angry, sad that he hadn't told her, betrayed that the two of them conspired like that, jealous at Monique, and sick, just sick. She ran inside.

At first Mark went to run after her, but his feet wouldn't move. Monique brushed her hand on the inside of his elbow and said, "You don't have anything to apologize for, Mark; it's carpooling—it's not like we've done anything wrong."

Monique's hand felt strange on his skin, in a "that's really nice, no stop it!" kind of way. He agreed with the factual side of her statement, but they had done wrong. They'd hidden the whole thing from Jane; they'd been deceptive. Sure, at first it was her fault, he reasoned at the time, because of her unreasonable overreactions. But that was no excuse for failing to behave like a man. He'd been hiding and lying.

So here it was, his whole marriage, his relationship with Jane, all of it hanging on a thread. He suddenly became super aware of his world: the bitumen road to his left, the robinia trees in rich green foliage along the driveway, Monique standing behind him in her sheer summer dress, the fence between their properties so solid-looking but unable to hold the two of them apart, the concrete under his feet, the white sports car he loved, the pool, the house, the wife, Jane… solid and fragile. In his kaleidoscope mind he also saw Jane's dad in recovery, Lauren starting her new degree, Gyan in all probability becoming his son-in-law, Monique, her children, Art, the promotion he was headed for… promising and flawed. This was it, this was the start of the fight. "But do I fight for her, or do I fight with her?" Mark wondered out loud.

"What?" Monique queried from behind him.

"Never mind," he whispered. Time stretched.

Jane wouldn't speak to Mark at first. In usual fashion, she was overreacting and felt the dangerous swell of emotions underneath her rational mind. It was like a dreadful undertow. Instead of fight, he produced flight. Mark left her alone, left her house, left her pool, left her Skype appointment with Lauren, left her wrath, and got in his car. He punched the go button. The engine barked to life, lean and mean and ready to go somewhere. The leather beneath his hands on the steering wheel felt solid and beautiful. Some craftsman had taken nine months to design that. Nursing the low front spoiler backward over the pavement he spun the wheel and floored it. This car was ferocious and so was his mood. As the time ticked away, he began to think more clearly.

It didn't really matter about the carpooling; that was just an inciting incident, and really, he'd been begging for a fight. He thought more clearly about the desire he felt toward Monique. It was like infatuation, or fantasy, and it had been waning as Jane had warmed to him again. His heart ultimately yearned for Jane, but nature abhors a vacuum. In any case, it wasn't her fault; he had never given her the remainder of his list of complaints. The longer he drove the clearer and calmer he became. He would not defend himself; he would not attack. He would drive home and be present to Jane. He would sit and listen—he would ask for nothing—and he would see what happened.

Eventually he pulled into the driveway. Mark approached the quiet, dark house. The car ticked and clicked behind him as it began to cool down. Jane had gone to bed. He made himself at home on the couch and began to get ready for the night when Jane crept into the room and whispered, "That's very sweet, Mark, but don't be ridiculous; come to bed. It was carpooling, not drug running."

He was surprised. Really surprised. Somehow he had built up her reaction in his mind as almost nuclear. Her voice was warm, understanding and kind, but provided no hint of more. Just simple acceptance.

*

In the morning, he did as planned, and waited for her to open the subject, which she did quite promptly.

"Mark, I just don't get it; I can't understand why… I can't… why did you hide this from me? I mean, what were you thinking?" Her brow was furrowed slightly, her eyebrows raised in a question. He shrugged his shoulders, waiting.

When he didn't defend himself, she continued. "The carpooling itself is, well… hiding it either says you're ashamed or you think I don't approve… " She waited a moment. He nodded his head once, not agreeing with either statement but suggesting, "go on."

"Well, you must know I don't approve, not because of the car, but because of Monique… " Mark almost interrupted with "or any other woman?" but thought better of it. He figured Jane would be all right with their other neighbour, Myrtle, who was sixty-five and cranky. He waited again, nodding slightly, looking at her.

"I mean Monique is… Monique is… well, she's dangerous. She's hurt, she's needy, and she wants company, male company. Mark, I'm afraid she wants you! That's why I took her out dating that night," she continued, slightly exasperated.

Mark ventured, "I was wondering about that," then stopped his interruption and looked at her in a way that said "and?"

"Mark, you just can't keep putting yourself in harm's way, darling; don't be so naïve. You live near her, you're in a self-coaching group with her, you end up in the spa together, you work right near her, you're probably having lunch together, and now you're carpooling with her."

Mark took a deep breath, went to speak, saw her face, and held his breath. She had more to say, she always had more to say, and most of it berating or belittling. So far she'd avoided that, mostly, apart from calling him naïve, but still… he was going to say "you're starting to sound paranoid," but gave her silent attentiveness instead. This hurt.

"A woman's heart slowly attaches, grabs bit by bit like Velcro. Now before you defend yourself," she said, holding up her hand in a stop signal, "I trust you, I do, in spite of your shenanigans at the beach, Mark, I trust you… but this is not about you. Well, it is, because you hid the carpooling from me, but in the end I think we're strong. It's what we do about her," she said, stabbing her finger at the house next door.

A long silence ensued and Mark tried to weigh whether it was time to speak or not. It seemed that it was, so he began slowly. "Jane, you know I love you, and… no, don't interrupt me, please… and I've been every bit the coward recently. I should have had more backbone; I knew it was wrong not to tell you and I chose that wrong. It has eaten at my soul ever since. Maybe I have been naïve and maybe Monique is a danger, but I don't really think any of this is actually about her. You're wrong about that and you're wrong about us being strong… no, wait, let me finish… Jane, none of this would have come up if you and I had things sorted out."

Jane couldn't wait anymore. *What is he thinking? This is totally about Monique; she is a seductress, she is coming on strong and Mark has to see that.* "Honey!" she began, "don't move the goal posts on me here, you've gotta see… " she raised her voice.

"I don't, Jane, because I think you're obfuscating, and I think we're both projecting our issues outside and away from ourselves. Jane, we're in trouble," Mark said desperately.

"Trouble?" Jane asked, a little hysterically, "trouble? I have no trouble, Mark, I'm perfectly happy. I have a great husband, a great daughter, a great house, a great life; what are you talking about?"

Mark gulped. He looked intently at the grain in the wood-table surface. *Is this the time? Is this the place? Should I raise the state of our marriage now? It could seem like I'm avoiding the topic, or blaming her for my actions, but that isn't it.* She became uncomfortable at his long silence and nearly went to apologize, then he began. "I think when we were married, our long list of opposite natures worked as attraction not repulsion. Our perspectives were so different and that was fascinating. But we have no common interests, except the recent cooking school. Somewhere along the line, my differences started irritating you, and you began correcting them until at last you had to correct every single one; every mistake, every choice you disapproved of, snipping and snitching and whining… " He caught a glimpse of her face, struggling and her mouth open to speak. "No, let me finish, please, because, Jane, this might be the end of it." He took a deep breath and Jane's face became very serious. *The end,* she thought, *the end of what?* She leaned back, pushing away from the table as he had, creating space between them.

"Jane, I know you think you're being helpful and kind, but most of the time it feels like your commentary just grates at my heart." He paused for a drink of water. He'd never been this honest before, and the stakes were getting high. "You are happy, yes, that's true because by some miracle of love I, and life, happen to give you most of what you're looking for. And thanks for the trust, by the way; I hope it's not misplaced. But mine… well, most of what I need just isn't coming my way. You've got safety and security, financial stability, family commitment, conversations and, until recently, honesty from me. You're happy. But Jane I need sex and physical affection, affirmation and admiration… heck, I get more affirmation from the guy in the car park at work. You know I want you to look your best, take care of yourself, and that's just not a priority for you—I get that. But I also need companionship and common interests."

As he considered his list, it was hard to take it all in. They had sex from time to time; he wasn't that insistent. True, they never hugged or kissed at the door, but they weren't into public displays of affection either. She admired him heaps, and boasted about him to her workmates constantly. She was very grateful for him. She couldn't get an internal reference for what affirmation might look like, and her employees had said she never praised them either. They shared the house, a child, trips, and a bed… of course they were companions and had common interests… well, he had her there. All the while he was watching her reactions, all played out on her face.

"Jane," he prompted, trying to interrupt her reverie. "Jane." Her eyes finally focused on the room, and on him. "Jane, you probably can't comprehend what life is like for me in this home but it's a gentle kind of torture. Even if I couldn't meet your needs, you could go outside, you can work and earn and be secure. My needs might be met outside… but you can see the havoc that creates… if Monique is a companion, if she admires and affirms me… if she hugs and appreciates me… it's so bloody dangerous, like you said. I need you to lean in, to come back from wherever you've been the last seven years. I'm not blaming you, really I'm not. My choices have been my choices, and very needy ones at that. My sources of dependency largely need to be inside me. I don't know what to say anymore."

Jane looked long and hard at him, not daring to speak for fear of hurting him. He had been bold, and honest, and truthful, and vulnerable, and manly, and she loved him, desperately loved him for it. She forgave him, truly and deeply from inside, but if she said that it would just seem like condescension. So she thanked him deeply for his integrity, and admitted that it was a lot to take in, and she also had nothing more to say. They were at an impasse, but at least an honest and vulnerable, on purpose crossroads.

*

Mark pulled into the car park near work. Yesterday he had texted Monique the suggestion that they go separately for now. Perhaps a more legitimate carpooling option will present itself, he thought. How were they to be friends? How were they to carry on with the group? What would he do about today's lunch appointment with Monique and Karen and the other members of his consulting team? He pondered all this as he walked to the section they were still based in.

Only a few more weeks and he could clock into another job. Back at the company office, they were putting in Request for Tenders (RFTs) for numerous government departments' work. Maybe then the relationship with Monique could return to its platonic state. In recent times it had become almost Shakespearean. He preferred intimacy, trust, and affection over intrigue, triangulation, and the intoxicating mixture of sexual attention and mistrust.

Lunchtime came around quickly and Mark headed for the cafeteria with a sense of dread. What did Monique think of him, of Jane? How would their self-coaching group handle this? As he entered the area, his eyes scanned the room for familiar faces. He was scanning for Monique when his eyes fell on Karen. She waved and sat down again as he moved toward her table. At almost the same time Monique made her way to the same table after they had sorted out lunch.

"Hey Monique," Mark ventured.

"Hey, Mark, nice to see you," she replied, looking down at the table. To divert the obvious awkwardness Mark asked Karen about her progress with the self-esteem material they'd gone over at his house and they laughed about his comments on there being too many people for the spa. The tension in Monique slowly uncoiled, and the three of them ate lunch and chatted about work, which was starting to become busy as people came back from summer holidays. Mark was about to ask Karen about changing gears in relationships and balancing work with friendship when Karen's pager went off. Mark stared with disbelief at the object she held in her hand. It was like seeing an old fax machine or something.

"Sorry. Crisis. They never use this system unless there's an emergency. Carry on," Karen said wistfully, and left. Mark's consulting buddies were a no-show thus far.

"Sorry about before, I didn't know how to start, this is… " Mark began.

"Awkward," Monique finished.

Mark was about to defend himself by attacking Jane's behaviour. But he realised she wasn't really at fault and besides, it was his decision to hide their behaviour from Jane.

"Mark, look," Monique started. "They were wrong in W*hen Harry Met Sally.* Men and women can be friends without having sex; we've proved that."

Yeah, but how close were we coming? How much risk we were taking? Mark thought.

She continued, "We're friends, right? There are factors that make it dangerous, I get that. When people are alone together for a long time in the office environment, when they go out together for meals, pouring out their hearts to each other, I get that too. But you know what? I've been leaning on you, of course I have, and most of the innuendo about us is my fault… Being single is hard, Mark… "

"What's being single got to do with it? How does that make you more dangerous? If I hung around with someone else's wife a lot, it would be the same, wouldn't it?" Mark asked, genuinely confused. He frowned.

"Mark, don't be daft! We spend a lot of time alone together and we have to guard our hearts, be careful. I like your company, I need someone to talk to, but that pressure would have come off if I'd found more friends. A boyfriend. He could have joined us and balanced things out." Monique's brow furrowed this time to match Mark's. *Men can be so stupid sometimes. Can't he see it was my fault?* She felt horrible about it. Monique moved the remaining food around on her plate and Mark sat thoughtfully for a moment. She looked up to catch his eyes. There was at least compassion there if not understanding.

Lunch break was over. As they walked away, Monique began to consider her own needs and where she was feeding them from. Though no one could hear what she said, Monique found comfort in the self-knowledge that flowed from lunch with Mark. *I'm lonely. I need a boyfriend. I'm under pressure. I need support systems. I've been quite unstable: afraid, angry, edgy, and probably depressed. I'm getting better after time with Karen but… I need to do better, get better, and I just don't think I can do that without Mark and Jane. I think I'm going to have to talk to Jane,* she thought. *I value that relationship a lot, and I'm not about to blow it up over carpooling.*

Resolving to do that, she remembered a proverb she once heard:

"If you want to go fast, go alone. If you want to go far, go together."
African Proverb

Karen couldn't remember when she'd subscribed to the *Journal of Neuropsychotherapy*. Nor could she remember what that word even meant. The current issue had been emailed to her and whilst the cover article was attractive, she knew the material inside the journal would be… dense. Heavy going even. She sat staring at the topic, depicted by a Latino or mixed-race woman lying on a coach talking to her therapist. The words, "The neuroscience of talking therapies" certainly caught her attention, and then suddenly she remembered.

She subscribed to a podcast called, *Shrink Rap Radio* by Dr. Dave. It was one of her favourites and Dave seemed to get access to the very best thinkers in psychology. In any case, some years ago she had heard Dave speaking about neuroscience and therapy in a very down-to-earth way. It really encouraged her to subscribe. Many episodes gave her a treasure for her work. Karen's mind wandered to recent topics the podcast covered like relationships, communication, and the effects of aging. Internally she started debating the merits of reading the journal or finishing up for the day. It had been a big week, with crisis after crisis. She decided to take her work laptop home for the weekend and read the journal there.

Karen pulled into her driveway, taking in the vista: the large elm trees lining the nature strip, drooping with green foliage and providing shade for the cicadas, who were making a din with their rattlesnake-white noise-jet fighter sounds. She opened the front door to a dark house and shivered. Karen still hadn't got used to being alone and the weekends her children were with her ex were especially difficult. It was certainly not an acrimonious divorce; in fact quite the opposite; they were still friends and he was very kind. It's just that he'd been unfaithful. Numerous times. She couldn't tolerate that.

Now that he was gone she'd fastened two white boards to the walls; one in the corridor for the kids and her to leave instructions to one another and one in the living room, where she wrote notes for herself. To an observer those notes might not have meant very much, but for Karen they acted as an anchor, a visual reminder of conversations, a book and a podcast to be researched.

In the top left-hand corner of the living room whiteboard were some notes about sympathy and empathy. The definitions snagged her after a counselling seminar. One note read, "Sympathy: feelings of pity and sorrow for someone, sharing a common feeling." Under sympathy Karen had written, "nothing to do with professional life and opinion, maybe useful in friendship." Beside it was, "Empathy: really walking in someone's shoes, understanding their perspective." Under empathy she had written, "dangerous to say you get how they feel 'cause nobody ever can."

In the top right-hand corner of the board were some notes about life experience. She had read a book by Oliver Sacks on neurology, which had led her to an article about something called qualia. Her notes read: "Qualia are the raw 'feels' of conscious experience: the coldness of cold, the yellowness of yellow and the sticky feeling of honey." Beneath that she had written, "qualia are absolutely personal, idiosyncratic and unique" and from here a red line lead across to empathy and a question, "who can understand your understanding, really?"

Karen had formed a useful metaphor to use with clients, and she said it to herself just now: *if your friend were sinking in quicksand, sympathy is joining them there; empathy is throwing them a rope, and apathy is standing by to watch them drown.*

In the centre, below the other writing, she had jotted some notes a friend of hers from the Queanbeyan Racing Club had told her about horse training. The word "pacing" was underlined. Underneath, it said: "two horses, who's leading? Moving up to, alongside, matching stride. Slowing, they slow and are in sync." Karen read that for the hundredth time and wondered if it was possible to really get in sync with someone, to walk with them, listen to them, be present, and have them feel like you "feel" them, and that you "get" them?

She placed her unopened laptop down on the coffee table, wandered into the kitchen, and hit the playback button on her answering machine. When were they going to integrate this into her Apple Watch? The messages were from her mother, a colleague from work about drinks on Friday, *Oops, totally forgot that* she said to herself, and Monique reminding her about the weekend. Gyan and Lauren couldn't come down, but would Skype instead. Karen smiled for once today, a real smile, not a professional smile. She poured herself a pear cider, grabbed some cashew nuts, and wandered back into the living room. Settling down into the leather wingback chair facing the whiteboard, she stared at it some more.

She recalled a time when, in the middle, she had once written a range of therapeutic practices: being present, active listening, understanding, compassion… and methods of therapy further down: psychotherapy, CBT, REBT, and this new field of cognitive neuropsychotherapy. But she'd rubbed all that out. It didn't fit somehow.

Sitting in her chair, she fancied that Sherlock Holmes could probably work all this out in his head. The modern Sherlock, of BBC fame, preferred to make elaborate diagrams on the wall of newspaper clippings, map segments, and red twine linking ideas. Unlike him, she needed more blank space outside her head. Karen couldn't bring it all together in there; she was more spatial. The voice of her ex echoed in her head. It was him that ultimately stopped her writing anymore, endless versions of ideas being replaced in a panoply of psychology. He'd said, "You're just writing down fancy words for good relationship, Karen; for God's sake, stop trying to make it all so academic."

She sighed and opened her laptop. Is that what she was doing? She sipped her cider as the computer whirred into life. Was it just her or did all laptops and computers slow down? Mildly at first and then dramatically after a year, finally becoming digitally retarded, like her ideas. What was she searching for anyway? She clicked on the journal and started reading a work by Dr. Pieter Rossouw. Then she stopped. How many times had she done this?

A website, a book, a journal, a podcast… wrote down all the good ideas on that board in front of her, only to erase them later. *What is going up on this board? she thought. Why should I care, why? I just do, I just am, and that's all right. I'm not trying to write a book or build a website. I just want to improve myself.*

She went back to the neuropsychotherapy article and focused on it. Karen could speed read 450 words a minute with eighty-percent accuracy, but she preferred to walk leisurely through a good book. She was taking the second strategy this time, relishing and enjoying the read; hovering, pondering, and listening.

Her note pad read:

FINDING 1
Neuroscience says talking therapies are the preferred strategy to facilitate lasting brain change. Change is facilitated through the unique qualities of talking strategies.
* A talking therapy is a structured conversation with someone who is trained to help a person deal with their feelings, explore their thoughts, beliefs, behaviour and mood. *
FINDING 2
The person listening is more important than how much of a specialist they are, the knowledge base they draw from or any bag of 'tricks' they might have.
* Listen, a special kind of listen. It has to be active, present listening so the person knows you understand what they've said, that it matters. *
FINDING 3
We are most effective when we have a high-functioning alliance with someone. That takes three things: rapport, trust and understanding.
* Rapport: get a quick connection, calibrate where they are at. *
* Trust: be open, straightforward, self-assured. *
* Understanding: pay attention, hold eye contact and being clear on the exact nature of the conversation. *
FINDING 4
We are most effective when we engage the mirror neuron system: the ability to express a warm and empathic style and to match pacing.
* This is a two way street. It is two people experiencing 'I understand!' which is empathy and 'I am understood!' which is pacing. *
FINDING 5
Excellent outcomes are made through great facilitation – establishing framing, safety and control for the person you are talking to.
* Frame the conversation properly, make sure they feel physically, environmentally and psychologically safe. Ensure they feel like they're in control and can direct the conversation. *

There was a lot more in the article of course, about neuroplasticity, length of treatment, ideal conditions, cortical blood flow, and neural pathways, but Karen was content with what she'd captured. She stared at the notes for a while, glancing up at the whiteboard, then put the computer down on the table, and went to make herself dinner. As the chicken and vegetables cooked in the wok and the brown rice with quinoa bubbled away beside it, she was beginning to see something.

Rossouw, the article's author, was writing in a therapeutic environment, a psychologist and their client. But his principles were fundamental to human relationships too, *Well, with a bit of a change in language*, she thought. Here were five findings about best practice for talking therapies which led to the greatest neural change, and after six weeks of therapy created lasting neural change. That was awesome. But the practices could really be used by anyone. With dinner in hand she trundled back into the living room, put some of her favourite music on ,and pondered in her "Sherlock" chair. *This puzzle is just about finished, she thought. This will be the last time I write something up there.*

She took the notes and drafted them up on the board, simplifying as she went, and linking up to the three notes already there: sympathy/empathy (linked to finding 4), qualia (linked to findings 2 and 3) and pacing (linked to finding 4). Stepping back, she smiled. Now this was going to be useful.

Where to test it? she wondered. She could hardly road test on Monique. Perhaps a married couple? They rarely came in to work together. Send an email out to people asking for volunteers? She had a list of past clients… that might work. She took her plate back to the kitchen and stared at the timber floors as the dishwasher started. Then she thought about the group meeting this weekend and whether they'd be willing to have a go. So she called Jane on her mobile and after chatting for a while, asked about how new ideas came into the group. Jane was curious and asked her why. Karen shared her tentative "relationship neuroscience" ideas. Jane loved it and asked her to make some notes for them.

Karen did that. She sent an email to the group along with some actionable items:

Action items

Pick a person or a key relationship that you would like to work on. Don't pick the hardest one you can think of because you need to practice some skills. When having a conversation with them next time consider:

- **Framing:** be clear on what the conversation is about. What would you both like to get ou E.g. If they're crying about school… Do they want sympathy, a listening ear or solutions'
- **Safety:** are they comfortable physically (room, seating) and emotionally (confidentiality, privacy) and environmental (light, temperature).
- **Calibrate:** how are they sitting? How are they breathing? What words are they using? W their emotional state? Watch now for changes as you go along.
- **Rapport:** establish a real connection as quickly as possible. There should be ease and

laughter, openness of heart and a syncing of the two lives.

- **Pacing:** what speed are they running verbally, what temperature are they running emotic Get up to speed, match and then see who's in charge of the flow.
- **Trust:** be honest, be open and true to your opinion even when it might possibly offend th say what you see, that's what good friends do. Do it gently, kindly, respectfully.
- **Understanding:** pay very careful attention to the conversation, get a bearing on the subje the focus, the direction of the conversation and go with it.
- **Empathy:** Try to get into their shoes, to see it from their perspective, understand the stor but realise qualia (experience) is unique to them. You cannot know how it feels for them
- **Active listening:** repeat key phrases back to them for clarification, in summary, making s you understand where they are at.
- **Being present:** be exactly where the balls of your feet are. Don't keep looking over their shoulder for someone else, or at your watch. Look them in the eyes.
- **WAIT:** ask yourself, 'Why Am I Talking?' Try to listen twice as much as you normally do when you speak try to make at least half of it questions and curiosity.
- **Actions:** try to resolve your encounter by asking what are we up to, have we come to an conclusions? Have we made any progress? Do we have any actions to take?

CHAPTER EIGHTEEN: WHAT EVERY BODY IS SAYING

"75% of all communication is non-verbal"
Susanne Jones

Jane had been following the study of her athletes and had concluded that belief and self-talk certainly did alter performance. Her test case was a cyclist whose performance dropped off at the same time as his marriage turned into trouble. It made her think of her own. Was her marital happiness, or lack of it, affecting her performance at work? Almost certainly.

Aside from biomechanics, the actual hard-coded body movements involved in the athletic actions, her reading and research had widened. She had started to examine what other indicators, aside from performance, might show early signs of performance degradation. Jane had read material on Olympic teams' mental preparations, including visualization, meditation, and mindfulness, self-talk, and positive thinking, goal setting and flow state. That list alone surprised her because they'd been over all this ground in their self-coaching.

At present she felt like she'd wandered off into the sticks. She read a study about the way people judged others by the way they walked, but ended up concluding that actual walking style said little about personality, mood or performance. That led her to non-verbal communication. Were there any cues in the way an athlete trained, spoke, interacted, wrote, or non-verbally communicated that she could use? On the wall in front of her she had posted an A4 tree diagram with four branches:

- Language: speech, writing;
- Non-language: vocality, pitch, tone, timbre, volume;
- Physical: proxemics, kinesics, stance, gait (also described as non-verbal)
- Situation: belongings, clothing, makeup, music, room (or context signals

Jane knew full well that hunching over like a turtle made it impossible to feel awesome, and standing tall released chemicals that assisted mood. But the question here was a) what sort of mood was ideal for performance, and b) what stances to adopt for that mood. She had interviewed the karate team and learned that "a little bit of anger" fused with "centered, balanced mindfulness" was needed to win. Engendering that aggression and ignoring the victories won thus far in round eight was a real trick because it was natural to feel a bit chuffed, or even cocky about winning seven rounds.

Staring at the wall with some sense of despondency at all her wasted effort thus far, but still maintaining some hope of finding treasure along the way, she packed up her things and headed for home.

It was Mark's turn to prepare the evening meal, so after cleaning up the yard late Friday afternoon, Jane excused herself, went inside to shower, change and head across to the hospital. The doctors had said her father was ready to leave. He hadn't exactly made progress as much as his symptoms had stabilised and he had remained coherent and conscious. Jane didn't care; he was up and soon he would be out.

She entered his private room. *How did he afford that*, she wondered, and looked around for him. He was such a strange mix of personality. He dressed like an earl, even on the weekends, yet his bedside table was strewn with debris. There was a wallet, lolly wrappers, a half-read book, an iPad, receipts from who knows where, an ear-marked magazine, coffee-stained paper, and a half empty cup of tea. Great wardrobe… poor housekeeping. It must have driven her mother crazy. Jane heard a shuffling noise behind her and came around slowly.

"You look like crap, Dad," she said without thinking.

"Why, thank you, and good morning yourself," he quipped in return.

"When do they let you out?" she asked, straight to the point. "The doctor should be round soon. When do they let you out?" he retorted, crossing his arms.

"Oh, you're in fine form; ready to come home, I see. I mean, go home." Jane breathed in sharply, hoping he would not take advantage of her mistake, and covered her mouth unselfconsciously.

"Why, thank you again." His eyebrows raising. "Yes, I would love to come to your home. My, how you've changed; it must be pity coming through," he said, smiling innocently.

"Dad, you can't come home, aren't you due somewhere?" she asked.

"Well, now that you come to it, I'm not. Being in the state I was, unable to correspond with my landlord to let them know of my plans or condition, my previous commodious accommodation was leased when I failed to return. So if I could stay a day or two, I shall get that sorted out," he asked, appearing to be at once both vulnerable and needy. Instead, to her eyes, he was reptilian: plotting, planning, and conniving.

Jane puzzled for a moment, full of turmoil and stress. She frowned, her brows furrowing. Looking to see if she needed a little push, he added, "It's not as though your neighbor pushes your father into a coma every day. Lend me a hand?"

Jane found herself in the unusual position of feeling for the unfairly accused party; not for him, but for Monique, and for herself, being used for his advantage. It was a tactical misstep on his part.

"Fine, Dad, a few days—that means house hunting on the weekend, packing Monday, on the train Tuesday, you understand?" she said with strength and more than a little determination.

"Understood. What's for dinner?" he jostled, getting his things together.

*

Lauren arrived back at her digs after dinner with Gyan. She looked at the clock, *Boy, it really is late,* she thought. Late in the semester and early in a new course, they tended to bring in experts to galvanise students with a "wow" factor. Today had been no exception. The Psychology School leadership series this year had included all manner of experts and professionals. Today Lauren had been thrilled to meet body language expert Joe Navarro, former FBI operative and now trainer for many security and policing agencies. He was playing some kind of role in an emerging "homeland security"–style super-department. Navarro had come to fame reading people's responses in interview situations. Though he was no neuroscientist, he used the subject matter in his daily work.

She had raved to Gyan about Joe because he came from a very different point of view than many experts portrayed in the media or drama series. He was not combative, but instead worked to build rapport and trust with the interviewee. Then instead of attempting to make sense of every single body movement, nor even clusters of movement, providing a dictionary of what each movement meant, Joe took a step back. His highest-level filter was one of reading comfort or discomfort: brain stem, systemic response to environment; do they feel safe or unsafe?

Lauren had told Gyan several stories about when self-comforting came to mean "I feel unsafe," and Joe's response was simply to ask himself "Why?" or "When did that start happening?" This did not lead to a "He's lying" conclusion. He would simply ask questions around that point. Gyan found one anecdote quite funny. Joe had seen signs of discomfort and self-calming, asked the lady about it and found she was busting to go to the toilet. As her meal with Gyan extended into the late evening, Gyan had rather brutally excused himself and said he needed sleep. Seeing Lauren's face full of hurt, he assured her they could talk going down to Canberra on the weekend. He thus executed a reasonable recovery, though he secretly suspected Lauren knew it was a calculated manoeuvre.

*

True to his word, he picked her up early the next day. They snaked their way out of Sydney in the long-weekend traffic. Even on a Saturday morning the flow of traffic was heavy, due in part to the rainy conditions and people's collective decision to avoid the Friday-night rush. Too many had made the same choice. Gyan invited her to continue from where she had left off last night, with the brain stem, the girl going to the toilet and safety. Lauren referred to her notes from the seminar, flicking to the section on the limbic system.

"You recall we've already learned about the limbic system? When we learned the three-layer model from MacLean… and mum applied it to Dan Pink's motivations?" she asked. He nodded. "Well, Navarro looked at the four basic response patterns: freeze, mate, fight, or flee—which occur in that order."

She had drawn a flow diagram of sorts and held up her notes, but of course he couldn't look at them, he was so focussed on driving.

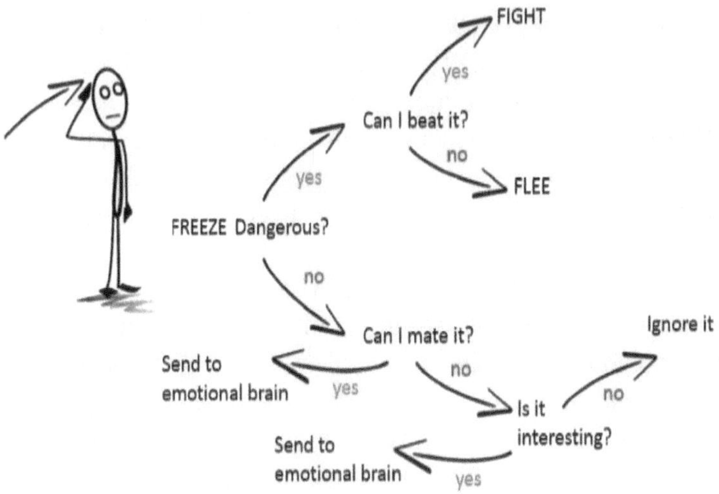

Scratching her head, she pondered how to get him to understand. She read them to him, gesticulating the flow with her hands. When he nodded understanding, she continued to read to Gyan from her notes.

Each of these limbic responses have a different effect on the body. They all fall into the safe/unsafe categories. In the body we may find unfiltered responses, real reactions to how we feel inside, which is where the emotional brain or the limbic responses come in.
The freeze response will manifest in stillness, or cessation of motion. The person may hold their breath, or interlock their feet around the legs of the chair. They may hunch down, or retract their head (into a turtle position with shoulders raised) and avoid eye contact. These are fear and self-protection responses drive by feeling enervated.
The flight response will manifest in foot pointing (toward the exit), leaning the torso away, tilting the head away. You may observe blocking actions: leg blocking when crossing the legs, double arm cross over the chest, closing of the eyes or placing objects between self and others. Fear will also energise the individual to distancing behaviours.
The fight response will manifest in chest puffing, standing up straight, nostril flaring, fist clenching, jaw clenching or violating another person's space. There may alternatively be a verbal exchange – argument (heated or calm) to replace physical threatening. These are attack responses, even when an actual attack does not occur.
The mating response manifests in foot pointing toward, torso directed toward the person they're interested in sexually, an open and comfortable stance, leg crossing when standing, open eyes and dilated pupils, 'anti-gravity' behaviour of the feet and hands, preening, head tossing and hip movement. These are attraction responses. Joe says this is the fourth 'f'.

Gyan pondered all of this in silence for a while, chewing slowly on a piece of gum, his jaw muscles grinding away as his brain started making connections. Unaware of Lauren's discomfort waiting for him, Gyan finally and carefully said, "I get that brain-stem responses can be seen in whole-of-organism reactions (safe or unsafe… comfort or discomfort) and that limbic system responses can be seen in body movements in four categories, the four Fs… but… " his voice trailed off. He rubbed his chin absentmindedly and she waited to see if he would continue. "But, it seems to me that he's just jumped to a list of specific body movements and actions he accused others of listing."

She waited a moment, so as not to appear too defensive. Despite the air-conditioning, she felt the cabin was still warm and rubbed her glistening palms on her thighs. "Yes, well, that would be my fault. I just read you my notes, my condensed list of things I heard. I'm the one who made those lists. He would say they are indicators, signs pointing to something. Our job is to ask "Why." not to jump to "she loves me" or "he's lying" conclusions!"

Gyan rubbed his chin again, smooth from shaving this morning, trying to decide whether it was safe to overtake an L plater. "Okay, point taken; maybe I should read the book. So, tell me what else you learned, like for example why was an FBI guy who's helping the as-yet-to-be-formed Homeland Security at your uni anyway?"

"Well, you know we're in the middle of studying behavioural economics? Well, as part of that we read *Nudge* by Thaler and Sunstein and learned some cool stuff about the way our environment helps or hinders our decision-making. I think they call that decision architecture… " she began.

"Sounds like programming or maybe manipulation to me," he said tersely.

"Yeah, I s'pose it kinda is, but programming of our unconscious. Well anyway a classmate brought in a book called *Snoop* by a guy in America somewhere, and he looks at the way our personality reflects itself in the environments we create for ourselves. Anyway, I reckon our professor had set all this up before because he announced that among the speakers coming this year was Joe Navarro," she concluded, smiling.

"You haven't actually answered my question yet," he said pointedly.

"Oh, right." She paused. "Well, there are three parts to the course. The first is behavioural economics proper: how the transaction or the decision architecture influences or nudges things along; it's the environmental part… Another part of the course looks at the communicator, the paralanguage: distance, touch, time, cultural symbols… The third part is the physical characteristics of the communication: pitch, tempo, volume, eye movement," she finished, satisfied with her summary.

"Sorry, I still don't see where Joe-boy fits in. He's on body language, limbic system, you know… " Gyan said, checking the fuel gauge quickly and making a mental calculation of litres per 100km and the distance to the next service station.

"Well," she stared, rolling her eyes a little defensively, "I guess there's a fourth part."

"Behaviour between the parties during interaction?" he questioned, shrugging. "It's really part of the communicator… well, okay, no, because it's about both of the parties and their limbic behaviour." He thought of elaborate presidential welcome ceremonies in Japan, or welcome-to-country dances in New Zealand.

"Yeah, we're interacting and affecting each other with our words and our movements—the body reflects much of what we're really thinking and feeling—unconsciously signalling that information to others. Body language is totally part of economics, and the neuromarketing field takes to it with a passion," she concluded.

"Neuromarketing's a crock," he said sharply, unnoticing of her cringe. "Most of it is nonsense, just using the language and not the science, jumping to conclusions, inventing cause-and-effect links where at best there might be strong correlations," and his heated judgements died in his throat, realizing it wasn't her fault. "What else you got there?" he asked, glancing over at her notes. "We're gonna stop for fuel and food at Goulburn shortly, so make it snappy." She couldn't tell if he was being playful or insistent. She read out loud some more.

Body language is important to building rapport (we learned about this before), in pacing and empathy and the way mirror neurons work e.g. see if the other person is remaining open to what we are saying, or is starting to withdraw. Matching body and language can help re-establish rapport. Really listening, being present too.

Joe says, "When reading body language, most individuals start their observation at the top and work their way down... my approach is the exact opposite... I learned to concentrate on the feet and legs first, moving upward in my observations." Navarro says the feet are the most honest part of the body, they are furthest from the limbic system. The face is closest and easiest to be manipulated.

Paul Ekman disagrees. He discovered the seven universal expressions of emotion in the face and even when lying, the limbic system gives away micro expressions. (It would be hard to get trained to read that though).

First impressions are almost instant. When we see a person the games begin with an assessment against our heuristics, our filters and stereotypes. Not a conscious process, and happens in 100ms. That impression is 'soft' for ten minutes, slowly being confirmed.

"Navarro said all that?" Gyan asked as they pulled into the service area.

"Well no, not all that," Lauren said somewhat ruefully. "I added my own ideas along the way, from our other texts."

"Well after lunch let's play a game," he said, "called 'how to apply body language to life'; how does that sound?"

Lauren perked up a little and after refuelling car and people, they drafted a list of ways her knowledge could be applied:

- In self-awareness as we walk through shopping malls and supermarkets. Are they using choice architecture to nudge our decisions?
- To the way we set our room, house, yard, entryway to make it welcoming.
- To job interviews, knowing our body language is being read by the others.
- In creating first impressions, they really do observe our clothing, colour choice, handsha facial expressions.
- In the choice of words we use in our emails, job applications, reports and conversations.
- In public speaking and giving a presentation, image selection, use of the stage, hand movements, examples we choose to get a laugh.

*

That morning Jane was back to trimming the shrubs lining the driveway, unsure whether it was the right time of year, but needing to do something to get into Mark's world. He had been sullen these last few weeks; the lustre of his new role in the advisory team had worn off and the weight of responsibility set in. At least that's what she told herself. Some deeper part suspected it was their relationship and that part had brought her out here to keep him company. During the day she'd handed him the hose to connect to the gurney, passed him the secateurs when he was up on the ladder, and squatted beside him in the garden weeding. His shoulders were slumped, his breathing like a sighing willow, his brow furrowed and dark like the soil they tended together.

Now, trimming branches near him, her mind naturally wandered to the analogous requirement of relationships to be tended to, watered, cared for, and trimmed from time to time. They had been more than trimmed, they were in the middle of winter and had shed most of their foliage. Her mind cast back to the night he came home, and how scared she felt that he could be so distant, so pushed away from her that he would sleep on the couch. She would never make him do that, and perhaps right there was the problem… he clearly felt she would. The next morning after that fight their conversation had been great. She was happy to have been heard, and to listen carefully to him. She felt, at the time, that they had good rapport and a healthy respect. But evidently that wasn't enough. What did he want?

It was as though he had stepped back to see what she should do, and she had done everything in her mind and power to connect with him: asking him how his day was, remaining present to him, making sure they found things in common like movies, walking the dog, eating out at his choice of restaurant. Was this a test? Was he trying to see if she was leaning in? Well, she was. She was glad for one thing, at least he was not leaning out anymore. The car sharing had stopped for now and Monique had not been over since the event. Was it that? Was he upset that Monique had become persona non grata? Did he pine for her? Jane didn't think so. He never mentioned her, though silence told her nothing. Several times she had asked him straight up what was wrong, and he only shrugged his shoulders as if to say, "I don't know" or "Whatever." She was left to flounder and her worries mind filled in the gaps with fiction.

For his part, Mark just couldn't believe how ineffective their discussion had been. He had tried to be as open and honest about his side, about his needs as he could, and she seemed to readily accept it. She had nodded and smiled and been very accommodating and he now saw why. She had no intention of changing! But instead of being frustrated or angry he simply felt disappointed, resigned to the ongoing failure to act. Day by day he watched and waited and hoped, very quietly, for an expression of love, a hug, some affection, a kiss, any advance… and was bitterly disappointed.

My need for love comes in physical ways; her need in emotional ways, he thought. *It seems she can neither think in physical ways nor consider or even be aware of my side!* In the first few days after their fight, after the emotional turmoil had calmed down, he had approached her in bed and she had said, "You know, any time you want, all you have to do is ask; I'm up for it" and he recoiled inwardly for some reason. In the ensuing days he had come to form a theory about his reaction. To his mind, asking him to ask for sex made her the master and him the slave; her the giver but only if he came begging. *Imagine,* he thought, *if her greatest desire was for me to parent and I came along and said, "You know, any time you want me to, all you have to do is ask,"* and he would only offer parenting when asked. Good grief!

So there they were, at an impasse, he with knowledge and her without; his needs going unmet and hers happily fulfilled; she perplexed and his resentment building once again. Mark had decided upon three things:

1) Detachment is what allows people to hold their power in the face of opposition, as they are not needing the permission or approval from the other person. The risk (which he was facing right now) was in pushing people back, or standing up to them you may fracture the relationship… and it just might need fracturing.

2) We become free of attachment or neediness when we can see the behaviour for what it really is, rather than being controlled by it. The risk here is that the other person may not perceive reality or face it, they might blame, guilt, shame, or feel persecuted and misunderstood by you.

3) Low-quality ways to meet needs tend to be external and other-oriented. High-quality ways to meet needs tend to be internal and self- (or God-) oriented. The risk here is being more vulnerable to the attention and affection and love and embrace of others if he was unable to meet his needs internally.

Something had also changed in the tenor of his relationship with Monique, and he certainly no longer felt like she was singing her siren's song. Or if she were, he had become more impervious to it. Still, they were meeting clandestinely at work. It was always in a crowd and always "by accident." At work he was more inclined to stand tall, to walk happily, and to crow about his accomplishments.

So went each of their thoughts that day. Click, clack, click, clack went the shears, and as the branches fell between them in the afternoon sun, so did their hopes of reconciliation. It was quite a picture for Lauren and Gyan as they turned into the driveway. mum and dad separated by branches, he with stooped shoulders and half turned away and she leaning over looking expectantly to him.

*

It was Karen's turn to bring the food to the gathering tomorrow. Having sent everyone her material on strengthening relationships a few weeks before, she was also going to lead the discussion and felt chuffed that they'd accepted her so readily. Their semi-regular meetings had taken a pattern: they reviewed their actions from the last month, their personal progress, the material, then answered questions. The round tour always concluded with someone bringing new material which included an action list. Because of the ebb and flow of life the gap between meetings could be a week, a fortnight or a month. Karen appreciated more than a week to practice what they had learned but hated month-long gaps because she lost momentum.

For the coming meeting Mark had taken a bit of a risk and invited Art, who had become something of a mentor to him as well as a boss. Art was delighted to be invited, and expressed genuine interest, since Mark had consistently debriefed him with the learnings. Art could see some commercial benefit, an edge or advantage, in being a management-consulting firm armed with human behaviour and performance skills. Unfortunately, this weekend, he couldn't come.

Since Mark's suggestion that they document the journey, the team had carefully collated the research, the references, a case study or two (usually their own), and the action lists for each subject. They joked about it making some kind of website or podcast series or book one day. Mark was being a little less ambitious than that, and compiled a PDF document with links out to the material on the Internet. He sent this to Art in hopes of getting him up to speed.

Overnight Mark and Gyan had concluded they really didn't have anything new to bring to the group. Lauren had spoken to her grandfather about his hospital stay and showed more genuine concern than Jane had. He kept to himself, like a wounded dog sleeping under a tree. Lauren had asked her mum about her week, and after the general she got specific about her frustrated search for performance indicators on and off the "track."

Lauren got very curious and told her mum all about her own learnings in behavioural economics.

"With a bit of fudging I think we can make something to bring, Mum," Lauren enthused, "well maybe not to your athletes, though let's see, I mean for tomorrow." Along with Lauren's stickman diagram and notes, book references and some ideas from Jane, they added a potential action list:

Observing others

- Pick a form of non-verbal communication to start watching. Only pick one like the eyes, t face, the voice, the body, clothing or environment.
- Ask yourself what is the baseline? Everybody behaves differently by default. Is their voic high and pitchy normally? Do they sit cross legged as a matter of course?
- Watch the behaviour of someone in as natural an environment as possible. It would be p if they can't observe you observing.
- Ask yourself, 'Is what I'm seeing self-comforting or comfortable?' think about whether it s they are nervous, fearful, uncomfortable… or relaxed, happy and open.
- Look for the context, what happened just before that, who were they looking at, what did say, what was said to them?
- Once you know, have a go at determining what limbic response followed: freeze, flight, f mate?

Becoming more self-aware

- Now do the same thing, but for yourself. Instead of using the same focus, choose a cont which to become self-aware of non-verbal communication:
- What does your room/apartment/house say to visitors?
- Observe your body language in a social context like work, sport, home, social outing.
- What do your fingernails, handshake, clothing, handbag, shoes do to your first impressic
- Become aware of the choice of words you use in our emails, job applications, reports an conversations. Watch formal and informal, and play with changing adjectives to see how people respond.
- Now observe your gestures, walking, use of space, stance, gesticulations and hand movements during a conversation, giving a presentation, public speaking.

In the public arena

- Become aware of nudging and decision architecture. Walk through shopping malls and supermarkets. Observe shop design, the placement of product, the colour of signs, the fragrance used.

CHAPTER NINETEEN: THE CHEMISTRY OF EMOTIONS

"Emotive circuits have reciprocal interactions with the brain mechanisms that elaborate higher decision-making processes and consciousness."
Jaak Panksepp

Mark stood in his backyard staring into the pool. The bottom was coated with a fine layer of dirt. He shook his head. How many times had this happened? Sometimes the wind blew dust, but more often it was the rain overnight. Rain was supposed to bring cool moisture and refreshment, but in his city it brought dirt. Sometimes, no matter what he did in his life, things got in; they just did. This waxing and waning magnetic attraction he felt toward Monique was, he originally supposed, entirely his own battle. But in time he realised, and at first blamed, Jane's part in their marriage. Eventually, he learned, Monique played her own foxy little role. But behind it all, there was also the environment, the stress at work, the chance meetings at work, an argument with Jane and, just like the rain, in came the dirt into his emotional pool. He kicked the pool cleaner back into the water with a splash. It would vacuum the pool in time.

Mark turned and was surprised to see his father-in-law watching him from the verandah. He was finally booked on a flight tomorrow morning, after numerous excuses and adjustments to the schedule from two weeks ago when he'd agreed to leave within a few days. Mark was actually sad to see him go. He felt sorry for the old bugger, regardless of what had happened in Jane's childhood. Jane had gone to work early, as had Monique. He was going directly to a client and didn't have to leave until then.

"Got a minute to chat?" Jane's dad called out. Mark nodded and got coffee for them both. Sitting on the verandah was pleasant enough in the morning before the heat kicked in.

The older man fidgeted a little, momentarily unsure of where to begin. "Mark, I haven't been around much. Lauren's all grown up now and, well, my relationship with Jane hasn't been all that great, so I don't have any right to pass comment or even give you my wisdom. But I have some general observations to make if you'll let me?" He looked wistfully at Mark.

"Sure, buddy, why not; what have I got to lose?" Mark said, attempting to be cavalier about it.

"Well, that's kind of the point, isn't it? You've everything to lose," he said wryly. "If you go on being a bonehead you'll lose her, then Lauren and Monique both."

Mark gulped uncomfortably; the cavalier façade was cracking up. "Go on," he said.

"It seems to me your marriage has reached a plateau, which I suppose they all do; heaven knows mine did. You get bored. You start comparing what you now have with what it was. It ain't as exciting, she's not as attractive, neither are you, but I suppose we can't see ourselves, now can we? In any case we seek excitement, challenge at work, work too hard, hang out with friends, drink too much, eat too much, spend a little more time with other women, who somehow start to seem more attractive… how am I going so far?" Jane's father looked at him sideways. Mark was hangdog, considering the "general observations" as being remarkably specific.

"So," he continued, looking at Mark, "It's a vicious cycle because then she starts feeling insecure, and throws herself into work to prove she's your equal, or undermining your work, or just not noticing your accomplishments much anymore, or not caring, and now we have two negative feedback loops."

"How'd you come to be a relationship expert; I thought you sucked at it?" Mark said tersely, feeling a bit defensive.

"I'm no expert," he rebuffed. "Just on the other end of the train ride you're on. It's a wreck. Listen, Mark, I'm all for independence, egalitarian relationships, equality for women, but the issue here is that instead of working together, you're tearing it apart. You got some hot-looking lonely neighbour ready to play ball next door but what you don't realise is that when she sees it go to hell here, she imagines it's her next, and she'll never let you do that to her as well."

"How the hell can you know Monique wants me?" Mark said, too loudly, Jane's father watching intently as Mark's cheeks reddened, either with anger, shame, or indignation, he thought. He took a breath. "'Cause I got eyes, Mark; it ain't that hard! Oh that, and being smacked into a coma while you're off down the beach! Anyway, this isn't about her, or Jane; it's about you. Do you even know what you want? Do you remember why you fell in love with Jane? Do you know what, in all of this, is worth fighting for? Because until you do, your poor mind is going to go round and round the plughole, being sucked down to the lowest common denominator… your most base instincts and needs." He watched Mark intently for a moment to gauge his reaction, but he was hard to read.

They sat in silence a long time before Mark ventured, "Listen, thanks, you took a big risk just now and I respect you for that. I'll think about what you said… but I gotta go to work." With that Mark stalked off inside, collected his things and headed out the front door. His chest felt tight, his breathing was shallow, his mind continued racing. Mark had to work hard not to speed in his absentminded distraction. He couldn't stand the thought that this had all become so obvious that a near stranger could call it, and worse still… that it had become about him. What Jane's dad failed to see, he reasoned, was Jane's almost complete neglect that started this. Or did it? Had he started the neglect of her with his career? Did it matter?

As his wide rear tires chirped under acceleration these thoughts swirled round and round his confused mind. There was one inescapable observation central to them all… knowing what he wanted and knowing how he felt were two very different things. The baser instincts did indeed seem to drive him so long as he had no bearings. He suddenly became aware that he was in the vicinity of the client, and started to look for the right street and parking. In this part of Deakin where the client offices were, two-hour parking was hell to find. Mark eventually found a park, and ducked upstairs to find Brad tapping his foot at the end of the corridor. Brad was the consummate CEO type: a good-natured ease and almost robo-cop sense of purpose, drive, and strength.

Mark had been serving Brad's company for three months now, off and on between weeks at Defence. He had been doing a mix of scoping study and evaluation of project purpose for him. Mark brought the human-performance element to this largely engineering and biomedical company. Two weeks ago, toward the end of their current assignment, Brad broached the question of Mark's firm offering executive coaching. Mark had taken it to Art, who very cautiously said yes, so long as the task and objectives were clearly defined.

Mark was confident he could take it on, although he was neither trained nor practiced at coaching. He figured at its heart coaching was staying curious, asking the right questions, and letting silence do the heavy lifting. He and Brad had good rapport, Mark was not shy to ask tough questions and they could do conversation. They had taken to walking at lunch time together to break the long days and Mark was a natural at coaching-style conversations, until today.

"No walking shoes, Brad?" Mark asked.

"Nope. Thought we'd sit it out, Mark, look at the sky," Brad answered, gesticulating out the window. Mark nodded. He'd missed the threatening gloom of storm clouds coming over in the car.

They chitchatted for a few minutes before Mark kicked off with, "Cool, so what's the most important thing for us to talk about?" They sat in Brad's sumptuous office in deep leather chairs that sighed when you sat in them.

"Emotions I think. I'm concerned about Felicity," Brad said. Mark paused, breathless. That was deep, quick.

"Okay, but just so you understand, since Felicity isn't here, I can't really coach her. We can really only discuss your side." Mark looked at Brad curiously.

"Oh, no, don't misunderstand me. It's something she said to me, so no, God no, we're talking about me." Mark leaned back, relieved as Brad continued, "She said she'd never seen me cry, and said humans are supposed to cry, and she was scared for our son; you know we have a young boy? Great. So Felicity wants me to figure out why I have shallow feelings." Brad got up and started pacing in front of the glass windows overlooking the Brindabella Ranges. They looked blue today nestled under the brooding dark of grey clouds.

"Do you have shallow feelings?" Mark asked, wondering to himself where the line between consultant/coach and counsellor/psychologist might be. It was like walking on a balloon surface, like a jumping castle, with everything shifting under him.

"I don't think so," Brad started, shaking his head and continuing to pace. "I yell and scream with passion at a Brumbies game, I holler and hoot with joy the days I get to go horseback riding, I experience gut-wrenching fear every time I have to land the corporate jet, I get real angry when we lose a tender, so… I've got plenty of dimension. But I never cry in a chick flick, or get taken in by those rom-com's which Felicity loves, and come to think of it, I haven't cried since I was a kid. Maybe that's what she means?"

"It's worth asking her what she means, but since she's not here, and we can't guess accurately, why don't we talk about what it means to you?" Mark asked, feeling the ground become firm beneath him. They talked for about thirty minutes about Brad's childhood, and found no deep or meaningful moment at which he resolved to stop crying. He couldn't determine any class of activity which might make him cry. Physical pain such as a broken ankle, emotional pain such as his first divorce, and loss like the bankruptcy of his first company had all failed to bring tears. Mark vaguely knew of research on emotions… *I've read things like four hundred and something emotions but only five or six basic ones?* So he offered to go do some research, and maybe bring back something that could explore Brad's range further.

"I don't want Dr. Google though, Mark; you know I'm not gonna pay good money for something I could just find myself," Brad said, ever the direct communicator.

"Sure, Brad, no self-diagnosis crap, but still you know I have the time to find stuff you don't. Some of it's sure to be on the Internet. But, yeah, I take your point." Mark shook hands and moved off to the elevator.

In the room, in that last moment he had been confident, but now Mark felt that the whole conversation had been out of his depth. That was his first coaching or consulting conversation to end without actions to take or a resolution of the problem. He felt a bit like a failure. He drove back to the offices of his consulting firm, the morning's conversation with his father-in-law filed away and the current topic of interest—emotions—in his conscious mind. Car park, stairway, security door, corridor, a nod and smile to his workmates and he was at his desk typing into a search engine. His first inquiry about "lack of emotions" and "unable to cry" turned up loads of references to alexithymia, a malady of shallow feeling and inability to name feeling; he found stuff on trauma and "locked in syndrome", which appeared relevant to the abused. Even more unhelpful were the pages of information on sociopathy and psychopathy.

Well, wait a minute, thought Mark. It was possible Brad was a psychopath… only one in a hundred killed, many of them were successful businesspeople… and so Mark was taken off into the world of corporate psychopathy (Snakes in Suits, they were called), shallow affect (expressed emotion) and the Hare psychopathy checklist. By late afternoon he had determined that a) it would be impossible to broach the subject with Brad, and b) it was very unlikely that Brad was a psychopath. Charming, yes. Flagrant and maybe unfaithful, probably. Shallow emotionally, well, not if his testimony was to be believed, though psychopaths tend to be good liars too. Violent to animals as a child, unlikely. Without conscience? Absolutely not. Brad had made sure his company's profits donated to a charity dedicated to rescuing women from sex slavery in Thailand.

Mark sighed and held his head up in his palms. The day was gone. Most people had left the office. This would have to wait for tomorrow. The thoughts of Jane's dad and his confronting message gradually seeped back into Mark's mind. Along with it, a cascade of random memories. For reasons Mark could scarcely comprehend, as he brooded on it he became engulfed in grief and an overwhelming sense of loss. Tears flowed easily and steadily down his cheeks and he began to feel like he was losing it. Mark just let it come, hoping that no one would take notice or offer unwanted consolation.

The tears eventually stopped and as Mark wiped his face he wondered, *What was that all about?* and *What am I so sad about?* Possibilities marched across his mind like so many circus animals: *poor relationship with my parents? Choosing this job? Missing my calling as a coach? Not having more children? Something about Brad? Something about emotions? The deep ache I feel for Monique? My resolve not to make anything of it? Some childhood thing?* His mind slowly oriented itself toward Jane.

Suddenly Mark could feel the hot tears brooking once again at the rims of his eyes. It was answer enough. Jane. *What the hell? Jane?* Bewildered, he sat trying to figure out why his soul might be so distressed while tears rolled down his cheeks afresh. He asked his unconscious what this all meant, and a singular, sickening, unbelievable image flashed hot into his mind's eye. A thought, a truth, a line of reasoning becoming crystal clear to him, upon which all the threads of his evidence would hang.

There was movement behind him and Mark spun around to see Art standing quietly in the corridor behind him. To their left the open-plan office stood all but empty. Art waited for Mark to speak, looking intently at his puffy eyes. When Mark didn't speak, looking instead like a frightened child plotting revenge on a schoolyard enemy, Art ventured, "Hey, Mark, you look terrible… are you all right?"

*

With her father finishing his packing in his room, the house was empty, and so was Jane's heart. Mark wasn't home yet and hadn't called either. Jane stared into her third glass of wine for the evening. She liked it because it took the edge off. She hated it because it was damaging to her health in these quantities. She seemed powerless to stop, but she wanted to stop. Jane fingered the glass bowl she held, the remnants of peanuts in the bottom. "It used to be a couple of days a week," she said to no one in particular. She used to have a glass a day. A health magazine helped there, with a story about long-living Italians. Then it was two a day, thanks to Tim Ferriss. In his book he talked about having two glasses of red wine a day. Last night, between two movies and a bowl of popcorn, she had a whole bottle. Jane experienced guilt, then recrimination. Yet here she was getting into it again.

"Probably self-medicating," she suggested helpfully, feeling the dullness of mind and feeling that always accompanied drinking. "But medicating what?" As if by answer, her father walked in unwelcome. She frowned as he sat down across from her and offered, "Me… probably. Well, me and your mother, and all that happened. That and your miserable marriage."

She scowled. Thoughts of her childhood rising unbidden to the surface of her mind; no, it wasn't that. Nowhere near. She'd long ago dealt with that disappointment, and why should it start her drinking now? The silence dragged between them, but he waited, as though knowing he didn't really have the right to parent her now.

"Why are we so self-obscure? Why can't we see our self, our deepest recesses, what motivates us?" he asked, without addressing her.

When she didn't answer he ventured, "I think it's only opaque if we pretend not to know what's going on. Your neatness is driven by a desire to control. You find the word control offensive so you deny it." Even then she winced at the word. "You have 'issues' with your parents, and these manifest themselves a hundred different ways, but you pretend you've dealt with it… "

"Honestly, what happened to us was decades ago! That's got nothing to do with drinking more and more this year, Dad!" she said, deflecting the conversation without knowing she was doing it.

"Doesn't it?" he asked. "These things take ages to come to the surface, decades, especially if we push them away, submerge them deep down… but what do I know? I'm not a psychologist, now, am I?" he added sarcastically, a sneer manifest on his upper lip.

They fell into silence again until she turned to face him more fully and said, "What do you mean my miserable marriage?" There was heat in her words, edged with accusation. Her father held her gaze, he was about the only man she knew who didn't wilt before her fury.

*

Lauren sat on her couch trying to read her textbook, but her mind kept going back to the way Gyan had behaved toward her in the car two weeks ago.

Travel to Canberra only took a few hours, but it was torture to watch him struggling to be human, to show some affection. He was like a robot, he was like a driver attempting to select the right gear and crunching it, or selecting the right emotion and getting it wrong! She replayed the interactions again and again without much relief. Her mind was snagged on this particularly trying set of events, and all of the related emotions.

She threw her book onto the coffee table, and it landed with a loud *thump*, surprising her. She determined to go over to Gyan's place and confront him about it once and for all. She pedaled the well-known path to Gyan's parents' house and knocked on the door, ready for a fight. But there was no answer. She knocked again, and then decided to look around the back. Finding the door open, she snuck inside and looked around. Then she proceeded to Gyan's bedroom.

Through a crack in the door she could see he was fiddling with something on the floor. He knelt there toying, jostling with something she couldn't see. Opening the door quietly, she moved toward him and put her hands on his shoulders, a move she thought might start a conversation gently. Instead he nearly jumped out of his skin, yelping in a way that made her think he was guilty.

"Jeez, Lauren! What on earth are you doing! I could have really hurt you!" he said in a high-pitched voice.

Lauren wasn't having any of it. Surprised by the reaction and pumped with endorphins from the ride over, she simply reacted with, "Whatcha hiding, Gyan? Hmm? Why the shock, buddy? I might have been your mum or dad, for all you knew!" Her eyes fell on the object he'd been playing with, a small blue-coloured box covered with felt.

"No, you couldn't because they've gone to see my uncle in Thornleigh, and it's none of your business… well no, actually it is your business… but not now," he retorted.

Cocking her head to one side, she said, "Whadaya mean? My business? I'll tell you what my business is Gyan and that's your behaviour! You've been acting strange these last few weeks and I've just about had it! I know you smart people struggle with expressing your emotions sometimes, but this is ridiculous… it seems to me you've clearly been wrestling with your emotions, what they are and how they work, and it feels to me like you're trying them out on me."

Gyan had causally flicked the object toward his bed and stood between her and it. "Well, that's very observant of you, though I protest that courage is not an emotion; it is an experience or outcome. Indeed, I question the very premise of emotion for it may simply be a label we use for a state… But yes, nevertheless I have been trying to be brave, also not an emotion, and muster, or gather, the courage to ask you a difficult question."

"Well, I'm wound up now, Gyan! I'm hopping mad and fit to bust, so if you don't mind, get on with it!" Her voice was screechy and loud, angry, and exactly the opposite of what he was after and Gyan winced.

"I really don't think the circumstances are right… I feel that the mood, the feeling or the timing, is wrong for my question," Gyan said defensively.

At that moment Lauren, having calculated the distance between her and the object, decided it was within her reach and leapt around Gyan to grab it from near his bed. In doing so, she both burned her skin on the carpet and knocked him down. He yelped in surprise, then deftly snatched it out from her hands. In doing so, the lid clicked open and the contents spilled onto the floor.

Out fell a glistening diamond ring.

They lay there in a breathless tumble, he with a mixture of embarrassment and dismay and she with rapidly deflating anger and shock.

*

Mark paused, wondering how much to tell Art. He then decided to tell him everything, including the conversation with Jane's father this morning, and his moment of crying and clarity just now. Art drew up a chair and sat down to listen intently, reserving judgement and trying to find something redemptive to say.

Eventually, when Mark had expended his energy, Art said, "Listen Mark, I'm no counsellor, hell, what do I know about relationships either? I'm twice divorced, but listen… your reaction, your fear, is perfectly reasonable. Now, while I'm not exactly sure what conclusions you're reaching, I do know this… people don't think clearly when they're emotional. From what you've told me along the journey you've been on, we filter reality, right?" Mark nodded. "So when you think something is true, you discard evidence, you make stuff up, you cobble a world together that makes sense… you join the dots so it makes your picture right, yeah?" Mark nodded. "Now, I don't know if you're doing that right now or not, but I'd be real careful about taking a 'position' and firing off shots at anyone just yet."

Mark scratched his jaw, then pitched back, "I appreciate that Art, really. But what should I do instead? I was going to go hunting for evidence just now…

”

“And you’d probably find it,” said Art, “we always do, but what does it mean? I think your father-in-law had it right: answer the first question first. What do you want? What’s worth fighting for?”

“Well, that’s the question, now, isn’t it,” Mark said, much more calmly. He could literally feel his emotional brain dialing down and his rational brain powering up again.

He and Art shook hands, and before he headed for home, Art finished with, “Listen, Mark, just treat your evidence with curiosity, stay fluid, just ask questions, and don’t fire conclusions, okay?” Mark nodded his agreement, then drove into the massive, gathering storm, a thunderhead ten-thousand feet high overhead as it swept in from the Brindabella Ranges and hammered Canberra, the rain pouring down in torrents and wind lashing the streets. Huge trees bent before the wind and water, groaning to breaking point just like the storm water drains beside them.

As he drove, watching the raindrops on the other side of the glass, images and conversations came to his mind’s eye. A disposable Chinese container left on the bench with two plastic forks in it; Jane’s attacks on his character—probably born of guilt or shame; her emotional and sexual distance from him; her late nights and higher-than-usual quantities of dinners out and away from home—as the credit card would testify; her increased drinking; her gracious acceptance of him coming home that night from Lake George, and even the very belated discovery of his car-pooling which by rights should have been discovered on the first or second day. He really only had one single question to ask her.

Simple but devastating.

Having arrived home, he braved the gap between the car and the house through the rain. Mark mounted the stairs, entered the house with confidence, and saw Jane and her father seated opposite each other, locked in some kind of battle. His question rose to his lips, but before he could ask it, her dad hit her with a powerful punch: “Jane, are you having an affair?” Jane dropped the bowl and it smashed on the floor among the peanuts. There was silence.

“Dammit!” Mark said out loud. That was *his* question.

The two men waited for an answer. She didn’t deny it, and she didn’t attack back with her own accusations about Monique. Instead, tasting the ash of a dying marriage in her mouth, she submitted to Mark’s ensuing barrage of questions and observations. She corrected Mark’s slight factual errors, and added new scenes and stories to his montage, painting herself completely into a guilty corner.

Jane couldn't tell why, but instead of coming undone, she switched to lawyer mode and punched holes in his theory from end to end. Then she switched sides and played her own accuser. The truth is, she said, she had both motive and opportunity. Mark's case was strong on innuendo and circumstantial evidence but weak on factual evidence of infidelity. Jane neither confirmed nor denied her guilt but instead allowed Mark to treat her like a criminal and see if she could be acquitted. Perhaps she wanted to be acquitted; perhaps she wanted to be found guilty. Perhaps she wanted to see if Mark was going to fight for or against the marriage: bring it back from the dead, or bury it.

She felt a hollow, guilty pleasure knowing the truth and not admitting it. Either he was a very cunning bastard, accusing her when she had walked the same line as he had, or he was clueless and thrashing out at her. Either way, she had to know if he still wanted her, if there was anything left for them. Then the storm of his pelting questions were exhausted, the living room littered with the metaphorical slick of their watery deaths.

Mark retreated to the master bedroom with the issue unresolved. The timber floor squeaked just at the threshold, and the door turned not silently on its hinges. He felt taunted by Jane, someone he thought he knew very well. If even half of what he suspected was true, it made her twice the liar he slept with yesterday, and just as guilty as her. But she was actually still exactly the same woman he had slept with yesterday.

With the bed taken, Jane had a decision to make. Did Mark want her there or not? He had made absolutely no sign to her. In the end, she decided, *I have to ask the same thing of myself that I asked of him. Do I have the fight left in me? Am I going to "phoenix" my own heart? Can I come back?* Standing at the bedroom door she slowly opened it, listening for his breathing to change. It didn't. She undressed and climbed into bed carefully, waiting. Thinking him asleep, she decided to speak quietly anyway.

"Mark, I love you, I still do. Just like you said that day cutting the hedges. I have it in me to fight for this relationship because it means the world to me. No, you mean the world to me. So here's the truth. I haven't been unfaithful, at least not in a physical sense. I started seeing Sean a bit more at work, we went out for drinks, even went out for dinner a couple of times. I was sorely tempted, Mark, and he offered too. But I couldn't. I didn't. That Chinese container you found was me and Dad, that's all. But I'm glad you care and that you fought… I'm really glad. I know I said I was leaning in before, but I wasn't. I've been leaning out. I'm so sorry."

Whether in his sleep, or still awake, she never knew, but she could have sworn he whispered, "Me too."

*

In the morning the storm had cleared, the air was fresh and smelled like wet earth and eucalyptus. There were leaves in the pool and sticks and twigs across the driveway, fallen from the trees. There was a sense of destruction and newness. Inside, Jane was preparing to take her father to the airport and Mark ate his breakfast in silence.

He wasn't due to see Brad till early next week, but he wanted to find answers to those emotions before the weekend. Jane was going to tell Monique she was welcome to the group and clear up any tension, Karen had expressed she was coming over and Art had even said to Mark he might have time this weekend. Mark texted Lauren about their plans, but had no reply.

So he decided to work from home today, and track down some leads he had on research for Brad. He picked up the phone, dialed Brad, and left a message that said, "Hey Brad, Mark here, been thinking about you and deep emotions. I reckon all your examples are what I might call 'hard' emotions. I'm wondering about 'soft' emotions to encounters and people. Things like love, sorrow, care, and regret tend to happen under less-than-spectacular circumstances. Anyway, I'm hunting some exercises down. Wondering if you'd be up for a trip to an fMRI machine to look at your amygdala and responses to pictures. Cheers."

He kissed Jane goodbye as she headed off to work. They had resolved both to talk and to work harder on the marriage, as soon as her dad was gone. Jane figured she might even come home after lunch, so they could get started right away. A small, new hope had blossomed in her heart, a cautious and hope, but it gave her strength to try.

After saying goodbye to Jane's dad, Mark got right online and looked for feelings, emotions, mood, state, and drive.

He discovered that what state you were in (a whole of being experience) was quite different from mood (like being energized, optimistic, depressed, or careless). Drive (to seek, find, learn, or love) is also different from emotion (love, joy, hate, or anger).

One site explained that all emotions were states – made up of physiology, biochemistry and neurology (not so different from Ian Snape's model about state). What this site did, however, was offer the idea that one could elicit how that state was arrived at. After all, something preceded you feeling angry, for example (a slight from a workmate). Something preceded that (a predisposition to being slighted) and something preceded that (the reason you were sensitive to being put down—e.g., bullying at school).

"Pretend you are from Mars, and you've never seen this emotion before," said the author, "Break down the path to that emotion in stepping stones you can explain to someone, because this very path carries you to that emotion every time." It was a useful idea Mark supposed. Steps to making a state. He'd done that in the car, and he'd even taught his lawyer client how to do it. So Mark accepted the supposition that emotions could be built, or at least the path to them could be discovered. And if discovered, then alter one step and… you'd be somewhere else.

He searched for a model of basic emotions—the core of human reaction—and found the five, six, seven, and eight basic emotions models. He wrote them down on a page under the heading "emotion or feeling," seeking to understand more about them. He found a website devoted to understanding the neurochemistry of emotions, and added a column headed "neurochemistry" to write down the various combinations beside his emotional ladder. He was forced to add yet another column for the results of an emotion—what happened on the outside: the actions, the body language, and the physiological changes. These he called "results."

Then he came across the remarkable work of Jaak Panksepp, an affective neuroscientist who did a lot of his work with mice and mammals. Jaak uncovered seven basic driver systems, seven basic neural circuits in the limbic system which, when fired, set off emotions in a cascade like Mark had written down already. Jaak's list did not line up neatly with Mark's list though because one of Mark's "emotions" (disgust) began in the gut, not in the limbic system. Mark's table ended up looking like this:

Limbic System	Emotion – feeling	Neuro-chemistry	Results
Seek – pursue	desire – reward	serotonin + dopamine	well-being, control, learn, pay attention
Play – learn	joy – happiness	dopamine	pleasure, movement, compulsion, reward, growth
Care – connect	peace – empathy	oxytocin	relaxation, care, empathy, connection

Lust – reproduce	love – belonging	testosterone + oestrogen + vasopressin + oxytocin + serotonin	attraction, sexual desire, potential
Rage – protect (fight)	anger – envy	adrenalin + catecholamine	energy, strength, speed, power, victory
Disgust – reject	guilt – shame	Gut-brain bile + more benzodiazepines	contempt, distastefulness
Grieve –avoid	sadness – depression	norepinephrine + serotonin + MAO	arousal, attention, experience of pain
Panic – flee	anxiety – anguish	Lack of benzodiazepines + adrenalin	freezing, anchoring, potential diminished, loss
Fear – freeze	worry – horror	corticosteroids (esp. ACTH)	resilience, stress, fatigue

"So, for example," Mark said to the screen in front of him. Sometimes talking out loud helped him learn and remember, "… there's a neural circuit: neurons firing together to create my fear response, in particular my freeze response. That very same circuit also underlies the emotion I would call worry. Worry and horror as emotions are based in the hardware of fearing and freezing. Neurochemically it is corticosteroids setting this off—particularly ACTH, which, well, I don't know what that even is! And the result, my outcome, is a stress response and eventual fatigue."

"What I find weird is that joy and happiness sit on learning and play according to Panksepp. Well no wait, just start at the start, like that other website getting me to step by step find my way to the emotion or state. Play leads to (is the step before) play! My school wasn't hardly fun at all, yet here in my brain the act of learning is hardwired to the activity of playing. We got that screwed up all right. But, so, joy and happiness are the next step beyond that. Now that's cool!" He poured himself a fresh cup of tea and went back to the computer thoughtfully, with Brad in mind. He drew a pathway for Brad, using his table and drew:

The limbic grief circuit

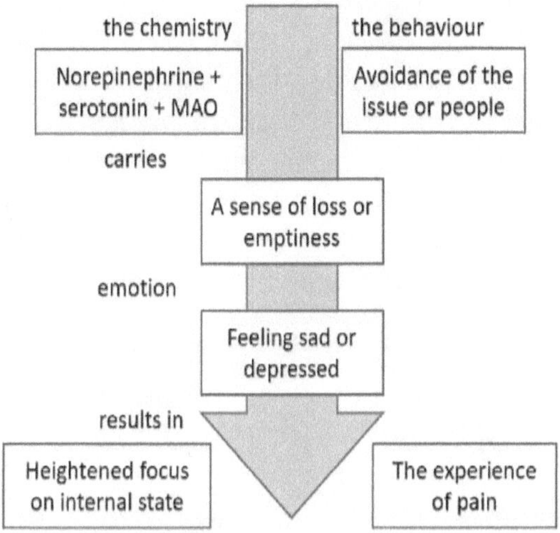

It appeared to Mark that Brad was failing to demonstrate sadness for a number of reasons. Working backward he might be avoiding past memories, he might be staying clear of grief as a baseline circuit or, working forward he might be on antidepressants, or lacking that triple combo of neurochemicals, or spending his arousal, attention, and experience on everything else. "Too busy living to be sad?" he asked.

"Okay, so that's all interesting," Mark said to himself. "Fascinating, even. But so what can we do commercially with this table? Actually, not commercially; how about creating alternatives for coaching ourselves? How about opening up limitless options when it comes to the way we react, respond, or limit ourselves like Brad has, not being able to cry?" One piece of research he came across showed the feedback and feedforward nature of these loops. Smiling makes you happy and being happy makes you smile. Physiology, environment, reactions, choices, perceptions, chemistry, food, rest, and a range of other things are effected by, and affect emotions. A classic example comes from the research on bipolar disorder. They found that people with bipolar slept poorly, and those who slept poorly were more likely to exhibit bipolar traits and behaviours. The first line of treatment slowly became sleep training (including medication) and the result was often a reduction in symptoms.

Anxiety comes upon people with anxiety disorders, but conversely its trajectory could be learned and headed off in much the same way as migraines. Even for those experiencing the onset of an anxiety attack could, with practice and training, speed the cycle up and make it pass rapidly. One testimony Mark read took a two-day disabling attack down to thirty minutes. This was only possible because the "outward" results of the emotion could be played backwards and used to drop the amplitude of the anxiety. Mark thought of Lauren and her CBT journey. He doodled on a piece of paper.

The limbic panic circuit

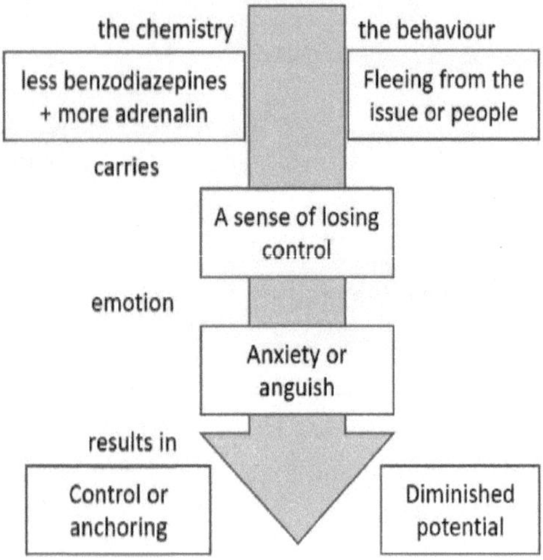

Starting at the other end, and creating a positive feedforward loop it can be run as:

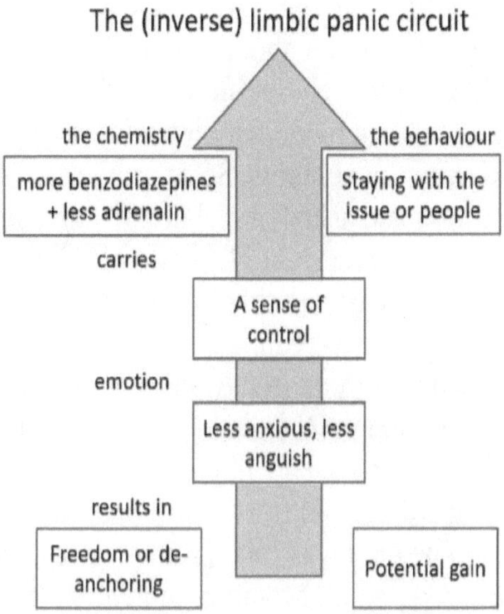

Such a chain was absolutely useful, if you knew which of the eight emotions you were dealing with. Of course he wasn't a psychiatrist, and couldn't access injections or tablets of whichever neurochemical was lacking or was needed. He did have access to a couple of rather scientific chefs who might be able to help him put together meals which added all the basic ingredients for neurochemistry. They had hinted at this sort of effect in one of their classes after all.

Mark finished up his research by downloading an emotional addiction questionnaire he found in a work-life balance course called A Balancing Act, so that he could give Brad something to start with next week, and the guys this weekend could try it out for him. There were, in this model, only seven core emotions, but he was okay with that. There were seven question sheets each tallying to 100 points, and you could build a radar diagram showing how well-balanced you were across the seven. He already knew Brad was short on sadness.

*

The week was ended, the day was done, and Jane came home early. They interacted awkwardly, like a pair of divorcees meeting at a bar for the first time, checking out each other's pasts and motives. As Mark moved into making and serving a meal, Jane unwound, once again with a drink and started to share snippets from her own morning sending her father away. Over dessert they agreed that Mark should share his emotions research, and something hit Mark like a truck. He should invite Brad! It was risky, mixing business with pleasure, but maybe Felicity would come too and meet the girls. They might make up the numbers. So Mark took a risk and called.

Brad answered first ring, and asked him about the message he'd left, and Mark talked him through the research. The clincher for Brad was knowing Karen would be coming; at least a psychologist could unpick him if the content didn't. He and Felicity were in.

Mark and Jane shopped first thing in the morning, deciding on lots of carbs. They brought Coppia sourdough, Nutella babka, American cornbread, Eritrean injera, English crumpets, and all the accoutréments with them. Fruit platter, real chai, strong coffee, and fresh fruit juice were put out, and they were ready for guests. The pool was clean, the spa was closed, the deck was ready, and the guests straggled in. Monique came first, looking sheepish, and Karen confidently strutting next; Art and Sean arrived at the door at the same time, exchanging a glance that said, *"Have you been here before; no, me neither."* Mark and Jane had talked at length about Sean last night, and Mark was the one who suggested he come regardless of the difficulty with Jane. He did this partly as a placation for allowing Monique to come, and partly because he figured the only way to secure Jane's affections against any suitor was to love her right. That was his job, not Sean's, and taking him out of the day solved nothing.

When everyone had been introduced, Mark walked the group through their illustrious past, mainly for the benefit of Sean and Brad. After brunch, Gyan and Lauren came in via Skype and before anyone could really discuss anything Gyan blurted out their news:

"Dear everyone, we wish to announce that, against my parents' better wishes and perhaps my fault at not previously asking Mark his permission, Lauren and I are getting engaged to be married!"

The room was at first silent, then erupted into applause as the news sunk in and Lauren's delighted and slightly flushed face beamed in the background. Mark wished them both well from the bottom of his heart, and Jane was absolutely delighted. The content of the day, despite being completely overshadowed by the news, still evolved into a healthy discussion about emotions, with Lauren showing particular interest in the questionnaires (for Gyan). Of all the interactions, perhaps Lauren's and Jane's were the most vehement.

Action List

- Do the emotions audit questionnaire: www.neurocoachingaustralia.com/resources/neurocoaching/emotions-questionnaire.pdf
- Once you have your score from the seven basic emotions, find out what area seems to l highlighted by your radar diagram, or which area of emotion strikes you as needing the r work?
- Is there an area that you have struggled with over the years?
- Go to the table contained in this chapter and draft for yourself a version of the process s as the one Mark did for anxiety. Then draft the same process backwards. Here it is as a example, if you are experiencing panic or anxiety, your journey, from left to right across table is (the arrows represent "leads to"):

Panic, flee (diminish) response -> anxiety
Emotion: anguish of mind
Chemistry: lack of benzodiazepines + more adrenalin

Result: freezing, anchoring, potential diminished, loss

- In reverse, if we are going to diminish or feedforward this cycle:

Gain, stand (potential increased) response ->
Result: de-anchoring, fluid freedom
Chemistry: less adrenalin – more benzodiazepines
Emotion: reduced anguish, reduced anxiety
Response: stay, calm

- What actions now occur to you as part of this feedback and feedforward loop?
- What can you work on as a result?

CHAPTER TWENTY: NEURO-ASSOCIATIVE CONDITIONING

"When you've exhausted all possibilities, remember this: you haven't."
Thomas Edison

Two weeks had passed in Canberra's late summer, more than enough time for the silver birch by Lake Burley Griffin to start turning, their leaves becoming green-yellow. Gyan and Lauren were preparing for a trip to Canberra to show everybody the ring. Brad and Felicity had made little progress; Art remained curious about the group; Monique had stabilised, got over her man-crush, and her inner darkness seemed much less threatening to her now. Jane sat opposite Karen, wondering if this was a therapy session.

"Don't get me wrong, I admire Tony Robbins and all. Fantastic as a motivational speaker and really does his homework on human behaviour… " Karen paused and took a deep breath, looking at Jane sideways, "but honestly, his lack of scientific rigor drives me crazy! *'A study says… '* What study for God's sake? For them, if it works, it's good enough. But not for me because it might work in the hyped-up atmosphere of a conference, or create a placebo effect when it's your guru helping you… but what do you do when your guru lets you down? What about when she's not there! No, no, we need the evidence base, the research to back his findings, otherwise we can't use them in the real world. Am I right?" She looked askingly to the rest.

It was time for Jane to look at her sideways. Karen hardly ever self-indulged with theoretical monologues. Their friendship certainly covered professional areas, but was mainly personal. This must be going somewhere. "You mean like that time-line stuff you did with Monique?"

"Yes, yes, the time-line stuff comes from a field of study called NLP, and believe me the field's rife with unscientific material, but it's also full of wondrous gems and jewels like that one—perfectly well-researched and backed not with raving testimonial but with evidenced clinical research. EMDR, the S-pattern, so many techniques like that. That's the trouble with this field: it's such a mixed bag, but I'd hate to throw away the meat just 'cause there are bones, right? I actually think NLP may contain the heart of this neuroscience-based coaching we've been playing at. We just have to dig up the research."

And with that, Karen went to move on. However, Jane stopped her abruptly. "Wait, you started talking about Tony Robbins; what's he got to do with NLP? He had little to do with John Grinder, or Bandler, or anyone else there, did he?"

"Right you are, though they say he stole a good deal of their ideas. Right, no. I mentioned him because I've been reading about his version of NLP, which he called Neuro-Associative Conditioning. Again, that field has turned to mud in many ways, but in the beginning Tony taught, based on Korzybski's work, that a person's experience is not reality. Experience is a mere representation of that reality and as such, cannot be changed. Another way to say that is: perception is real only to the perceiver. Now Robbins acts on this belief or way of understanding, on our perceptions and experiences, with two levers: pleasure and pain. I think that's a bit too simplistic. As you showed us before (in your show down with Daniel Pink) we know you can act on it with seven if you like: pleasure, pain, reward, punishment, self-improvement, self-direction, and transcendent purpose, right?"

Jane nodded gently, encouraging her to go on, "Well, Robbins taught that everything out there has an internal representation in here, the territory out there is mapped inside our head. Everything on that map is associated with good/bad, right/wrong, pleasure/pain. So if you want to change the map—and your experience of things—you have to change what's associated with it."

"Seems fair enough," Jane said. "So we can control our experience of reality?"

"Well, I wouldn't say control. Interact with, adjust, amend, upgrade, but not control. Remember we're dealing with neurology and the unconscious. What interpretation is best for you? Is your interpretation serving you well? Do you need another one?"

"Okay, influence, change… just bear with me and forgive me if I'm getting ahead of myself here, Mark, but sorry… but we have slowly formed negative or painful associations with our internal representations of each other. If we are to change our relationship, we must also change our experience of each other."

"Yes, Jane! That's right!" Karen enthused, failing to hear the hint of irony in Jane's voice. Jane just didn't believe it was that easy.

"I'm going to keep reading on the subject, and find out what science has to say about Robbins and Korzybski. Are outside things and internal feeling associations mapped this way—at a neuronal level? Can they be changed? What are the best ways to associate and disassociate? Anyway, that's my work… and as our time is nearly done, how about you tell me what self-work you're going to do?" With this Jane proceeded to summarize their hour-long conversation and some actions she could take.

*

Brad scratched his stubble as he considered the results of the survey Mark had emailed over. The radar diagram showed he was balanced in all emotions apart from sadness. Apparently he and sorrow, depression, loneliness, and the blues were not friends. Indeed, not even remote acquaintances. *How could that be a problem?* he wondered. *Being happy is what everybody wants, right?* So he was paying a management consultant perfectly good money to tell him he needed to be sad? Madness in the extreme!

As he began to pen a reply to that effect, another email came in from Mark. It simply reminded Brad that sadness as an emotion sat upon the circuitry of grief and avoidance, and built up arousal and attention. Mark's terse note concluded, "The less we are acquainted with grief, the less we are companion to avoidance. The Titanic might have learned something from that." Brad had to smile at Mark's prescient advice. He'd just saved his contract! Brad pondered a moment longer, thinking how in the end a failure to deal with grief ended up creating grief; failing to avoid resulted in accidents. "What am I pretending not to know?" Brad wondered out loud, parroting the question he'd heard Mark use more than once.

He knew several things for sure: he was not going to get any further with diagrams and discussions. He was also not going to any chick flicks or rom-coms with Felicity. Lastly, book learning would not touch his heart. He needed an experience. He thought through all his favourite experiences: eating out at new restaurants, riding his horses, flying, doing adrenaline sports, and boxing… he knew they would not bring him to tears anyway. *What's the point of trying to be sad?* he asked himself. "I'm just going to take life as it comes and see what happens." But that sounded too much like piking out.

So he rang Mark. "Hey, Mr. Consultant-man; how you doing?" he started, smiling.

"Hey yourself, Mr. Business-man; did you get my email?" Mark retorted.

"Clever, very clever, I thought. Hit me right between the eyes. But Mark," he said, getting right to the point as always, "what's the point of trying to make myself sad? Is that really going to work?"

"Nope. But that's not really the point; you're not even open in that direction. Joy and sadness are all around us, in the simplest things. There's a beggar on the street, a child squealing with delight, the fragrance of a freshly baked muffin, the storyline of a Shakespearean play… these are all avenues to the soul. Some of them you just don't take. My advice to you right now would be open up to the world, embrace the parts of it you've been cold towards."

"You mean go and see a bloody tragedy," Brad said with resignation.

"Well, yes and no. How about be open to submerging yourself in the experience instead of watching and analysing it all the time. To quote CS Lewis in his final book of the Narnia series, you're so afraid of being taken in, that you can't be taken out, Brad."

Brad mused on that. He knew the scene from his childhood, the dwarves sitting in a hut, huddled out of harm's way and the lion, Aslan, trying to bring them out into paradise. But they wouldn't come. Too afraid of being taken in. Always calculating, never participating.

"Okay, Mark, I take your challenge. Participate, don't just observe. Well, I think the only thing for me to do is go and see the Book Thief. It's on at the playhouse next month. I'll take Felicity."

"By the way, don't forget, you owe me a trip to the fMRI," Mark prodded.

"Book it in," Brad said and smiled. Perhaps he'd get to see if sad was missing from his brain.

*

The thing about working for yourself as a psychologist in the military, thought Karen, *is you have no birds of a feather with whom to flock.* Karen needed to chat with some academic psychologists, and most of the ones she knew were at Canberra Hospital and the ANU. She put a call though to her friend August, who agreed to have lunch. So she drove over, picked her up, and went to an eatery in New Acton. August was a rotund, humorous woman, whose chins jiggled every time she laughed. She was also the sharpest, most widely read psychiatrist Karen knew.

By the time the waitress at ABaker had taken their order, they were all caught up on the minutia and Karen had filled her in on the internal representation, perceptual-experience conundrum; the stuff she'd been musing with Jane about. August asked if she'd seen any of the work done since Penfield's homunculus: a map of where the parts of the body were mapped to in certain areas of the brain. Karen had heard of it that, yes.

Auggie asked about the phantom limb syndrome work by VS Ramachandran, who went on to explore synaesthesia.

"You're getting way ahead of me, Auggie; sorry, can you go back?" Karen asked.

"Sure, sure, sorry. Penfield was the neurosurgeon who discovered somewhat by accident that touching the somatosensory and motor cortex when the patient was awake during brain surgery produced sensations all over the body. Years of experimentation resulted in mapping hundreds of places on the body to specific neurons. That map produced a homunculus, or little man; just Google it. So yes, external things really are mapped into neurons in our brain, at least every aspect of our body." August paused to eat her burger while Karen picked at a salad. She went on, "Phantom limb syndrome, the phenomena of amputees feeling their missing limbs as though they are real, and indeed experiencing real pain in those lost limbs became part of what neurologist VS Ramachandran explored. He found for example that the neuron for one tiny spot on the upper arm sat right next to the neuron for a spot on the upper lip on the opposite side. Stranger still, the neuron for table sat right next to the area we use to determine where our body begins and ends. As a joke he learned to integrate a table into his hand! Perception literally is reality to the perceiver. You can imagine the same is going on for synaesthesia too. Neurons getting crossed over, pathways being larger than they should." August paused to see what Karen might want to ask and as she did the waitress took coffee orders.

"That's all about our body, right, and a table, but does it hold for inside us, and emotions, and everything outside?"

"Well, you know the mirror neuron system matches and represents the emotional state and intention of others, right, just as it tracks and matches the emotional state of a crowd in football. Two researchers, Rizzolatti and Maunsell, determined that not only does an apple have a neuron, but other systems determine everything else about the apple—weight, calories, desirability, colour, and the representations of reward and expectation for that object. So, basically, yes."

"Right, so the million-dollar question, Auggie: can you change them? These neurons, their associations, can you repair, adjust, or augment them?" Jane asked anxiously.

August thought for a moment, then smiled. "Well, I can't give you scripture and verse, but yes, of course you can. Consider a child who develops a phobia of a dog, and gradually it makes links across neighbouring neurons to become "all dogs.".That child can get over her aversion, her reaction to dogs, and the therapy usually involves a) thinking, b) talking, and c) taking action. There might also be gradual exposure therapy."

"I've heard of a method of taking one association, say an old relationship, and stripping it of negative associations, or of taking one and mixing it with another to make the object even better." And then Karen realised her relief that science probably did back the theory.

"I don't know who else, apart from neurologists, might have studied this, but surely someone in the practitioner field has done so," August said. Karen was to later find out, they hadn't.

Whilst the session had been interesting, Jane felt a little ripped off. She had no problem with medical professionals making small talk, or interjecting their own story or research, so long as it was relevant to the case at hand. Otherwise she was paying for them to think out loud.

*

Jane had just finished a session with Karen. Karen felt bad about taking so much time out of her counselling session going on about other stuff, and rang her at work. Jane picked up and curiously asked what was going on. Karen explained that she had just been to see August, and would drop by Belconnen library to collect a couple of things she thought Jane would find interesting. Could she drop by work, have coffee, and catch her up? Jane said sure.

Forty-five minutes later they were sitting together in the cooling afternoon sunlight. The grass had already slowed its growth as the season turned cooler. It hadn't been mowed for two weeks. Outside the grounds of the café, a group of pentathletes were shooting at targets way down the field. Jane could just see their Fitbits and knew the data would be part of her work next week. Karen brought their coffee over to the wire ladder-backed chairs. She dropped a book and a magazine on the table and asked how Jane was doing.

"Crying for no reason," she replied. "I think I'm going nuts."

"How's Sean taking it?" Karen asked quietly so as not to prejudice workmates.

"I dunno, he moved on pretty quickly, leaves me thinking he only ever saw me as a short-term prospect. Hard to respect a guy like that."

Karen then brought Jane up to speed on her conversation with August, explaining that she should read the book, and the article she had marked in the magazine. Jane promised she would review it, and asked if Karen was going to come on the weekend?

"Wouldn't miss it for the world! Are we going to have a go at this stuff?" she asked.

"Well, let's see if we can operationalise the research," Jane prodded.

"No need; we know the research backs Robbins' NAC and the NLP approach to internal representations. Neuroscience says neurons associate and change the way we think."

"We'll see," Jane said. And they left it at that.

*

Two days later, Jane flew down the expressway to home, wondering if Mark might consider seeing a counsellor together and, as she did, she began to cry. Tears fell down her face and a deep sob welled up from her chest. The emptiness of the distance between them felt so large, and no bridge was offering itself to her. Could neural representational systems be helpful to her questions about marriage and her treatment of Mark these last twelve months? When had she switched from faithful and loyal to out there dating Sean, for God's sake? When did her internal representation of Mark change and how could she change it back?

Jane wept all the way home, until at last she arrived at the driveway. The hedgerow stood proudly, neat and trimmed, the lawn and pool in perfect order. That's how Mark coped, lining up everything in his outside world, and if he was hindered from doing so, he could really get antsy. Truth be told, she did the same thing when she was trying to avoid something. Entering the house, she would find the paintings all straight, the closets tidy, towels folded, and kitchen cupboards immaculate as she had left them after furiously cleaning up. That's how she coped.

She hopped out of the car just as Gyan's Volvo pulled up. He waved, and Lauren leapt out to embrace her mum, her heart skipping a beat with tactile joy. Even though she had known something was off between her parents, Lauren had no clue the depth to which their issues went. But now she noticed Jane's puffy eyes. It wasn't hay fever; it was grief. *Oh God,* she thought, *it's worse than I thought.*

While they gathered their stuff and brought it into the house, Lauren wondered what to say, and chose to ask a simple question. Once Gyan was locating them at the end of the corridor, she asked, "How are you and Dad doing?" Innocuous enough, but it triggered howling from her mum. She collapsed in on herself and dropped to the couch to cry, and Lauren looked on, stunned. When she had gathered herself enough, Jane gave a simple outline of what was happening, without denigrating Mark at all. As she listened, Lauren could feel her lifelong image of Mum and Dad, and of marriage, being shaken to the very foundations. How ironic that she and Gyan had come to celebrate the beginning of a new marriage when her parents were perhaps facing the end of their own. She quietly wondered, and hoped, that they were exaggerating. Surely things couldn't be that bad?

Lauren asked Jane about work, and instead of answering that, she told her about the conversations with Karen. "A person's experience is not reality but a mere representation of that reality and as such, could be changed at any time, or at least that's what I'm hoping for," Jane explained. Lauren knew exactly what she was talking about. Her own image of her parents, her internal representation, and therefore her experience of marriage, had been changed that very hour.

Lauren looked down to the coffee table at the cover of *Phantoms in the Brain* by VS Ramachandran. Underneath it was a 2012 copy of the journal *Current Biology* Karen had borrowed from the library for Jane to read. On the cover of the journal Lauren could see a list of articles including "Measuring Internal Representations from Behavioural and Brain Data." Nodding down at them quizzically, Lauren asked, "Is that what that's about?" and her mother nodded. Grateful for the diversion, Jane explained about phantom limbs, neuronal representation of external objects, maps in the mind, the homunculus, and the territory outside. Jane tried to think of a relevant example, and rested on Monique's struggles. "I admit I'm a bit hazy on exactly how to do what I'm about to tell you—I haven't tried it myself but here's the theory. When Monique was married she had an internal representation of 'man' and 'husband' and 'marriage,' but as time went on she had to change those internal definitions. Structurally her brain adapted, the neurons making different connections. As she learned what kind of abusive man she had married, the neurons for man connected to violence and self-defence. However, her experience of all men was also affected by her experience of that man. That neuronal cluster reached out and connected with the group representing men. Along comes my father in a threatening setting and bam her unconscious takes him out. She has been working on changing that map, and it changes her experience of, and treatment of, men. Does that make sense?" Jane asked. Lauren nodded.

"You know as well as I do that not all abused women make that connection, some remain ardent and passionate toward finding another man. Not all broaden their connection to the category 'all men' either. They can separate their experience of 'him' from their experience of 'them.' It's incredibly personal. But the point is the literature seems to indicate that we can change those associations, sometimes with as little as a few minutes of considered thought," Jane said.

Jane stopped, realising simultaneously that Gyan had joined them, and that she was oversharing. Gyan smiled, casually put his arm around Lauren, and when Lauren asked how that could be, when Monique's map was built up over so many experiences, he said, "Darling, one, if they can be made in a moment, they can also be dissolved in a minute. But if they are well-formed and established, it will take more work to undo. Neuroplasticity is not like acid, destroying the fibres; it is like a spider making and later eating its web." He was not being condescending, and neither did she take it that way. She asked again how a spider might eat the web, how neuronal maps might be dissolved—by what method.

Another thought hit Jane as he said this. "I almost forgot, one of the practitioners in this neural association and conditioning uses pleasure and pain to change people's associations. We can change what's associated with them, removing violence from man for example, and replacing it with trust."

Lauren said, "But why would Monique want to do that, Mum? She did meet and marry a violent man. Surely she must keep the lesson? Surely she keeps the wisdom, right?"

Gyan replied, "Yes, yes, she would keep them, perhaps only the good things. Monique needs to re-associate if she is to have another man. I would surely like to experience those changes. From what I know, those maps are rich and well-supported by sight, smell, emotion and many other forms of information which gives us handles, or leverage, for playing with them. Like Jane, I have only read, but they can be moved, merged, blended, improved or wiped out through mental processing. In an article I read about motor ideation and task execution for second-year biology, a bunch of scientists used an fMRI to watch a person change their somatosensory representations of card play, the colour of a carrot and where their hand was. A company called Omneuron has helped people reduce their experience of pain by mentally manipulating a computer-generated flame inside their fMRI. As they do it, the internal representations change and the pain diminishes." He drew breath, realising that really Jane owned the conversation and not he. She nodded for him to continue. "Jane, surely we can use this very information without the need for having an fMRI. Now we cannot produce a flame that changes in response to our thoughts and cortical blood flow, but surely we can use metaphor, or visualisation, or our imagination?"

They discussed this possibility backward and forward until Mark came home. He put on a brave face, smiled, embraced his wife, and went to the bedroom. He had been as devastated as anyone. As Gyan and Lauren prepared the evening meal, they chatted to Jane about Saturday and the impending meeting of "the group." It was Gyan and Lauren's turn to cater, and it would surely be both tropical fruits and Indian food, though Lauren had drawn the line at curds.

Mark eventually joined them, and over dinner they toyed with the idea of playing with their own neuronal maps and internal representations. Mark glimpsed hope in the idea. His experience of Jane had changed, and their kisses tasted like ash now. Unable to read Mark's thoughts, Gyan suggested that perhaps this was a path to dealing with phobias too. Lauren hoped it might lead to dealing with allergies and intolerances too, but the others doubted it would. With dishes cleared and the kettle on, they stacked the dishwasher and moved into the lounge to experiment. It was all Jane and Mark could do to stay focused. They both switched to "work" mode.

Jane suggested they all think of something they wanted to change, something not too difficult which might be easy to change. So they all thought of something: Lauren, her parents' marriage (which proved difficult to change); Gyan, the concept of emotions (which proved too nebulous for him and not somatic—which ironically would have worked for anyone else); Mark chose the event of rubbing oil on Monique's back; and Jane thought of her leg issues when running. They each closed their eyes and imagined these items, how they looked, felt, smelled, and then tried to change them. Nothing changed.

Gyan made a suggestion. Someone should lead another person through. If it worked, the other two could copy. They grabbed a hot drink and returned to the experiment; Mark paired with Lauren, and Gyan stood with Jane watching. Mark instructed Lauren to visualise the issue she had chosen (Lauren had downgraded her first attempt to anxiety over schooling—still a very difficult issue, but no worse than back pain). She got nothing. So he told her to make it a metaphor, a shape of some kind, and immediately a spiky sphere materialised in her mind's eye.

Mark asked her not to share anything out loud, figuring that verbalising would hamper the internal change. Then asked her to distinguish its colour (she saw it was black and yellow), its size (was like a balloon), its behaviour (was inflating and deflating slowly), and other attributes. Finally, he asked where it was. Lauren waited for a moment, and as she stood there Mark whispered to the other two, "I wonder if it can be inside or outside?" Lauren could clearly see it inside her now.

Mark was a bit stuck. How to change it? He knew autogenic experiences were far superior to changes forced by someone else. So he asked open-ended questions like, "What would you like to have happen?" and "What happens next?" and "Do you want to add or take anything away?" The result was, after about ten minutes, Lauren's spiky ball was much smoother and lumpier, smaller, and had moved to just outside her. Linguistically speaking her experience of anxiety had become less volatile, less harmful, smaller in volume, and passed outward, no longer insider her. This was powerful change.

They celebrated together and suggested more improvements. For example, since neuroplasticity took days not minutes, Lauren should continue to imagine the altered balloon, and over a week notice any change in her experience of anxiety. Gyan suggested that if working with just one object didn't work the way it had with Lauren, they should think of two. The others seemed perplexed.

"Well, I'm just thinking about people who have synaesthesia, they mix together two channels, two items. We might make them cohere, and this might make it a richer experience."

"Or, they're working with something they want to decommission, like I was," Lauren interjected, "and the element still has parts they want to keep, like anxiety has an upside you could use. You know, like it protects you… a second element could be used to keep any good aspects."

They all thought that was a great idea, and paired off to experiment with it. By the end of the evening the four of them were satisfied that the images, the metaphors, were actually creating change. It was unclear how much was placebo effect, how much was altering the unconscious, and what fruit would be born in the weeks to follow. But it was a start. At least for Mark and Jane, their state had changed and they were able to stand near each other.

One thing niggled at Mark, who was thinking about Brad and his missing emotion. He asked the group, "Can this neuro-associative conditioning work for something we don't have?" Without betraying confidences, he used the example of someone with alexithymia (the inability to feel or express emotions), trying to find that connection. Jane suggested he ask Karen tomorrow. Gyan felt that if the connection were not there neurally, and if they had not experienced this thing somatically, it was unlikely they could imagine it well enough to make a neural pathway.

"But," he said on second thought. "Everyone has the emotional equipment, the base circuitry, so surely you could build from play to joy to learning for example. And everyone, even psychopaths and those with autism, have experienced emotions, even if shallow. This alexithymia I know nothing about, but they probably have emotions, right? They're not robots; they're just damaged. Well, damage can be repaired."

It occurred to Mark that Brad had actually been sad in his life, and perhaps all he needed to do was work on that emotion, and see what the connections were. Bring it up, imagine it, shape, and place it, then look to see what's connected. Something might come up spontaneously, like an image, smell, movie, story, person, place… who knew? So he resolved to try it.

Tomorrow Monique would come with her kids; Arthur had committed, as had Karen (who would surely be pleased with the topic). Jane had invited Auggie, but she was in Sydney this weekend, and Brad's invitation was extended again. He and Felicity were coming. Jane was the one who gathered their notes in preparation for the following day.

Action list:
To help you dispel any doubts you have that there are real neural maps in your head which dictate your experience of the outside world, take a sneak peek into your neural representation systems (e.g., with phantom limb syndrome). Do the exercises created by Questacon, the Australian Department of Innovation:
http://www.neurocoachingaustralia.com/resources/neurocoaching/hands-on-perception-activities.pdf

- Pick any item, object, emotion, interaction, person, place, or thing to play with. At first dc choose anything hard or deeply emotional or disturbing (i.e., for which you are seeing a psychologist). Find a quiet place, stand or sit, and imagine that object. Does it have forr Does it have attributes like shape, colour, size, weight? Whereabouts is it, inside, outsid near, or far? See if you can change something about it, and test how that feels.
- Now pick something a bit harder, something you wish to change your experience of. Do same process as above and investigate with open-ended questions such as: what woulc like to have happen? And then what happens?
- If you have an issue that is negative, you wish to diminish, remove, or destroy it, then ch a second object or subject you can transfer the best parts to. Nothing is wasted in exper and life, so find a new home for the positive intent.

- If you have an issue that relates to lacking something, an emotion, capacity, inspiration, wisdom, or whatever else, start with what you have. An experience, a gem, a nugget, ev is someone else's. Find it (as above) and then explore what else might be connected to Then change the connections—rewiring and re-placing as necessary.

CHAPTER TWENTY ONE: ACCESSING YOUR METAPHORS

"Metaphor sits at the interface between the conscious and unconscious"
David Grove

Brad went to the theatre and although the event was moving, he did not begin to cry. Not that he expected to either; nothing was that easy. He certainly did submerge himself in the experience instead of watching and analysing it all the time. He would later tell Mark that this deepened his experience, especially of Felicity, and he was more present.

A week later when they met for coffee Brad stared out the office windows at the autumn rains driving in from the mountains. The clouds looked like a five-tentacled monster, with its arms spread wide over Canberra. The sun stood behind the clouds, casting pink and yellow rays of light like searching fingers up into space. The effect was a double array of reaching cloud and light. *The hand of God, ready to tip the world, he thought.*

"I reckon we just ditch the effort, Mark, and let this happen naturally," Brad said, turning to face him.

"I don't disagree. We've made progress though, and it feels to me like you're being more aware, more present, and more vulnerable," Mark agreed. "What's your week with Felicity been like?"

"Our discussions constantly seem to fall to an emotional level, and she tears up. I hate it when she gets overwhelmed by that… "

"What do you do when that happens?"

"I bring it back up to a rational level."

There was a long pause as Mark tried to track what had caught his attention. There was something about the way Brad spoke that seemed… helpful. Fall to emotional… up to rational… surely that wasn't actually a real thing. Mark had no idea what to do about it. He took a punt. "Did you notice what you did just there? You metaphorically placed emotions down and intellection up, even though they don't exist in that way."

"Hmm, no I didn't notice. What about it?"

"Well, can you tell me more about 'down' for emotions? Why down?"

Brad scratched his chin and pondered. He couldn't really say why, and told

Mark so.
"Well, you put rational up; is up good, bad, right, wrong, better, worse, or what?"
"Oh, rational is better for sure; much more reliable."
"I see. Nice set of stereotypes you're running there, Brad; can we explore them?"
"Sure, but rational is better."
"Okay, but has rational ever let you down?"
Brad said not that he could remember.
"Even in a situation that calls for emotions? Like love, seduction, sex?"
Brad pondered for a moment then a lightbulb came on. "Yeah sure, being overly rational has got me in trouble plenty of times with Felicity, especially when I argue an emotional issue from a rational perspective. I just come off as being a right fighter, and I end up sleeping on the couch!"
"You up for playing with this?" Mark said, picking up some of their learning about internal representations from two weeks ago.
He wondered if flipping layers might do something. He struggled to think of a way of letting Brad do this himself, so he opted for guided coaching instead of pure self-directed learning. After asking Brad to find a place to be, choose a posture (he chose to stand) and think of an event with Felicity, he said, "In your mind, can you see Felicity and yourself?" Brad could. "How are you in relation to each other?" Felicity, being shorter than him, was lower. "Now you're having that discussion where she gets emotional; what do you observe?"
"She's dropping, like she's on an elevator going down; her head is at my feet level now." Brad found this quite funny.
"Okay, now instead of bringing her back up to rational like before, I'd like you to imagine changing the rules. In this world rational is down and emotional is up."
Brad winced and got vertigo as he suddenly fell below Felicity in his mind. Emotions were ascendant. "This feels really weird, like gravity backward!" Brad exclaimed.
After checking he was okay, Mark proceeded. "Well, since these are the new rules, and remember we're just playing, right, how do you get to Felicity?"
At first Brad tried to bring her down to rational, but it wouldn't work. In his world up was ascendant, and he was always ascendant. "Up, I have to go up,"

Brad said, somewhat desperately, wrestling against what this demanded of him. Mark noticed what he thought were beads of perspiration dripping from Brad's chin. "All right then." He gritted his teeth. "We'll do this her way."

Mark gently encouraged Brad not to do it her way, but to do it his way. Not her nature but his. In Brad's mind he slowly rose, very slowly, and at the same time experienced a kind of melting, dissolving, and aching. It was then Mark realized those beads of moisture were tears. Brad opened his eyes, surprised by the wetness of his, cheeks and was slightly embarrassed.

"Do you want to leave it that way, or switch back?" Mark said. Terrible coaching, he knew: offering two alternatives instead of an open question. He could just as well have asked, 'What would you like to happen next?'

"Mark, this is doing my head in; how is this even possible?"

"Maybe doing your head in is necessary for this other part of you to grow more?"

"In that case, let's leave it the way it is."

*

Karen and Jane sat on the balcony of the café overlooking the AIS turf. The sun had been blotted out by the cloud and most of the patrons were heading inside to avoid the rain. The two of them had just got done reviewing their progress with internal representations and exploring internal figures. It was a mixed bag, with some things changing easily and other things not changing at all after significant visualisation and effort. Jane had done a bit more reading in neural change since the weekend at the coast when Gyan had come. She told Karen their learning on neuroplasticity, since Karen had not been around during that time.

"The basics, as I understand it, are that it takes three days to make a new neuron or alter the structure of an existing one. Six weeks will give you a stable neural network or structure. Ten-thousand repetitions will make the new network stronger than the old one."

Monique's structures for responding to threat from men were much stronger than that, having been practised for a lifetime. She surmised that this must be what was going on for Karen and herself: the lighter structures changed easily; the longer, more practiced, and therefore stronger structures might need a bit more work.

Karen agreed that could be a possibility, raising the example of Todd Sampson learning to tightrope walk in Series 2 of *Redesign my Brain*. It took him eight to ten weeks, and even then he fell off on his first attempt to cross between two buildings. That fear took quite some reworking. But it was possible.

Then it was Karen's turn to share. She told Jane about an exciting three-day seminar in Melbourne she had been to this week. James Lawley and Penny Tompkin had designed a form of therapy called Clean Language, and also Clean Space. It was clean because the therapist only used a basic set of nine clean questions and none of their own content.

Jane found it a bit strange and asked who used it. "GlaxoSmithKline, Yale Child Study Centre, NASA Goddard Space Centre… places like that," Karen said ironically. Only the best then. Jane asked more about it, and was told that the results were often a form of hypnosis, a psychoactivation of the interior of a person's unconscious. As they chatted, Jane was looking for something they could work with in their self-coaching group. They didn't have three days for training everyone in clean coaching. "So how do they get a person into their unconscious, shining the light, exploring what's going on down there?" Jane asked.

"Well, of course clean questions, but the key really seemed to be using metaphor."

"Did they come up with one or did they keep asking till one turned up?"

"No, that's the beauty of it: when the person has come to describe what they want as an outcome, say, for example, 'I want to think more strategically,' the coach would ask, 'And when you think more strategically, what is think more strategically like?' See how asking a person the 'like' question immediately demands they come up with a metaphor (or a simile). They'd say, 'Well, it's like a tower with a hundred layers,' or something like that."

"Wow, I love it. Generating a metaphor, self-generating a metaphor; that's awesome!"

"Yes, but that's not the half of it, Jane, because that tower is an object—see—just like we've been playing with in internal representation only instead of being a geometric shape; it's a building. So we go in and explore. Now, of course, it's just imagination, right? But in some ways this metaphor is a linguistic object, a real thing, a neural representation of that person's 'strategic thinking'. It almost always results in the person exploring inner space, going inside those objects, and when change takes place in there, inevitably change takes place out here too. Beliefs, attitudes, feelings, and even physical pain. There was one lady there, and after she explored her metaphor the sun rose over the scene and she decided to come out. That evening at dinner she told us that her lower back pain, crippling for twenty-three years, had suddenly dried up. James matched the story with others from the UK and his coaching journey."

They revelled in the synergy of lessons being learnt, and decided that exploring metaphor, and the objects created by them, would certainly be part of the weekend lessons.

*

Gyan dreamt very little as a rule. But this night as he drifted off to sleep, he fell into a restless sleep and dreamt. He was in a narrow street in Sydney, near the university. The street used to be paved with cobblestones but had been redone with tarmac at some point. The gutters, however, remained in the original style. Gyan walked along the street and he appreciated the geometric design of the stones. But something tugged at him, annoyed his sense of order and perfection, because the stones weren't all the same size and there were errors. Gyan hated errors. As he stood there, counting stones on one side and then on the other, the earth began to tremble and shake. Gyan turned just in time to see a wall of water pouring down the street. It hit him, washing him down the nearby drain.

Gyan felt no fear and no surprise at this impossibility. He simply fell and fell and fell into a landscape. This one was vastly different from the one he'd left. He was in India, near his hometown, wandering down a familiar yet strange dirt road. The dusty soil stirred beneath his feet as he walked, drifting in puffs across the cebu chewing grass by the road. Ahead of him was the familiar shape of a Hindu temple with layer upon layer of concrete rising into the sky. The outside of the temple was painted in fading beauty and colour. Gyan felt a pang of emotion as he looked at the open symmetrical structure. He loved symmetry. The temple was a 64 grid *padas* design, after the most sacred template.

As he approached, he noticed that this temple, annoyingly, was not entirely even. There were many variations off the square grid. The geometry of circles, diamonds and squares layering toward the sky were not in a symmetrical pattern however. This was most irregular, and he would have to address it somehow.

Each layer of the structure was festooned with flower wreaths for the gods depicted in statue. This temple appeared to be dedicated to Shiva. As he drew near, the largest of the statues turned toward him and addressed him in his native language. She, the goddess of war, told him he had a problem… many problems in fact, and they were all to be found in this temple.

"Visit, if you dare. Enter the place and find yourself, Gyan," she said. Although by tradition the temple was not sacred, for it was not built exactly according to Hindu design, and the holy place was not considered *bramah*, for it was not perfect, it was still *his* place. Gyan did enter and walk through to the very middle of the building. Like the centre of all temples, this was the place to where he should come and meditate on things. Gyan didn't like to meditate. It annoyed him. And there was the point.

Suddenly he was awake and his dream, if indeed it was that, did not evaporate into the morning light. It stayed with him, almost conscious, like a waking dream. It was most curious to him, and he wrote the entire experience down, in case it did disappear. He told the dream to Lauren, who had no idea what to do about it, but at least the meaning was clear… the street and the temple both annoyed him for the same reason… their failure to adhere perfectly to order. To Lauren's mind at least the temple seemed much closer to home for Gyan, almost as if it were his to consider. For him it was more about the centre of the temple, and being able to meditate there, or not.

*

Because this coaching work no longer seemed to fit within the standard definitions of her work, especially now they were looking at metaphor and internal-object exploration (which sounded clunky to her, really), Jane decided to research it after work hours.

Karen had given her the workbook from the Clean Language seminar. From it came the first entry in her journal on this topic which read: "A metaphor is a figure of speech in which a term or phase is applied to something to which it is not literally applicable in order to draw resemblance." Jane was sitting in her wicker chair on the back verandah at home, a shawl drawn around her shoulders because the late afternoons were getting cool. She pondered that resemblance is the bridge, the way the mind connects to an experience or event and draws in emotions, feelings, state, and the unconscious.

Jane now went to the most obvious next place, books. Perhaps the best known work in the field was by Lakoff and Johnson, called *Metaphors We Live By*. Rather than buy it, Jane simply borrowed an electronic copy from the local library and flicked through, reading the salient pieces. It was a rather dense work, with a literary focus.

Johnson defined metaphor as, "Understanding and experiencing one thing in terms of another." The key word there seemed to be that using the metaphor actually changed our experience of a thing. Mark had told her about the incident with Brad, though she didn't really know whether that coaching experience was true metaphor or not. But up for rational and down for emotional was actually how he experienced it mentally and somatically… until Mark switched it on him. So far as she and Mark knew, even two days later the effect remained for Brad. It was slowly changing his experience of Felicity and of emotions. Well, then it probably was a metaphor because rational and emotional are not, in fact, up or down.

She wrote a few other notes from the book then went looking for another at the library. She found *I Is An Other: The Secret Life of Metaphor and How it Shapes the Way We See the World*, and decided to borrow that as well. In the opening paragraphs she learned from the author and researcher James Geary that we utter one metaphor every ten to twenty-five words, or six times a minute!

Holy smokes, that's a lot! Jane thought, and then immediately recognized that was a metaphor.

She read a few more pages and realized that she'd not actually read the Lawley/Tompkin manual, yet and decided to go back and start there again. Such was her skittish mood and method, but even then she didn't open the manual. Her eyes were tired and she wanted a cup of tea. Whilst making preparations, Mark came home. Things between them had been confusing since deciding to have a go at remaking the marriage. They had fierce and wonderful sex again, as if physically fighting for the core of their connection… while at the same time contributing almost no romance or emotional love to their relationship. Conversations were at times deep and at other times transactional.

They exchanged a brief kiss, Mark considering whether to take it further and Jane being tempted away from her study. The moment passed and Jane watched him wander off to the bedroom, empty-handed as it were. *Metaphor again*, she thought. She made tea and sat down under self-discipline to read the manual.

James Lawley and Penny Tompkin had evidently learned Clean Language from a New Zealand psychologist by the name of David Grove. His study of effective counselling and psychology techniques had led him to design a very few simple questions to use, which left the client to contribute all of the remainder of the content. Grove's research explored the way in which people perceive and experience the world, how they make sense of it. Jane read that,

"There are three fundamental ways of making sense of the world: sensory, conceptual and symbolic. Each of these domains has its own purpose, logic and type of language." So Jane wrote down the summary of those three:

1. **Sensory:** we experience the world through the five senses, and when we code memory and experience we do so in a sensory-rich way. This can include direction, orientation, aspect, dimension and position.
2. **Conceptual:** we categorize, group and assemble our experiences, giving them labels such as "work", "family" and "recreation", which do not, in fact exist. They are concepts, and the labels define our experience of them.
3. **Symbolic:** a growing number of cognitive neuroscientists believe that both sensory and conceptual frameworks are superseded by metaphor.

*

Between the dream and now, Gyan had truly taken time to explore his dream. It was nearing mid-semester break and the burden of assignments and essays had peaked last week. In the final week of lectures, he had found time to walk into the gardens of Sydney University and explore the temple of his dream. "Visit, if you dare; enter the place, and find yourself," Shiva had said. His rational mind said there were no gods, and as such this was a cultural representation of his land, his people, his upbringing. His emotional mind said, well, yes, that is all bosh and what do humans know anyway, and there might just as well be a spiritual life for all he knew.

He sat down. He knelt down. In one sense he was on the grass in the Garden in Sydney and in another sense he was inside himself kneeling. In any case, he had gone there, *there*, to the centre of the temple and knelt to pray, or meditate, or whatever. But he couldn't, he just couldn't, because the building was imperfect. And while he was there Shiva came in her sword-wielding, passionate fury and asked him this question: "Gyan, can you accept this building? Can you walk these streets? Can you see this place and all who worship here, and love them? Because if you cannot, then Gyan, you cannot love yourself! For they are you. I give you this gift, this observation: how you do anything is how you do everything."

How those words haunted Gyan. Day and night they followed and questioned him. They sounded almost Buddhist, and frankly, coming from a war goddess, somewhat ridiculous. Some other part of him, less spiritual, and less inclined to believe simply explained the apparition as his unconscious self. Those words came to him from another time and place, and were being raised now because he really did have to face himself. Either way, spiritual or psychological, Gyan was beginning to realise that the road, that university, that temple, that goddess, and that war were all him; they were all inside him. Like a landscape. And that self was now calling to him. "If you cannot love this place, then you cannot love yourself."

Was a tendency toward OCD bound up with a tendency to self-loathing? He guessed it probably was. That and the intrusive thoughts, like these ones, he could not make go away. Lauren had told him about her definition of perfectionism: having no standard at all. He certainly knew that feeling, always striving to be better, to have a tiny margin, more… why? Why the struggle upward? What was he trying to prove and to whom?

In any case, it was time to head to Canberra again, the distance seeming to shorten with each trip, and see the gang to discuss a new topic. Gyan and Lauren had packed the night before and set off with coffee in hand to eat up the three-hour journey with conversation.

*

Jane had just got done reading the books and manual and had happened upon one last piece of research: *Clean Language: Revealing Metaphors and Opening Minds*, by Wendy Sullivan and Judy Reess. She'd really only scanned to the end of chapter three, where she read that the aim of David Grove's methods was to "grow the person's metaphors, to help them to discover and explore their internal metaphoric landscape, reach deeper levels of rapport with their unconscious minds, transcend limiting beliefs and behaviours, and find resolution and healing."

There was a knock at the front door and Gyan stood there holding Lauren's hand. He looked exhausted, as though he hadn't slept the night before. Lauren was also looking rather drawn. Jane asked them if they were okay, and Lauren entered the house saying, "Gyan's having issues. He's working on stuff, and I guess I'm just tired now." Before she could think about whether her comments were hurtful or not, Gyan launched into a full explanation of his state, lack of sleep, tiredness, soul-weary exploration, and need to debrief. Jane listened, while all the while Gyan remained on the porch, not coming through the open door.

Jane asked, "Gyan, what's the soul weariness about? Why sleepless nights?"

Then it dawned on him that she hadn't been in the car, hadn't heard the dream or the hallucination of Shiva. Entering their house he noticed, perhaps for the first time, that it was not symmetrical either, but it hadn't bothered him at all before. In fact, most buildings were not. In any case, he went on with his debrief, covering the dream, temple, goddess, and challenge to enter, and about the streetscapes and dirt roads of his soul landscape. At this, Jane jumped. The language matched completely what she'd been reading, yet Gyan was exploring it without any help or assistance, and all because of a dream. *How many of us do that accidently?* she wondered.

She didn't feel comfortable trying Clean Language or Clean Space coaching on Gyan. But she was up for a chat, was able to ask questions, and was fairly confident she could take Gyan through the "internal space." After they were settled, she offered Gyan and Lauren a hot beverage and the chance to destress in the hot tub. They gladly accepted both.

With everyone settled in the hot tub, Jane made her offer, and was disappointed when Gyan declined. "No offence, Jane, please, it's just that I have some work to do on my own first. I don't really know what I'm dealing with here. But I'd be happy to raise it with the group as an example at least."

"Well, it's funny you should say that because I was going to raise the issue of metaphor and landscape this afternoon anyway."

Then Jane brought them up to speed on the seminar Karen had been to, the metaphorical upside-down experience Brad had with Mark, and the books she'd read. They all agreed that Brad and Gyan's experiences were highly instructive—especially to prove that this phenomena was real and not just imagination. They showered, changed, and started making preparations for the group to come. Mark arrived back with all the supplies for a feast and Monique came over with the kids. Brad and Felicity arrived with Karen and even Art managed to make it.

When the eating and drinking had begun, and before the session began, Mark dragged a whiteboard into the living room and asked them all to be seated there.

"Hush down, everyone," he started. "Now, I know not everyone was here at the start of our journey, which is why we've collected the books, resources, and action sheets together. I think it's safe to say that we've stayed away from following gurus, but at the same time we have received from many, many wise and intelligent people. I'm fairly confident we have stuck to the course of making sure everything is backed by the research, but also works in the real work, more or less, for all of us. What I was hoping to do was draft the roadmap for the newbies among us."

"Hey, Mark," Gyan called. "Now is a really great time for this review because we started out forty-two weeks ago. The number is divisible by three and also by two. Furthermore, we have covered, including this week, twenty-one subjects—a number which once again is divisible by three, and on average it took us two weeks to cover each topic. Nice symmetry!" He laughed, and Lauren was the only one to join him in that laughter. The rest would understand when they heard his temple dream.

"Great points, Gyan, thanks. So maybe we do a whole of journey time-line. Looking back, I think we were trying to go too fast, and we could have covered these sessions in a year, allowing for holidays and so forth. Nevertheless, here's our journey of trying to find out how limitless we are, to heal our wounds, to build our strengths… to face our demons and rise above our failures." And so he began to write on the whiteboard:

1. The Art of Self Coaching—the Artist's Way, journaling and mindfulness. The Gallery experience.
2. The Coaching Framework—finding choice, being responsible, escaping oppression. Backing ourselves with internal resources. The Coaching seminar.
3. Establishing Relationship with the Unconscious—somatic signalling, building rapport with self. The Racetrack.
4. Changing State Changes Everything—fluid intelligence, state made of biochemistry, neurology, physiology. The French Movie night out.
5. Flow State and Creativity—surviving a meltdown, getting in the zone, high performance and The Rise of Superman book.
6. Building a High-Performance State—Ian's model, circles of excellence, brain training games and apps.
7. Goal Setting and Attention—BHAGs, SMART goals, be-do-have, start with why, outcome/intention/consequence.

The board was full, so Mark waited while people wrote down or photographed the contents on their phones. Then he cleaned off the board, turned around, and Mark looked sheepishly across at Art. "The next thing which happened was my resignation, which Art did not accept, for which I am now grateful." Then he started to write:

8. Learning About Learning—schools reinterpreting D and F as "not yet," quad-loop learning, 10,000 programs and the Action Learning course.
9. Being Flexible About Neuroplasticity—Jane's dad in a coma. The coast trip. Neural change, third-person strategy, watching Todd Sampson re-runs.
10. Who Split my Brain?—time-lines, croc/monkey/human brain, the suggestive power of words, "oh crap to okay" and the Mark Goulston seminar.
11. The Mind-Body Split—Descartes' error, the Divided Mind, three brains, hypnotism, breathe in/breathe out. Cooking school!
12. Healthy Motivation—seven kinds of motivation: Motivation 1.0, 2.0 and 3.0. The Seminar at AIS Gym with Dan Pink.
13. The Magic Effects of Sleep—sleep hygiene, massive damage from not sleeping, improved performance from sleeping. Gyan's lecture.
14. Reframing Perception—Speed dating, perception is reality, perceiving stress, Lauren had a really hard…

To this last point, Lauren unashamedly called out, "Trip to the hospital, you mean?" She told enough of her story that Brad, Felicity, and Art could be caught up. The board was full, and Mark wanted to point something out. When all eyes looked up, he said that every time they had found something, it caused a little journey of research and discovery. By the end of that cycle, many of their findings had been laid to one side, or would be used again later. He felt that the journey forward would go on being like that. Not everything they found would work, and not everything they researched would ultimately relate to them or be usable by all of them. But he encouraged exploration without criticism. Instead, use judgement and decision. Everyone agreed. Once more after photos and notes were taken, he erased the board and continued.

"Now, Jane, you're doing today's session; give us a title and a one-sentence summary of the stuff we're going to look at." She did, and he wrote it under the bullet point 21.

15. Enigmatic Personality—ABCDE in CBT, amygdala hijack, stop beating yourself up, self-talk. Mark designs 'Who's at Your Table?'
16. Where Self Esteem Comes From—face or flee our reality? Past versions of ourselves are with us today. Jane does a stand in Lecture for her friend.
17. Deepening Relationships—what relationships are made of: neural change, listening, rapport, bilateral contribution, empathy. Karen's research on qualia.
18. What's Every Body Saying?—body language, non-verbal cues, safety, comfort/discomfort: monkey brain is in charge! Joe Navarro's seminar.
19. The Chemistry of Emotions—emotions sit on limbic-system drivers, produce neurochemistry that are felt as feelings. Mark gets turned upside down!
20. Neuro Associative Conditioning—internal representations of external reality, associations, positive and negative can change. Karen reads Tony Robbins.
21. Accessing Your Metaphors—metaphors sit between conscious and unconscious. We can access our internal landscape. Clean Language seminar.

From here Jane took over. She wiped down the board and began to share all that she and Karen had learned: that metaphors occurred a lot in everyday speech, that they often conveyed meaning beyond the speaker's conscious intent. If explored they could take a person down into a landscape of objects even more rich than internal representation. She shared several of her own observations about metaphor turning up in conversation and gave her own example of having said to Karen that a holiday "would be such a fairy-tale adventure right now," and when asked, "What kind?" gave Karen all sorts of rich, nautical themes. Karen had explored that metaphor with her, and finally asked how all that related to the idea of a trip. Many things jumped out at Jane, like the freedom of it and the less-than-safe nature of an adventure. Jane then confessed that for her life had become too "grindstone" and not enough fun.

Then it was Gyan's turn to bring out his dream and daytime experience of Shiva's question to him. While he was sharing it, Gyan spontaneously realised as he told the story that the symmetry, or lack of it, was a metaphor. He desired things to be perfect, to work perfectly, but they never did. His proposal to Lauren for example was messy, but lovely. His OCD tendency and need to control represented his need for control, but things were never in his control, thus Shiva's invitation to come and meditate in the midst of mess.

Art raised his hand to make a suggestion. "Gyan, I don't know you very well, and I think you've been very brave today. I just want to acknowledge that before I offer any advice, okay? Well, in your first dream a wave washed you down the drain, but the ordered disorderly cobblestones remained. And when you got to India, the temple was ordered, mathematically beautiful, but not symmetrical. Could it be that you need to develop the capacity to live amid this chaotic order? What I mean by that is that fractals are mathematically ordered but chaotic. Trees, grass, babies, life is incredibly well-ordered, but natural and not synthetically beautiful. I guess I'm saying you seem to desire a kind, or order, that isn't really here." It was the most profound, hard-hitting thing anyone had said to Gyan. He accepted it. Until he could do that, he could not embrace the messiness of the rest of life.

From here the group broke up to discuss metaphor with one another. Jane had already put together a hit list of to-dos and was handing them around when Monique stopped the show. "I don't know how everyone else feels, but despite the mathematical exactness of twenty-one lessons learned, I still feel like I'm a long way off being a finished product. I have a lot to learn, and I don't think I've mastered even the first thing we learned: journaling! I'd like to suggest we either start the whole thing over so the new friends can learn with us, or we carry on finding new things to add to our lessons log."

And everyone agreed.

*

The chill was coming to the city, and the early morning air breathed like cold water. Inside Mark and Jane's house the two of them nestled by the fire, letting it warm their bones, and rekindle their relationship. The dog lay there too, on its side until there would come a familiar knock at the door; he would wag his tail and Monique would take him out for a walk. Preparations for the wedding with Gyan (and his family, and their family) was quietly driving

Lauren crazy, but Mark was confident she would get through. She had new tools to deal with stress, a whole lot more self-awareness, and Gyan was truly a great catch. Mark looked into Jane's eyes with fresh admiration for her. Middle age was treating her well, and the running kept her lithe. Behind those eyes was a burning intelligence and a healthy sense of self-worth. She had come out the better of her father's visit and so had he. Mark had now decided what to fight for, what he wanted.

The group itself grew by number slowly until it finally divided and made more groups. They would stretch out across this city like the hands of the storm cloud in the autumn sky. When Monique finally found a worthy boyfriend, she moved to his place in another suburb and started a second group. Art carried it to work and started one for managers. Karen became involved in a coaching psychology group, and started a group there. Gyan and Lauren started a group with Ming, Clarity, Jeremy, Paul, and the members of the book club… and so the story went on. They were limitless. Their learning unbounded. Their journey without end.

Their journal of session notes was eventually put together as a book, put up on academia.edu, and linked off to the resources they used.

Action list

- If you don't already, start journaling your dreams, whether they are meaningful or not.
- Spend the time to sit before them and examine them.
- Start to observe and watch the metaphors being used in your everyday interactions.
- When one strikes you as being particularly meaningful, examine it and see where it lead Why this turn of phrase? What meaning does it carry for you? What else is connected to
- Listen to the metaphors being used by others and be curious about them and what they mean, and ask and see where it leads.
- Pair up with someone else to discover what they want, stated as an outcome (a positive want X"), and then explore the outcome. When you feel it is fully formed, ask "And when what's that like?" This turns it into a metaphor.
- If you wish to, you can continue to pursue the metaphor until it becomes a landscape.
- We strongly advise you get training to proceed to Clean Language and Clean Space, as technique is very powerful and the questions content-free.

EPILOGUE: SECTION THREE

"As humans we all have immense potential but most people go through their lives with that potential untapped."
Sir Ken Robinson

So, there we are—the final third of the learning has slotted into place. Much has happened in the neurocoaching community since they made sleeping a focus fourteen weeks ago. The end of summer has proven very hot. Lauren has learned CBT to bring her anxiety under control. Mark and Monique walked dangerously close to an affair while Jane and Mark struggled watching their marriage fall apart. In the end it was Jane who was actually driving the partnership apart with her clandestine dating of Sean.

Jane's father finally emerged from his coma, much wiser than before, and more circumspect about his knowing-it-all. Gyan finally worked up the courage to ask Lauren to marry him and she said yes. Several others joined the group, including Karen, Monique's psychologist; Brad and Felicity, Mark's client and his wife; and Art, Mark's boss. The diversity of the group has enhanced their ability to gather data, experiment on a broader range of people, and intensify the feedback loops. The group started to tap the massive potential they have inside them, and realise much of their experience of the world is totally subjective, internally generated, and changeable. This realisation came at the hands of science, not just experience, as we shall see.

15. Enigmatic personality. Lauren learns more about Albert Ellis and his approach to the stream of consciousness and personality. This lead to an examination of self-talk and how our perceptions are formed by what we say to ourselves. Karen explored various forms of reframing after her conversation with Mark Goulston. Monique is confounded by her propensity to attract the wrong men and wonders if she's putting it out there. Lauren, Gyan, Mark, and Jane watch the movie Inside Out, and gain perspective on their emotions. Mark designs the "Who's at Your Table" exercise to have a structured conversation with himself. So what were out sources?

Primary: *1. Self-talk:* The layers of quality for conversation with self comes from Shad Helmstetter, *What to Say When You're Talking to Yourself*

(1990).

The material I use here is mainly from Chapter 9. *Psychology Today* published an excellent blog on self-talk and catastophizing called "Six Ways to Stop (Mentally) Beating Yourself Up" by Sarah Best, Jul 30, 2015.

2. Personality theory: Albert Ellis, Mike Abrams, and Lidia Abrams wrote *Personality Theories: Critical Perspectives* (2009). The quote in this chapter comes from page 526. The text discusses a great many other topics, but gives you the strong link between self-talk and the development of personality.

Secondary: *1. Who's at Your Table?:* This exercise, very useful for developing internal personalities and a robust set of conversations, was developed by Greg Bellingham from the Tarrodale Institute, 2012. By the way, I also have clients who are paranoid-schizophrenic sufferers and this exercise still works for them. I simply invite them to find a way to allow and exclude those fictitious or false members of their personality. One of them had these members, God and Satan, push their chairs back from the table.

2. Self-talk: Shad Helmstetter continues his work on self-talk, this time from a neuroscience point of view in *The Power of Neuroplasticity* (2014). Self-talk has at least three other applications: as a self-regulatory activity, Kross, E., et al. (2014). "Self-talk as a regulatory mechanism: how you do it matters," *Journal of Personality & Social Psychology*, 106(2):304–324.

As a drive for motivational style, Damon Burton et al. (2011). "Motivational styles: examining the impact of personality and self-talk patterns of adolescent female soccer players," *Journal of Applied Sport Psychology*, 23(4):413–428. It is also core to our performance at tasks and success (Chris Neck and Charles Manz, (1992). "Thought self-leadership: the influence of self-talk and mental imagery on performance," *Journal of Organisational Behavior*, 13 (7):681–699.)

Tertiary: *1. Emotional re-exposure reframing*. Elliot Krane, a paediatric anaesthesiologist from Stanford, who works with amygdala hijack. An alternative method is

2. Response/behavioural reframing proposed by Jeffrey Schwartz, a neuroscientist and expert in neuroplasticity from UCLA. REBT was invented by Albert Ellis, *A New Guide to Rational Living* (1975).

Emotional neuroscience. Matthew Lieberman found an almost exact negative correlation between the activity in the amygdala and the prefrontal cortex. When one powers up, the other powers down. Lieberman, M.D., Eisenberger, N.I., Crockett, M.J., Tom, S.M., Pfeifer, J.H. and Way, B.M. (2007). "Putting Feelings Into Words: affect labelling disrupts amygdala activity in response to affective stimuli," *Psychological Science*, 18(5):421-428.

16. Where self-esteem comes from. Jane's dad is still in a coma, but wakes up and prepares to move home. The enlarged group, including Karen, invited Sean and Dave (who never come). They get to know one another. Monique is curious about whether people (women) can put out signals men catch onto. Jane plays stand-in for her friend at college and prepares a lecture on self-esteem. The basic findings are that you can face reality and build esteem or flee reality and erode it. Carpooling becomes an issue as Mark and Monique spend more time together.

Primary: The psychologist William James coined the term "self-esteem" and drafted one of the most enduring models for it in Chapter Ten of *The Principles of Psychology* (1913). I much prefer the model presented by Nathaniel Branden, Six Pillars of Self-Esteem (1995).

This journey of facing reality, stepping through the three stages, was identified by Stephen Covey in *The 7 Habits of Highly Effective People* (2000). He explains that the journey towards maturity goes from dependence to independence to interdependence.

Secondary: The story of Thom Porro comes from Susan Scott's *Fierce Conversations* (2002) pp. 76–77. When examining facing or fleeing life, very often the issue of neediness turns up. The coach asks about internal/external sources of affirmation which feed our six basic core needs, as identified by Tony Robins https://training.tonyrobbins.com/why-we-do-what-we-do/.

The research Mark refers to about the right hemisphere and multiple versions of ourselves comes from Jill Bolte-Taylor, *My Stroke of Insight: A Brain Scientist's Personal Journey* (2008) pg. 144.

Tertiary: *1. Cognitive bio-feedback mechanisms:* Very helpful to overcome our perceptions. Christopher DeCharms, www.omneuron.com, works with FMRI techniques to reframe pain perceptions for example. A technique similar to perceptual positions can be used to help a person adopt third person to reframe their experience. Diane Divett from www.refocussing.com specializes in this process. They also assist us in our experience of ourselves.

2. *Power posing:* The research Monique finds is Carney, D.R., Cuddy, A.J.C., and Yap, A.J. (2010). "Power Posing: brief nonverbal displays affect neuroendocrine levels and risk tolerance," *Psychological Sciences, 21(10):1363-1368.*

The contradictory report Mark refers to was conducted by Pablo Briñol, Richard Petty, and Ben Wagner (2009). "Body posture effects on self-evaluation: A self-validation approach," *European Journal of Social Psychology* (39):1053–1064.

3. *Rape:* Diana Russell, *Rape in Marriage* (1990). Nicholas Holtzman and Michael Strube coined the dark triangle personality in, "People with Dark Personalities Tend to Create a Physically Attractive Veneer" (2012), *Journal of Social Psychology and Personality Science,* 4(4):378-394.

17. Deepening relationships. Carpooling comes to a head and practical answers clash with emotional expectations. Mark and Jane run headlong into trouble and need to find a way of working on the relationship. Karen explores sympathy and empathy, qualia, and experiencing life. Then she hits upon the neuroscience of change, especially through a therapeutic relationship.

Primary: This chapter primarily relies upon the research of Rossouw, P.J., (2013). "The Neuroscience of Talking Therapies: implications for therapeutic practises," *Journal of Neuropsychotherapy in Australia*, Vol. 24:3–13. Karen recalls hearing Pieter speak on Shrink Rap Radio, which was episode 383. http://shrinkrapradio.com/383-developments-in-neuropsychotherapy-with-pieter-rossouw/. Sadly Pieter is no longer with us.

Secondary: The definition of talking therapy comes from the UK Mental Health Foundation. https://www.mentalhealth.org.uk/a-to-z/t/talking-therapies

Rapid and strong development of relationship relies firstly on establishing rapport and trust. It then relies upon the limbic mirror neuron effect—showing empathy and pacing yourself to the other, Rizzolatti, G. (2005). "The mirror neuron system and its function in humans," *Anatomy and Embryology*, 210(5-6):419–421.

Finally, it requires facilitation of safety and control. This is nowhere better demonstrated in the field of neuromarketing and the book *Pitch Anything: An Innovative Method for Presenting, Persuading and Winning*, Klaff, O., (2014). See mainly Chapter One.

Tertiary: Great relationships also require we understand what is being said, pay consistent attention, and hold eye contact according to Ackerman, S. and Hilsenroth, M., (2003). "A review of therapist characteristics and techniques positively impacting the therapeutic alliance." *Clinical Psychology Review*, 23:1–33.

18. What every body is saying. Jane is frustrated by her search to assist athletic performance degradation turnaround. Her father comes home from hospital and stays. Lauren gets to experience Joe Navarro and the power of body-language observation in the FBI. She draws a very helpful diagram showing limbic response to environmental cues. Mark discovers the power of being mindful, free of attachment, and neediness, and finding high-quality ways to internally reference approval.

Primary: Fundamental to personal development is the ability to read other people's body language, and then see your own… understand what it means and what you should do about it. There is no better text on this subject than Joe Navarro's *What Every Body is Saying* (2008). The basis of the book is understanding the four primary limbic system responses to environment: freeze, flee, fight and mate.

In his argument, Navarro contradicts the work of anthropologist and neuroscientist Paul Ekman, whose thirty years of work have found seven universal emotional expressed on the face. These appear naturally, or when repressed, in micro or subtle expressions. See his work *Emotions Revealed* (2003) and *Emotions in the Human Face* (1975).

Other books about environmental factors mentioned in the chapter include: *Nudge* by Richard Thaler and Cass Sunstein (2013), which includes decision architecture and Sam Gosling's *Snoop* (2009).

Secondary: *1. Body language:* in job interviews or first impressions, take a look at Robert Holmes' "Managing Body Language for First Impressions" (2014) on Pulse. Olivia Fox-Cabane takes the issue of body language in the direction of public speaking and improving career in *The Charisma Myth* (2014); see mainly Chapter 1.

2. *First impressions:* See Willis, J. & Todorov, A. "First impressions: Making up your mind after 100ms exposure to a face." *Psychological Science*, 2006, 17(7):592–598.

Tertiary: "The Brain-Training Secrets of Olympic Athletes," Carolyn Gregoire, (2014) http://www. huffingtonpost.com.au/2014/02/11/mind-hacks-from-olympic-a_n_4747755. Jane looked at Thoresen, J.C., "Body Motion Cues Drive First Impressions: Consensus, Truth and the Origins of Personality Trait Judgements based on Targets' Whole-Body Motion." *Durham Theses*.

19. The chemistry of emotions. Jane's dad has a remarkably frank conversation with Mark about marriage and emotional decisions. Brad enters the story and the CEO is struggling with emotional expression. Mark is forced into doing some research and discovers that emotions are bedded down on physical or instinctive circuits. Jane's dad has a brief but honest conversation with her about hiding darkness and pretending not to know what's going on. Poor Gyan is "discovered" hiding an engagement ring. Mark finds the ladders of connection between the base circuit, the reason it acts, the emotion is generates, the chemicals that cascade to create a state and the outcomes. This becomes helpful to unpack an emotion that is missing. Brad gets invited for the first time to the group.

Primary: I prefer the neurochemical model of emotion because it produces seven base emotions. The Swiss National Centre of competence in research allocates eight basic emotions: joy, love, sadness, fear, anger, disgust, shame, and guilt. However, disgust is a biological product of a gut reaction and probably does not qualify as an emotion per se. They would also say peace is a by-product, or outcome, of lacking emotional response.

Secondary: Affective neuroscientist Jaak Panksepp discovered the seven biological systems underlying emotion. Detailed in Affective Neuroscience: The Foundations of Human and Animal Emotions (1998). He identifies seek/pursue, play/learn, care/connect, lust/reproduce, rage/protect, grief/avoid, fear/freeze. To this I add disgust/reject (gut), panic/flee (heart). See Jaak Panksepp interview on Shrink Rap Radio about "the Archaeology of Mind": http://shrinkrapradio.com/329-the-emotional-foundation-of-mind-with-jaak-panksepp-phd/.

Tertiary: Neurochemistry of these combinations of afferent (felt) emotions and underlying neural circuitry is done well by physician and psychiatrist Michael E. Lara, The New Science of Emotion: From Neurotransmitters to Social Networks (2009). Heart Rate Variability (HRV) monitors are now being distributed to all hospitals in the US and will shortly be in Australia too. Developed by the HeartMath Institute, these machines indicate eight emotional states.

If this all seems a bit too weird, take a look at Thayer, J.F., Åhs, F., Fredrikson, M., Sollers, J.J., Wager, T.D., (2012). "A meta-analysis of heart rate variability and neuroimaging studies: Implications for heart rate variability as a marker of stress and health." Neuroscience and Biobehavioral Reviews, 36:747–756.

20. Neuro-associative conditioning. Karen is frustrated by the mixture of science and speculation in the field of NLP, and in the original neuro-associative conditions of Anthony Robbins. They explore the way in which perception is reality to the perceiver. This includes the way certain things are associated with and fired off by external stimuli. Brad is still working on emotional connection, particularly sadness and awareness. The internal constructs that define a thing can also be changed by thinking about them. Strangely enough, this takes a few in the group to phantom limb syndrome and internal representations.

Primary: Karen's initial discussion is based on the work of Tony Robbins, from his writings about neuro-associative conditions, much of which finds its way into Awaken the Giant Within (1991). Robbins himself relies on the field of general semantics, forged by Alfred Korzybski, who argued that human knowledge and understanding cannot surpass our neural and nervous system and our language. Since our minds, our brains, have no direct access to the outside world, everything is filtered through perception. He coined the term "the map is not the territory" to describe this. Everything outside is represented by specific neurons, neuronal clusters, and neuronal networks in the brain.

Phantoms in the Brain: Probing the Mysteries of the Human Brain (2008) by VS Ramachandran provides an excellent under-pinning to the idea that objects and even our own body only exists in our brain. Through manipulation or miswiring, phantom limb syndrome, along with phantom pain and zombie limbs, can ensue. This is because the cheek and the thumb for example are neighbours in the neuron map.

Secondary: Marie L. Smith et al., on "Measuring Internal Representations from Behavioural and Brain Data." Current Biology, 2012, Vol. 22, Iss. 3, Pg. 191-196. The company Omneuron in 2005 began in MRI machines working on brain-controlled pain. See deCharms, R. C., Maeda, F., Glover, G. H., et al. (2005). "Control over brain activation and pain learned by using real-time functional MRI." Proceedings of the National Academy of Sciences, 102(51):18626–18631.

Tertiary: Those maps are rich and well-supported by sight, smell, emotion and many other forms of information. They may also be moved, merged, blended, improved or wiped out through mental processing. The somatosensory cortex for example contains a detailed neural map of all our body parts, internal and external. Leonardo, M., Fieldman, J., Sadato, N., et al. (2004). "A functional magnetic resonance imaging study of cortical regions associated with motor task execution and motor ideation in humans." Human Brain Mapping, 3(2):83–92.

21. Accessing your metaphors. Mark finally gets a break with Brad's emotions when he turns the underlying metaphor upside down. Karen attends training in Clean Language and learns about the power of metaphor, and Gyan falls into his metaphorical landscape during a dream. Spoken metaphor arises from the unconscious, as do dreams. They are the language-representing structures below and for that reason when you change the landscape you change your experience of the world, perhaps in a more profound way than in IR.

Primary: *1. Clean Language:* By far the best course work on using metaphor is the clean language in coaching by James Lawley and Penny Tompkin, Symbolic Modelling Lite, 2015. James and Penny are clear that they started their work as a result of David Grove, a psychologist with a penchant for exploring human behaviour and personal development. If you're looking for the three forms of metaphor, go to Page 2.

2. Exploring the landscape of the soul: this is an area taken up more carefully in Clean Language: Revealing Metaphors and Opening Minds by Wendy Sullivan and Judy Rees (2008). Chapter 3 starts the ideas on landscape. Look at Chapters 12 and 13 to explore the idea further.

Secondary: The exploration of the role of metaphor was pioneered by Lakoff, G. & Johnson, M., Metaphors We Live By, 2003. Warning: this is more of a linguistics book than a coaching one.

Tertiary: Geary, J. wrote an excellent follow-up piece on how metaphor literally shapes our experience of the world in I Is An Other: The Secret Life of Metaphor and How it Shapes the Way We See the World, (2012).

We also find reference to Todd Sampson in Series 2, episode 3 of Redesign my Brain walking the tightrope and both succeeding in the end and falling off at the start. Note that usually Todd only allows himself two to three weeks to master the technology, including rock climbing blindfolded. But this particular episode took him eight to ten weeks to master. The contents of this book may take you longer than that.

www.ingramcontent.com/pod-product-compliance
Lightning Source LLC
Chambersburg PA
CBHW031444160726
47994CB00005B/1869
9798733113333